PRAISE FOR *COHERENCE*

"In my experience, it normally takes around five years for teams to operate at the level of trust and co-operation I was able to develop in my team. With the techniques in this book we did it in six months."
Warwick Brady, CEO, Swissport

"The business was underperforming and now we are winning. Part of that success has been the team coming together faster with Alan Watkins' help. This book tells you exactly how."
Peter Pritchard, CEO, Pets at Home

"After working with Alan and his team I see the progress we've made every day. The dynamics of our team are great. I feel very proud of what we've achieved, and the change is cascading throughout the business to our millions of customers."
Matt Simister, CEO, Tesco Europe

"I've read hundreds of leadership and business books over the years, and this one stands out from all of them. Not only has it given me the ability to consistently perform at my best, but has helped me greatly in my recovery from long Covid."
Marcus Hemsley, co-founder, Fountain Partnership

"If you want to perform at your best you need to know how to make this happen. Fortunately for me I met Alan Watkins, and I am sure others can benefit after reading this book."
Michael Drake, CEO, Cognita Asia

"I've spent millions on coaching over the years but Alan Watkins and Complete's understanding of leadership is at the next level. The insights shared in this book can help you transform yourself, your team and your business."
Simon Beard, CEO, Culture Kings

D1563474

Coherence

*The science of exceptional
leadership and performance*

SECOND EDITION

Alan Watkins

KoganPage

First published in Great Britain and the United States in 2013 by Kogan Page Limited
Second edition 2021

2nd Floor, 45 Gee Street	122 W 27th St, 10th Floor	4737/23 Ansari Road
London	New York, NY 10001	Daryaganj
EC1V 3RS	USA	New Delhi 110002
United Kingdom		India

www.koganpage.com

Kogan Page books are printed on paper from sustainable forests.

ISBNs

Hardback	9781398601208
Paperback	9781398601185
Ebook	9781398601192

British Library Cataloging-in-Publication Data

A CIP record for this book is available from the British Library.

Library of Congress Control Number

2021942792

Typeset by Integra Software Services Pondicherry
Print production managed by Jellyfish
Printed and bound by CPI Group (UK) Ltd, Croydon CR0 4YY

CONTENTS

LIST OF FIGURES

LIST OF TABLES

ACKNOWLEDGEMENTS

I normally skim past the acknowledgements in most books, so please feel free to do the same. This is really for the people mentioned here. It's so rare to be able to publicly thank the people that make our lives easier, more enjoyable and worth living. This bit is for all of you.

The first edition of this book incubated for the best part of 15 years and was eventually published in 2014. This second edition came about for three reasons: the publishers felt it was still selling well enough eight years on from its original publication that it warranted a new edition. The fact that the book was enjoying sustained sales was encouraging because I deliberately wrote it to remain relevant, rather than the book being topical for a few months before vanishing into the clouds of history. The second reason for this new edition was that so many people told me that it was possibly the best leadership book they had ever read and so I felt that it could continue to help them if I updated it. And the third reason for this new edition was I have developed and evolved my thinking on what was shared in the first edition. The precision with which we now explain the ideas contained in these pages has advanced so significantly, we felt it was time to re-fresh and modernize the narrative.

Like the first edition, this second edition could only happen because of the incredible support of many people. First and always, I would like to acknowledge my wife Sarah, who has been on the journey with me every step of the way. Sarah, your love, humour and big heart help me believe in the future. I am so blessed that we found each other. You enrich my life in every way with your inner and outer beauty. I would also like to say thank you to my four sons, Jack, Sam, Joe and Charlie. I love each of you for your uniqueness but most of all the beauty of your individual spirits. Others see your brilliance too. I know because they tell me. What more could a father ask for? You have all grown into wonderful young men and I couldn't be prouder of each of you and how you approach your own lives.

Over the last eight years the company I am privileged to lead, Complete, has grown and evolved to enable the delivery of the content of this book (and much more beyond this book) to a global client base in all market sectors. Many of my colleagues have been with me for a great deal of that journey and have shown incredible loyalty and commitment to the cause of reducing human suffering and accelerating human development. Thank you, Rebecca, Alan, Peter, Katie, Chris, Leanne, Gestur, Rachel, Pip, Ralph, Danish, Ollie, Yvonne, Tom, Dave, Claire, Nick, Ali, Bettina, Bevan, Paul, Debbie, Kat, Denise, Jon, Louise, Arcade, Ellen, Sophie and Hannah. It's a pleasure to work alongside you all. Fortunately, during the pandemic, we managed to pivot the business and continue to grow the team. What an incredible group of people we have as we move forward in pursuit of our vision and purpose.

In addition to the Complete team, I would again like to extend a special thank you to so many clients who have been open to the change and challenge we bring. You are far too many to mention by name and thank here, and I will do that in person anyway. I hope that our challenge is always compassionate – as we recognize that making the world a better place is a tough job. We always approach supporting you with a view that, as brilliant as things may or may not be right now, we can all always develop more, be more and do better. In fact, humanity needs this of leaders. I have learnt a lot from working with you all and the personal development that this has created in me is partly why we are here now with a second edition.

Very special thanks go to Karen McCreadie, who has edited this new edition even more brilliantly than the first edition. You make writing so easy for me and for that I am eternally grateful. You are also delightful to work with mainly because we get on so well but also because of how brilliant you are at what you do – and who couldn't appreciate such genius? When I wrote the first edition of this book, I mentioned that it would be the first of eight books, and we have now done ten together. And, as you know, we are not done yet. There are still plenty more to do, and having you alongside makes this part of the journey so much more enjoyable – thank you.

Lastly, I would like to thank Kogan Page for suggesting the time is right for this second edition, and I hope we can significantly outsell the first edition and reach an even wider audience.

The need for better leadership in the world has not diminished in the last eight years; if anything it's increased. So, we continue to dream of seeing enlightened leaders in all walks of life and pursue our mission to reduce human suffering and accelerate development. The clock is ticking and if we can, with others, wake up and grow up enough people, then humanity has a real chance to flourish. We may then be able to live in harmony with this beautiful planet that we call home.

01

The great performance myth

Golf often brilliantly demonstrates the performance myth. Jordan Spieth won the Masters in 2015. He was 21 years old. His return to Augusta the following year looked promising. Despite not playing his best golf, he was leading the field at the 10th hole on the final day. What followed was more a disaster class than masterclass – back-to-back bogeys, a quadruple bogey and a pitch in the water. It wasn't so much that Danny Willett eventually won, but that Jordan Spieth lost. Normally when something like this happens, which is quite frequently in golf, one of the commentators will lament, 'Ahhh. It's a funny old game' as though it is a complete mystery why these things happen. But Spieth has some spectacular company in the melt-down department. In the first edition of this book, I opened with a similar story of Sergio Garcia who, despite playing stunning golf throughout the tournaments, managed to lose the 2006 and 2007 British Open plus the 2008 PGA Championship on the last day of competition. Further back, Greg Norman was on course to win the 1996 Masters, but didn't. Tiger Woods and Phil Mickelson both had a shocker during the 2006 US Open. Rory McIlroy's final round at the 2011 Masters or Adam Scott's spectacular demise at the 2012 British Open all testify to the fact that even the most skilled individuals are capable of giving a disaster class on their day every bit as easily as they may give a masterclass.

Of course, this drop in performance is not unique to golf; it happens in all sports as well as in business. People consistently underperform in all walks of life, making poor or sub-optimal decisions so often that sometimes it's a wonder we make any progress at all. These mis-steps in business can have massive financial repercussions for the organization and for society too – we just don't normally hear about them or get the opportunity to witness them in real time like we do in sport.

But, contrary to most sports commentators' wisdom, there is nothing mysterious about the sudden loss of form, the precipitous failure, the calamitous shareholder meeting or the disastrous media interview. The reason it happens, on the golf course or during the strategy off-site, is that we simply don't understand what's really driving performance in the first place. This book aims to set the record straight and reveal the secrets that, once understood, will enable you to be exceptional every day.

To facilitate that understanding we are going to explore a number of scientific discoveries about all levels of the human system from a diverse range of research fields including medicine, cardiology, neurophysiology, evolutionary biology, quantum physics, signal processing and systems theory as well as organizational performance, sports psychology and emotional intelligence. In examining the many, largely agreed upon, 'facts' we will see that some astonishing conclusions become clear – conclusions that, as extraordinary as they may seem, consist of no more than pre-existing knowledge.

Whilst this book exposes the secret science of brilliant leadership, it's important to understand that these scientific insights have not been kept secret deliberately; it's just that the people who could benefit most from their appreciation and application rarely know them. This knowledge has been around for many years, sometimes decades, but each 'part' has usually only been known in academia or reported in obscure medical or scientific journals. Very few of these key insights have made it into mainstream discussion, and almost none are taught in business schools or published in business literature. And yet, when we integrate these insights, they lead us to a surprising conclusion about ourselves – we can be brilliant every single day. We can regain the energy we had 10 years ago and become much smarter, happier and healthier. We can be more successful, enjoy better relationships and have a greater impact on our business, our society and the world.

This journey is not for the faint-hearted. Most leadership books contain one big idea and a few interesting nuggets along the way. This book contains several big ideas in each chapter and the nuggets are large enough and frequent enough to start a gold rush. It brings together the critical business-related insights of the last 20 years so that we can finally appreciate the 'mystery' of performance, once and for all. And the first of those critical insights, as we shall see, is that our brilliance all starts with the quality of our physiology.

In business (and sport) it's all about results. Results are how we measure success. In business, most leaders are in pursuit of the same financial goals – more revenue, more profit, greater market share, a significantly improved share price and increased stakeholder value. The obvious place to look if we want to understand and improve our results is behaviour. What are we doing? What are the key people in our team doing? What milestones are being met, what gains are being made? It's behaviour that is most commonly addressed by the variety of 'business solutions' put forward by consultants and coaches. The standard approach usually involves assessing what is currently happening and deciding what needs to be done differently to improve results. Unfortunately, every manager already understands that knowing what needs to be done does not mean that it will get done. The answer to elevated performance does not therefore lie in behaviour alone. If we really want to improve performance and crank out our A-game every single day, we need to look deeper into what is happening below the surface, and not just focus on the visible behaviour and results (Figure 1.1).

There really is no mystery to performance: our effectiveness and the results we achieve start with something much deeper in the human system than behaviour – our physiology.

FIGURE 1.1   The integrated performance model

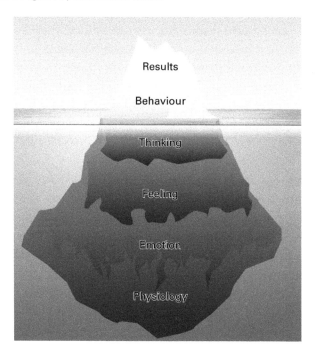

It's your physiology, stupid!

During the 1992 US election Bill Clinton's campaign strategist James Carville effectively drew the American people's attention to the largely ignored but critically important topic of the economy with his campaign slogan: 'It's the economy, stupid!' Bush senior had failed to pull the US economy out of recession and was busy fighting his campaign on other issues. Clinton won the election.

In the same way, many of the 'solutions' to business performance put forward by the coaching and consulting industry are ineffective or irrelevant, albeit interesting, while the real catalyst for elevated performance – physiology – is almost exclusively ignored.

Just think about it for a moment…

If we want to guarantee that people actually do the right things to deliver the results we want, we need to understand what really drives their behaviour. In order to answer that question, we need to peel back each layer of the human system, one by one, to understand the deeper drivers of performance.

First, what drives behaviour is thinking. What we think determines what we do. If I'm coaching a CEO and he thinks I'm an idiot or he thinks that what I'm saying is rubbish, he's not going to do what I suggest. Why would he? His thoughts about me alter what he will or will not do. Similarly, if I don't grab your attention in these opening few pages and make you think, 'Mm, this is a very different approach, I'm going to keep reading', you're going to assume this book is like every other leadership book you've ever read and you're probably not going to do anything differently. And if you don't do anything differently, you're not going to get different results.

But even if I manage to change what you think, it's still not enough. We need to go deeper to peel back another layer. For example, it's likely that most of the golfers mentioned earlier employed a sports psychologist to help them with their thinking or mindset. In business, you may even have employed some sort of psychometric testing to measure reasoning or analytic skills, or commissioned psychology-based coaching to help try and improve the quality of your thinking and that of your senior management team. But getting to grips with thinking isn't enough to change the outcome. Why? Because how we think or how well we think it is determined by something more fundamental in the human system, and that's how we feel.

How we feel has a very direct impact on how we think. There is, of course, a reciprocal relationship between thinking and feeling. How we think affects how we feel; and how we feel affects how we think. But if thinking and feeling engaged in an arm wrestle, feeling would win every time. This is why feeling, rather than thinking, is really the primary determinant of what we do.

A salesperson may think, 'I have to make 20 more cold calls to meet my prospecting quota for the week.' But if it's Friday afternoon and they don't feel like it, what wins? Thinking or feeling? Feeling will always out-gun thinking. Sure, we can force ourselves to follow through on tasks because we think they are important, but it's unsustainable. Consider our New Year's resolutions to get fit. There's a mountain of evidence about the results that can be expected if we do. We know it's a smart thing to do and we may be able to use willpower to force ourselves to comply for a week or two. But sooner or later – usually sooner – most of us will stop going to the gym because we just don't feel like it!

When Spieth started to drop shots, his feelings took over and no amount of thinking, or sports psychology work on his mindset, could halt or reverse that process. It is not easy to overwrite a feeling with a thought, whereas a feeling of 'worry' or 'stress' can dominate an individual's thinking all day.

In order to change the quality of someone's thinking, to drive a different behaviour, improve performance and achieve better results, we actually have to change the way they feel. Every good marketer knows that. People don't buy things because they think they want them; they buy them because they feel they need them!

Let's imagine you could change how people feel. It still wouldn't be enough to consistently change the game. Why? Because how we feel is determined by something even deeper in the human system, and that is raw emotion, or more accurately e-motion (energy in motion). The reason it is so hard to control or change the way we feel is because of the raw emotion that is occurring in our body without us necessarily realizing it. Telling someone not to worry is like closing the barn door when the horse has bolted. The raw energy pulsing through their body is already in transit – it's too late. And the reason this raw energy is coursing through their body in the first place is because, at an even deeper level, down in the basement of the human system, is their physiology – their biological reactions and processes.

What's driving our behaviour is our thinking, which is largely determined by our feelings, which themselves are the awareness of our emotions, which are made up of our physiological signals. And this is the real reason Spieth lost. His physiology changed; his emotions became turbulent and he didn't realize it. He couldn't feel it, but this physiological shift meant that he was unable to 'read the conditions'. This led to impaired thinking and poor decision making that ultimately cost him a second back-to-back green jacket.

There is no mystery. There was just a human being not functioning at his best because he didn't understand and therefore didn't control the myriad of internal signals and processes that need to be balanced in order to consistently perform at his best.

If it all starts with physiology, what is physiology? Physiology is just data or information streams that each bodily system generates all the time. As you read these words your body is taking care of a million little details that keep you alive – there is constant activity. Vast streams of data are being sent and received from one body system to another in the form of electrical signals, electromagnetic signals, chemical signals, pressure, sound and heat waves. We don't have to think about this information or put it in our diary – the human body is the ultimate performance machine. It just does its thing whether we are aware of it or not.

We all have this constant traffic of physiological information flowing around our body 24/7. But very few people understand its impact, and fewer still have learnt how to master this traffic and generate better-quality information flow that enables better-quality performance. Learning how to change the quality of signals in our system to deliver brilliance every day is the first skill set to develop as an Exceptional Leader. Hence enlightenment starts with awareness of your own physiology, as there is no change without awareness.

The performance myth explained

I am constantly amazed by how often well-meaning coaches or consultants continue to peddle the great performance myth in an outdated attempt to improve an individual's or a team's performance. All too often such advisors are dishing out nuggets such as, 'It's OK to be nervous before you start' or 'If you are not a bit nervous you will not perform well'. Such statements are based on the belief that we need to be 'psyched up' in order to excel. Other coaches may tell us the exact opposite and suggest that in order to perform at our best we need to be 'relaxed under pressure'.

Neither is true. Before giving a major presentation to city analysts or making a sales pitch to win a large corporate account, we don't need to be pumped up or relaxed. Neither of these determines success.

When we put our 'pedal to the metal' or hit the accelerator prior to an event, a meeting, a presentation or any performance scenario, we activate our autonomic nervous system (ANS). When we try to psych ourselves up, we engage the primitive 'fight or flight' response. The chemistry that drives the fight response is slightly different from the chemistry of the flight response, although they look quite similar. In flight our system releases adrenaline, which gives us a boost of energy so we can run away! In contrast, when we fight our body releases adrenaline's sister, noradrenaline, which readies the body for battle.

If, rather than psyche ourselves up, we tried to be 'chilled under pressure' we are activating the other main physiological response to a threat, namely the freeze, play dead or faint response. None of these are terribly helpful in a high-pressure business setting. Nevertheless, society has become obsessed by this 'relaxation response'. It is trotted out as the panacea to all ills, and is often advocated by coaching professionals to improve performance. The chemistry of relaxation is much less well known. While most people have heard of adrenaline, the 'accelerator fluid', very few people have heard of the brake fluid. When we freeze or faint, our body releases a chemical called acetylcholine.

In very general terms, heating our system up requires adrenaline or noradrenaline, and cooling the system down requires acetylcholine (Figure 1.2). But brilliant performance is not about relaxation or arousal. It's not about 'chillin' out', getting 'gee'd up', fight, flight or freezing! What

FIGURE 1.2   The assumed drivers of performance (ANS)

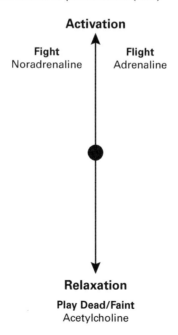

FIGURE 1.3   The real drivers of performance (NE)

really determines the quality of our performance is not our autonomic nervous system (ANS), it's our neuroendocrine system (NE). The NE system determines the quality of our emotional experience, whereas the ANS determines the degree of our arousal.

When we are on the right-hand side of the horizontal NE axis (Figure 1.3) our bodies are in a catabolic or 'breakdown' state. This state is underpinned by the catabolic hormones, particularly cortisol, which is the body's main stress hormone. There is a strong scientific relationship between cortisol and negative emotion. For example, people with brain tumours that produce too much cortisol often get depressed. And people suffering from depression show high levels of cortisol in their brain fluid. Consequently, increased levels of cortisol are likely to induce more 'negative' emotions. These negative emotions increase the cortisol still further, creating a vicious cycle and impaired performance. This is why individuals or teams often experience 'losing streaks' – it's biologically underpinned. High performance is extremely difficult when we feel negative.

In contrast, when we are on the left-hand side of the NE axis our bodies are in an anabolic or 'build up' state. This is underpinned by a range of 'anabolic hormones', particularly dehydroepiandrosterone (DHEA). DHEA is the 'performance' or 'vitality hormone', the body's natural antidote to cortisol, and is associated with more 'positive' emotions. These positive emotions increase the levels of DHEA still further, creating a virtuous cycle and enhanced performance. This is also why individuals or teams can experience 'winning streaks' – this, too, is biologically underpinned. High performance is obviously much easier when we feel positive. DHEA is the molecule that makes testosterone in men and oestrogen in women.

CORTISOL:DHEA RATIO

The ratio of cortisol:DHEA is widely seen as one of the best biological markers for aging. A high cortisol:low DHEA ratio has also been implicated in many of the most common diseases we face today:

- Obesity: cortisol increases fat on the waist.
- Diabetes: cortisol increases blood sugar.
- High blood pressure: cortisol disrupts fluid balance.
- Heart disease: cortisol increases cholesterol.
- Cancer: cortisol impairs immune function.
- Depression: cortisol promotes negative feelings.
- Senile dementia: cortisol impairs brain function.

A high level of cortisol impairs many aspects of performance, and consequently a business may underperform simply because the 'corporate cortisol' level is too high. Conversely, high DHEA levels underpin great performance. In fact, DHEA is a banned substance in the Olympic Games because of its performance-enhancing capabilities.

If we put the vertical 'activation' axis together with the horizontal 'state' axis we get the 'Universe of Emotions' (Figure 1.4). The interaction of these two critical physiological systems impacts performance. Known for years, this interaction was first described by James P Henry in 1982 while Professor of Physiology at the University of Southern California School of Medicine in Los Angeles.[1]

FIGURE 1.4   The Universe of Emotions

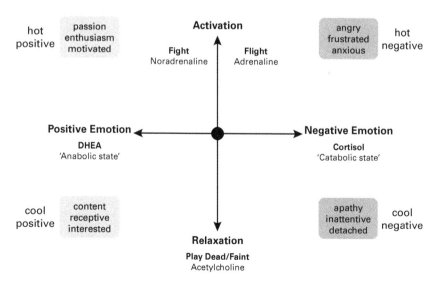

What really matters when it comes to consistent performance is whether we are on the positive left-hand side or the negative right-hand side of the Universe of Emotions, not whether we are in the activated top half or relaxed bottom half. Too often, the blanket antidote for stress and performance issues is assumed to be relaxation – or just reducing the level of arousal and dropping into the bottom half of the grid. People often ask if you had a relaxing weekend or holiday as though relaxation is always beneficial. This obsession is underpinned by a universal misunderstanding of how our physiology really works. There are two types of arousal – positive arousal (states such as passion or enthusiasm: top left) and negative arousal (states such as anger or frustration: top right). In addition, there are also two types of relaxation. It is possible to drop into the bottom half of the axis positively or negatively. Positive relaxation is characterized by feelings such as contentment, curiosity and peacefulness, whereas negative relaxation is characterized by feelings such as apathy, boredom or detachment.

The problem is that when we drop into these negatively 'relaxed' states we are still producing high levels of cortisol and other catabolic hormones that will seriously interfere with our health, our ability to think clearly and ultimately our performance. In fact, the dangers are often exacerbated because people in these negative states tend to think that they are all right because they are 'relaxed'. They are not all right – physiologically speaking, they are in real danger. At least when someone is in the top right quadrant of the Universe of Emotions, feeling angry, resentful or frustrated, they usually realize they are not in a great place and may be more inclined to do something about it.

Just because we have learnt to detach from negative feelings does not mean that the negativity has disappeared. It is still wreaking havoc with our physiology. It is therefore essential that we are able to distinguish whether we are operating in the top right or top left of the Universe of Emotions and where our senior team is operating from. This is critical to consistently delivering best performance. And when our team needs to recuperate, we must ensure we are in the bottom left not the bottom right of the Universe of Emotions.

Cultivate coherence to be brilliant

The real secret to performance is not relaxation; it is not even motivation. It is the ability to get over to the left-hand side of the Universe of Emotions and stay there. Living on the left-hand side requires us to develop a new way of being, a state of 'coherence'. Coherence is, in essence, the biological underpinning of what elite performers have known for nearly twenty years as 'the flow state'[2] – a state of maximum efficiency and super effectiveness, where body and mind are one. In flow, truly remarkable things are possible. Like the stonemasons of old, coherence is the 'keystone' that locks all the pieces of Exceptional Leadership together. It allows us to be at our brilliant best every single day.

Conceptually, coherence is a state of 'stable variability'. All healthy systems, whether the human body, a car, a society or a business must have variability. There are two aspects of variability that are critical to the optimum functioning of the human system, namely the amount of variability and the type or pattern of the variability. When a system exhibits a predictable pattern of stable variability it is a vibrant, healthy, living system. A lack of variability indicates a lack of health: brittleness, rigidity and an inability to adapt to changing conditions. Variability is therefore essential for the health of complex systems, whether we are talking about an economy or a human being.

When architects designed the Burj Khalifa in Dubai (as of 2021 the world's tallest building standing at 829.8 metres) they needed to create a design with the right amount of variability so the building would bend in the wind. If the building moved too much in the high winds of the desert, the building would be unstable and the people inside the building would feel seasick. Too little variability and the building would be too rigid and brittle so the first serious sandstorm would destroy it.

The same principle about variability is true in business – too little variability makes the business unable to adapt or pivot to changing market conditions. Similarly, if a leader refuses to change a strategy despite evidence that a strategy is not delivering, the business will start to fail and eventually fold. If you want a reminder of the carnage a lack of variability can create, just think of the music industry's refusal to accept that their market wanted to download music instead of buying a physical product. They were so focused on stopping illegal downloads that they ignored the fact that people were using and actively seeking to get their music in a different way. Had they demonstrated greater flexibility this could have been a major cost-saving opportunity, but it was missed as they chose to battle it out in the law courts instead.

At the same time, too much variability also makes the business unstable; it lacks focus. It becomes unpredictable, jumping from one new idea or strategy to the next. Struggling businesses often become overly flexible – diversifying excessively into new untested markets or launching untested products or services in a desperate bid to find a solution to falling revenue or diminishing market share. This 'throw everything at the wall and let's see what sticks' approach to business is costly and ineffective. Results become more erratic and unpredictable because no one knows what's expected of them anymore. It is, after all, very hard to hit a moving target.

A sign of health in *all* complex systems from buildings to business to biology is therefore the right amount and pattern of variability. When we achieve that balance, we achieve coherence. The principle of coherence is therefore a healthy amount of predictable, stable variability. And physiological coherence is the platform on which complete coherence is built. When we learn how to actively manage our energy levels and recuperate properly, we have access to the right amount and pattern of energetic variability in order to deliver optimal performance. If we can learn physiological coherence through the mastery of some simple techniques that I will share in this book, we can effectively turn the clock back to access the energy levels we experienced 10 years ago. Not only will we feel as though we have more energy, but we will use that energy more efficiently and recharge our batteries more effectively. In short, we will feel younger (Chapter 2).

This internal physiological awareness in turn facilitates emotional coherence because we become more aware of more of our emotional data giving us access to a deeper, richer vein of emotional expression. Remember, physiology is just data or information streams. Using a musical metaphor, physiology is the individual stream of notes that are being played all the time by our bodily systems.

Emotion is the integration of all those individual notes to form a tune. And feelings are the cognitive awareness of what tune our body is playing at any given moment. Is your physical system playing a coherent symphony or an incoherent cacophony?

Our body is always playing a tune – 24 hours a day, 7 days a week, whether we are aware of it or not. Problems occur when we're deaf to the tune we are playing, refuse to acknowledge that we are playing any tune at all or misinterpret the tune, thinking we're playing Mozart when we're actually playing thrash metal. This is hugely important and ignorance and misdiagnosis of the repertoire of emotional 'tunes' our biological systems are currently playing can have serious consequences for our health and emotional well-being as well as the success of our business.

Physiological coherence, facilitated primarily by cardiac coherence, therefore makes emotional coherence possible. As the most powerful organ, the heart can trigger coherence in all our other bodily systems until all the biological data streams are playing a coherent tune. When we learn to recognize and actively manage our emotions and improve our emotional literacy, we have access to the right amount and pattern of emotional variability. By learning to harness emotions so that we use them constructively and appropriately instead of suppressing them or ignoring them, we develop greater emotional flexibility and intellectual capacity and maturity, and this emotional coherence also positively impacts our energy reserves. The cumulative effect of physiological and emotional coherence will positively impact our health and happiness (Chapter 3).

Physiological and emotional coherence in turn facilitates cognitive coherence and gives us consistent access to more of our cognitive ability whilst also preventing brain shut-down. You'll probably have experienced brain shut-down or seen it in others when you are in a meeting and someone gets upset or overly anxious and either freezes like a rabbit caught in headlights or starts babbling nonsense. It's caused by chaotic physiology and lack of emotional variability. Brain shut-down will be explained fully in Chapter 4 and can easily be prevented through the cumulative advantages of coherence – starting with physiology.

But preventing brain shut-down is just part of the answer when it comes to improving intellectual horsepower. Real cognitive breakthroughs and superior cognitive processing are only really possible once we expand our awareness and develop our level of maturity as adult human beings. When we do both, we have full access to the right amount and pattern of cognitive variability. We are able to think more deeply and clearly; we can apply the right type of thinking to adapt to complex and challenging problems in real time. As a result, we become more creative, more innovative and better able to bring our 'A-game' to the table every day, not just intermittently. In short, cognitive coherence makes us smarter (Chapter 4).

This collective internal coherence then facilitates a vast leap forward in performance that begins to manifest in the external world through behavioural coherence. When we add a greater understanding of the types of behaviours that develop elevated performance and we understand the mechanics of performance, we have access to the right amount and type of behavioural variability. As a result, we do more of the right things, at the right time and have a wider range of behaviour open to us in our tactical arsenal, so success becomes more consistent and replicable. Or, as neuroscientist John Coates suggests, 'emotion and mood ensure conscious thoughts synchronize with body to produce coherent behaviour'.[3] Too often in business, we end up doing what we've always done or we end up doing something that is not what we thought we would do. In those moments, our thinking and behaviour is not congruent. And often the discrepancy is down to lack of energy, emotional upset or poor thinking. Once we gain physiological, emotional and cognitive coherence we are finally in a position to turn our attention to the key behaviours in a business that can transform results. When we do that, we will become more successful (Chapter 5).

If we are not constrained by low energy reserves, negative emotion, impaired thinking or ineffective behaviour, we will be more productive and more influential. If we develop our people leadership capabilities, we will be able to significantly accelerate productivity and performance because we understand what creates powerful working relationships and high-functioning teams. Coherent leaders appreciate that it's not smart to treat everyone the same because people are complex and diverse. Coherent leaders adapt their interactions and approach because they have access to the right amount and type of relationship variability. When we understand what makes people tick and appreciate their motives, we have far greater interpersonal flexibility, which in turn allows us to negotiate more effectively, make collectively coherent decisions and develop powerful teams and strong relationships. When we implement genuine governance up and down the business, the people in the business finally come together to deliver on a shared purpose.

Coherent leaders are individuals who demonstrate high integrity; they are people of their word who embody vast and stable flexibility in their behaviour and interpersonal approach, which is not only absolutely critical to future-proof a business but also inspirational, often resulting in the leader becoming much more influential (Chapter 6).

Coherence is the active ingredient in Exceptional Leadership, and amazing things are possible when we achieve coherence in ourselves, our teams, our businesses, our industry and society as a whole.

The evolution of Exceptional Leadership

When we review the sweep of human evolution from our early days as hunter-gatherers through the agrarian period onto the Industrial Revolution and the current information age, the feature that really stands out is the accelerated compression of time from one age to the next.

The hunter-gatherer age lasted 200,000 years, whereas the current information age is thought to last about 70 years and we are already (2021)

63 years into it. That's a massive difference and indicates just how much our evolution is speeding up. The business world we live in today is vastly different from the environment even 20 years ago, and the corporate environment of 100 years ago is almost unrecognizable.

American intellectual and development psychologist Ken Wilber suggests that there are two key processes in human development: 'waking up' and 'growing up'. First, we must individually and collectively 'wake up' from the delusion of control and power. In order to 'grow up' properly it is necessary to 'own up' to those parts of our nature that we dislike so we can re-integrate them. When we 'wake up' and 'grow up', this evolution alone can make a dramatic difference to how we 'show up' as a leader, which in turn can help us and our company grow up into a new, more dynamic and competitive future.

If we don't grow up in sufficient numbers, the extinction of humanity becomes a very real possibility. We must evolve, all of us, from where we are now to a more sophisticated level so we can successfully deal with the increasing levels of complexity and wicked problems humanity is creating for itself.[4] And in this regard, the world of business has a great responsibility. We will only succeed in the long term and build an enduring legacy if we all grow up and mature as human beings. We must be more open to input and receptive to new ideas, even from unlikely sources. The good news is that a new, more sophisticated leadership is emerging that is comfortable with change and, more importantly, can see what further change will be required if we are to flourish on this beautiful planet we call home.

As the corporate world moves from profit-driven leadership, through people-driven leadership, to paradoxical leadership and on to planetary-focused leadership,[5] we are essentially, as Wilber describes, 'growing up'. Planetary-focused or Exceptional Leadership has developed the ability to differentiate and make the critical subtle distinctions that the complexity of the challenge requires to drive wise solutions and deliver real game-changing innovation.[6] In fact, differentiation is a sign of increasing maturity. What used to work is no longer working or it's simply not working well enough. A planetary-focused Exceptional Leader is perpetually seeking to define and redefine the agenda to drive change and build his or her own future.

Such leaders also move beyond differentiation and are constantly searching for more complete, more coherent answers. They are concerned about maturation, sophistication and integration. They seek to define the next level of performance or capability and identify how this can be achieved through greater integration, given the current reality. They recognize that such leadership is a profound journey and requires them to reflect on their own potential to actually impair progress.[7] In fact, 'owning up' to this fact becomes a critical step in really 'growing up' as a leader. Having 'woken up' and 'grown up', if we now 'own up' sufficiently to the world we have created then we are well on the way to becoming the Exceptional Leaders the world now needs. And all of this change in us will determine how we 'show up' to lead.

But this journey is not just the journey of us, as leaders. Everything in life, including information and knowledge, follows the same evolutionary path: emergence, differentiation and integration. The primary challenge right now is to develop much greater integration capability if we want to overcome the wicked challenge we face today. The knowledge we need is available to all.

But the volume of knowledge can itself be an impairment. In fact, the volume of knowledge is so staggering that it has pushed many individuals, in all walks of life, into intellectual silos. The route to success for many is assumed to be only possible by becoming an expert at something. But the era of the expert is over. The cult of competency is past its sell-by date. What is now required is integration. It's time to integrate all the really insightful and important 'parts' of all the myriad complex systems, mined for us by experts, to create a more complete understanding of business – one that deeply comprehends that the whole is once again greater than the sum of the parts.

The planetary-focused Exceptional Leadership we need requires the integration of several scientific discoveries from disparate fields of research. Most of these fields are not normally associated with highly performing business. Many of these discoveries are common knowledge in their respective fields, and they are all robustly proven. These insights have, however, not made their way into mainstream consciousness and remain relatively unknown in the place where they could make the biggest positive impact – business. The 'parts' of this information are useful, but what is transformational is the integration of all the information. This integration, which I offer in this book, delivers a map to personal and collective brilliance – every day.

The Exceptional Leadership model

For the last 25 years I've been working with leaders in all market sectors and all geographies around the world. Most leaders spend most of their time focused on all the short-term performance tasks and operational issues that are necessary to drive quarterly results. This is not surprising, considering that business leaders are held accountable for delivering results today. It's what they get hired for and also what they get fired for if they don't perform.

In fact, according to an Equilar study, the median tenure for CEOs at large-cap (S&P 500) companies was just five years at the end of 2017, down from six years in 2013.[8] In other words, leaders often can't afford to focus on anything else, because it's the short term that they are predominantly judged on. A few brave leaders spend quite a bit of time focused on strategic issues, beyond their 'in-year' plan, and plan how to grow the company over the next three to five years. Few leaders invest significant quality time in cultural transformation despite the fact that most realize that culture eats strategy for breakfast. There may be talk of culture, values and organizational climate but the depth of understanding of such issues is generally still very shallow.

Hardly any leaders spend time thinking about their own awareness, their own individual development, the quality of their own thinking or their energy levels. And virtually no one we've worked with so far has ever thought about their physiology as an important leadership topic. This is also not surprising. These critical but lesser known and rarely discussed aspects of effective leadership are not taught in business schools, or if they are, they are skirted over in a matter of hours. They are not discussed in commercial circles and they rarely, if ever, appear in business journals.

It became obvious to us, working with C-suite leaders every day, that the model of leadership being used by most leaders was incomplete. And it was this incomplete view that was itself continuing to constrain a leader's ability to step change their own performance, as well as the performance of their team or their organization. What was required was a more comprehensive model, one that included what leaders already paid attention to and also embraced the other equally critical issues that must be attended to if the leader wanted to deliver sustainable results and build an outstanding legacy. Put simply, a more complete model for Exceptional Leadership was required.

In order to decide what that model should look like, the natural place to start was to look at the academic research. After reading many books on leadership, philosophy, psychology, performance and several other disciplines, it became obvious that the most complete picture that embraced the largest set of phenomena was the work of integral philosopher Ken Wilber and his well-known 'all quadrants all levels' (AQAL) model (Figure 1.5).[9] The AQAL model represents the core of Wilber's work.[10] Wilber himself had looked at all the maps of how the world was described by academics from

FIGURE 1.5   Ken Wilber's original AQAL model as it applies to business

	Inside	Outside
Individual	I Identity Self-awareness Thinking, feeling, emotions Physiology	IT Brain structures Leadership behaviour Personal plans Job
Collective	WE Values Culture Trust Team dynamics	ITs PESTLE context & themes Organization design Company strategy Business processes

many walks of life and what maps they used to describe their reality. Wilber's four-box model sketches the inner landscape and the outer landscape of human possibilities for both the individual and the collective. As such, it describes the inner and outer landscapes of individual leaders and teams as well as the interior and exterior reality of an organization.

The essence of his model is that there are four quadrants:

- Inside of I ('I').
- Inside of WE ('WE').
- Outside of I ('IT').
- Outside of WE ('ITs').

These describe three perennial domains – 'I', 'WE' and 'IT'/'ITs' – which are present in every moment of our day.

When a leader is in an executive meeting, the leader is thinking and feeling certain things, as are all the other individuals in the room. This is their individual inner 'I'. Those individuals are also having an interpersonal relationship, which may be strong or poor. This is their shared inner 'WE'. And they are almost always talking about the business as a series of observable individual actions (an individual 'IT') or a series of observable structures or processes (their collective 'ITs').

Wilber's AQAL model illustrates an objective world in the two right-hand quadrants of 'IT and ITs'; an upper left-hand quadrant invisible inner world of 'I' and a lower left-hand invisible quadrant of shared 'WE'.

I adapted this model by rotating it anti-clockwise and placing the individual at the centre looking forward into their rational, objective world. In doing so, we created a more commercially relevant frame that could help leaders better understand the breadth of the challenges they face and added the dimension of time that so drives leaders today. Standing at the centre of their world (Figure 1.6), front left the leader is focused on short-term commercial performance issues and front right are longer-term market leadership issues. Over the right shoulder, and out of normal vision, is the interpersonal people leadership world of 'WE'. And over their left shoulder is the inner subjective personal performance world of 'I'.

The reason we rotated the model and gave it a 3-D landscape is because that is how modern business leaders think about their world. Leaders stand in the centre of their own lives looking forward and they rarely see what's behind them ('I' and 'WE'). Instead, they are predominantly focused on the 'IT' – and then only the short-term 'IT' – most of the time. Most leaders freely admit they are suffering with an 'IT addiction'. Their thoughts are filled with what is 'IT' that I/we need to do today to deliver results.

Since 2010 Complete has successfully 'road-tested' this model with more than 500 global CEOs, including 70 per cent of the FTSE 100, some of the best CEOs in India, China and the Far East plus luminaries in the Fortune 500. We wanted to assess whether leaders were thinking about anything that isn't included in this model of leadership. We discovered that they are not.

As a result, we share this model extensively with clients and encourage them to think about the challenges they are facing in terms of the four quadrants.

Leaders pretty quickly acknowledge that their rational, objective effort in the world of 'IT/ITs' could be completely transformed with a transformation of their own individual 'I' and that the success of any individual leader requires interpersonal connectivity in the 'WE'. As countless failed businesses will attest, even if the strategy ('IT') is brilliant and the short-term results look good ('IT'), if no one trusts the leader ('WE'), he or she will never unlock the discretionary effort of their colleagues ('I') so the strategy will never get executed anyway!

To succeed in an increasingly complex world we must develop our ability to create impact in all four quadrants. Most leaders are pretty proficient in the objective quadrants of 'IT/ITs'. The source of the next stage of competitive

FIGURE 1.6 The Exceptional Leadership model

COMMERCIAL PERFORMANCE
- Drive revenue profit and EBITDA
- Develop offer, products & services
- Build scorecards, KPIs & metric tracking
- Create competitor radar
- Control operational risks
- Run performance & talent mgt systems
- Manage the business system

MARKET LEADERSHIP
- Clarify vision
- Set ambition
- Uncover purpose
- Identify strategic pillars and initiatives
- Establish effective governance

PERSONAL PERFORMANCE
- Energy, resilience and well-being
- Quality thinking
- Maturity and sophistication
- Personal brand (purpose, PoV etc)

PEOPLE LEADERSHIP
- Drive culture transformation
- Develop company values
- Build leadership teams
- Cultivate deep relationship ecosystems

IT

WE

I

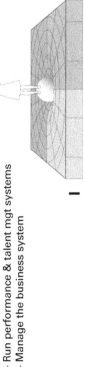

advantage, acceleration and growth is to be had in the domains of the 'I' and 'WE'. This means much greater self-awareness, maturity and emotional intelligence ('I') while also improving our interpersonal dynamics ('WE'). Outstanding leaders move effortlessly between and are coherent in all four quadrants. For a leader to be outstanding in all four quadrants requires vertical development across a number of different 'lines of development'.

Vertical development and 'lines of development'

The CFO of a major consultancy firm asked me to meet one of their execs, and contextualized the meeting by saying 'We need your help because we don't know whether we should promote her or fire her.' When I asked the CFO to explain, she said, 'The woman is one of our highest fee earners but she bullies everyone, so we now have five grievance procedures around her.'

'Don't tell me,' I said, 'you gave her a coach?'

'Well yes, I did,' the CFO said rather ruefully.

'And the coach taught her some skills in how to communicate more effectively?' The CFO nodded. 'And it has just made her a more effective bully, hasn't it?'

The CFO conceded that this is exactly what had happened.

This story aptly illustrates the difference between 'horizontal' and 'vertical' development. Horizontal development is really the acquisition of skills, knowledge and experience or, put more succinctly, 'learning'. These three things are very useful, but they are very different from actual adult development, increased maturity or vertical development. With 'horizontal development' the consulting executive had learnt and deployed a new set of skills, which meant she had simply become a more effective bully and more effective at manipulating other people. The exec wasn't any more mature as a leader.

If the coach had developed her 'vertically' it is likely that the exec would have realized the counter-productive nature of skilful bullying and she would have stopped doing it. With increased maturity, the exec would have developed greater self-awareness and an increased capacity to change her unhelpful behaviour.

Most leadership programmes, or coaching, focuses on learning rather than development. Most organizational 'learning and development' departments consist of a massive amount of 'L' and a miniscule amount of 'D' (if any at all). Vertical development is now recognized as, perhaps, *the* defining factor of future success.

Exceptional Leadership differentiates between horizontal and vertical development and is based on the work of four of the eight leading developmental theorists in the world who have written extensively on the subject of adult development: Ken Wilber, Susanne Cook-Greuter, William Torbert and Robert Kegan. Indeed, Kegan likens adult development to filling a glass with water. Horizontal development is about filling the vessel while vertical development expands the glass itself.[11] Not only does that allow us to take on more skills, knowledge and experience, but we are better able to create complex solutions because we have a broader, deeper perspective that can transform results and finally provide access to the potential everyone has been so desperate to find.

It is the integration of key insights, not normally found in business schools, which allows us to expand our perspective not just horizontally outward, through the accumulation of knowledge and experience, but vertically upward – giving us access to significantly more resources as a result.

In order to progress vertically, leaders need to evolve vertically across eight separate but interconnected and synergistic lines and levels of development (Figure 1.7). Whilst the developmental psychologists recognize numerous lines of development, we believe an exceptional leader must have sufficient altitude across all eight of these specific business-centric lines of development as a fast-track route to business transformation.

These lines of development help explain why people significantly underestimate their own potential. If we have no frame of reference that separates the key capabilities that need to be developed to deliver outstanding performance, we simply lump everything together and judge our current ability as a leader, effectively thinking in terms of just 'one line of development'. When we differentiate eight commercially relevant lines of development, it is easier to see that there is a great deal more potential yet to be unlocked. When an individual unlocks just one new level in one line of development, they can become unrecognizable from the individual who began the leader's journey. If they unlock several new levels across several lines of development, they can become a transformative force in an organization.

The benefits of unlocking new levels of development are non-linear and each line of development has a different number of available levels that can be unlocked. Moving from one level to the next in any line of development is not as easy each time. For example, development up the maturity line is initially pretty straightforward as we grow from a child into an adult, but the real magic occurs when we develop from an adult to a mature adult human being.[12]

FIGURE 1.7 Lines and levels of development

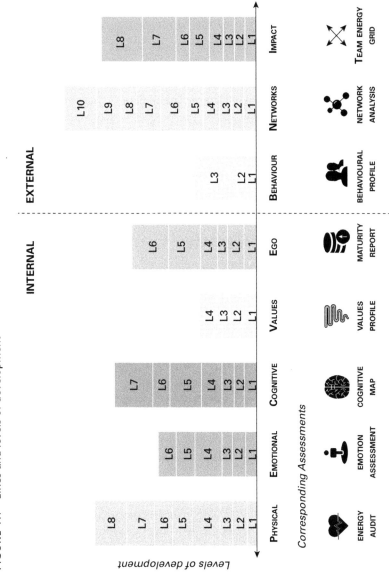

Unlike the physical development from child to adult, the maturity development from adult to mature adult is not an automatic process – it requires conscious effort and attention. Not all lines of development are equally valuable at all stages of a leader's journey. At Complete, we believe that the energy and emotion lines are especially important in the early stages of a leader's journey because, left undeveloped or ignored, they will stifle the early stages of high performance and success. This is why many of the initial developmental skills of Exceptional Leadership, which I will explain shortly, are focused on these fundamentally important lines of development. As you read about each skill, you may be tempted to dismiss them because they may appear too easy or straightforward. Don't be deceived; they have been very carefully tailored to be succinct and precise. These skills, when mastered, punch well above their weight in terms of energy, health, happiness, cognitive ability, peak performance and influence.

The skills and intelligences of Exceptional Leadership

Each chapter of this book builds and adds to the previous chapters. We will explore the initial skills of Exceptional Leadership to build a solid foundation that will, in turn, facilitate vertical development and transform organizational performance. When we understand all the elements of the integrated performance model, why they cause the challenges they do and how to avoid those challenges, we will transform our results. When we understand all the elements of the Exceptional Leadership model, what causes problems and how to avoid those problems, we transform our results still further. When we develop coherence at every level in all quadrants, we will be on our way to becoming a planetary-focused Exceptional Leader – capable of leading business into new, uncharted and profitable territory with a fraction of the angst, stress and pressure.

You may notice that there is a specific focus at this early stage on emotional mastery in the context of business success. This is not a repackaging of emotional intelligence but a new framework that packs a significantly more powerful punch. The reason these skills are so potent is that it still taught poorly and remains significantly underdeveloped in most businesses. It also offers the fastest and simplest way to elevate performance and achieve greater growth and success.

These skills build on each other from physical intelligence up through emotional intelligence to social intelligence (Figure 1.8). Ever since American

FIGURE 1.8 12 levels of emotional and social intelligence

INTER-PERSONAL SKILLS

12. Sustain positive relationships, drive success = Social intelligence
11. Awareness of the impact of your emotions on others = Social impact awareness
10. Awareness of others' emotions = Social intuition, empathy and rapport

PERSONAL SKILLS

9. Ability to make positive emotions your default = Optimistic outlook
8. Use raw emotional energy to drive self forward = Self-motivation
7. Ability to return to a positive emotional state quickly = Emotional resilience
6. Control emotions & manage stress = Emotional self-regulation
5. Label & discriminate emotions correctly = Emotional literacy
4. Awareness of emotions (feeling!) = EQ, emotional intelligence
3. Awareness of the concept of emotions = Emotional concept awareness

PHYSICAL SKILLS

2. Control physiology, esp. HRV = Physical management
1. Awareness of physiological state = Physical intelligence

developmental psychologist Howard Gardner proposed the multiple intelligence theory[13] and Daniel Goleman popularized the idea that emotional and social intelligence (ESQ) was more important than cognitive capability,[14] business has been interested in the concept of intelligence. In fact, there are now more than 200 different instruments that measure different dimensions of ESQ. However, having reviewed all of these instruments, it is clear that most of them only cover a fraction of the 12 dimensions of ESQ and many of these instruments are contaminated with concepts that have nothing to do with emotional intelligence. These different capabilities also need different assessment methodologies, as they can't all be quantified using self-report protocols. Our Complete app is designed to accurately assess all 12 dimensions over time using a much more nuanced assessment protocol.

Richard Davidson, Professor of Psychology and Psychiatry at the University of Wisconsin-Madison, suggests that the brain actually has structures that support six of the different dimensions of emotional intelligence.[15] The skills and intelligences of Exceptional Leadership therefore draw on academic research, embracing Goleman, Davidson and many others, while seeking to go further through 'commercial experience' so as to create a practical framework that can be applied to any business.

Ironically, of all these lines of development, cognitive is the least differentiating. Most leaders who have made it to the C-suite are smart enough, but this is the one that is most widely measured by the assessment industry.

Our view is that the entire assessment industry must stop focusing on descriptive assessments such as typologies, personality profiles and strength finders and start quantifying levels of development. Descriptive assessments were born in the 1950s in various psychology departments to understand human nature. They generate fascinating information, but they were never designed to predict the future and certainly can't predict whether a leader will succeed or not when promoted or appointed. In fact, the entire leadership literature suggest there isn't one type of leader or one personality that always succeed, so why do we keep measuring such things? Probably just habit and a lack of evolution in our understanding of psychometrics. In contrast, developmental assessment is much more predictive and not only provides compelling information but instantly creates a developmental path to improvement. We honestly believe that within five years descriptive assessments will be a thing of the past as more people recognize they don't deliver a real ROI.

Clearly, hiring great people is always going to be important, but it is unrealistic to expect, in today's global talent market, that we can recruit all the people we need to grow the business. Senior recruitment is expensive, fraught with difficulty and takes a lot of time. We believe it's wiser to embed a real talent development agenda deep into organizations – one whose goal is to grow Exceptional Leaders from within the ranks. That is the purpose of this book.

Notes

1 Henry, J P (1982) The relation of social to biological processes in disease, *Social Science and Medicine*, 16 (4), pp 369–80; Henry, J P, Stephens, P M and Ely, D L (1986) Psychosocial hypertension and the defence and defeat reactions, *Journal of Hypertension*, 4 (6), pp 687–97
2 Csikszentmihalyi, M (2013) *Flow: The classic work on how to achieve happiness*, New Ed Rider, London
3 Coates, J (2013) *The Hour Between Dog and Wolf: Risk taking, gut feelings and the biology of boom and bust*, Fourth Estate, London
4 Watkins, A and Wilber, K (2015) *Wicked and Wise: How to solve the world's toughest problems*, Urbane Publications, Kent
5 Watkins, A and Dalton, N (2020) *The HR (R)Evolution Change the Workplace, Change the World*, Routledge, London
6 Watkins, A and May, S (2021) *Innovation Sucks! Time to think differently*, Routledge, London
7 Watkins, A (2022) *The Leader's Journey*, Routledge, London
8 Marcec, D (2018) CEO tenure rates, Harvard Law School Forum on Corporate Governance
9 Wilber, K (2001) *A Theory of Everything: An integral vision for business, politics, science and spirituality*, Shambhala Publications, Boulder
10 Wilber, K (2012) Excerpt C: The ways we are in this together: Intersubjectivity and interobjectivity in the Holonic Kosmos, *The Kosmos Trilogy*, Vol 2, Ken Wilbur
11 Petrie, N (2011) *A White Paper: Future trends in leadership development*, Center for Creative Leadership
12 Watkins, A (2016) *4D Leadership: Competitive advantage through vertical leadership development*, Kogan Page, London
13 Gardner, H (1983) *Frames of Mind: The theory of multiple intelligences*, HarperCollins, London
14 Goleman, D, Boyatzis, R E and McKee, A (2002) *The New Leaders: Transforming the art of leadership*, Little Brown, London
15 Davidson, R J and Begley, S (2012) *The Emotional Life of Your Brain: How its unique patterns affect the way you think, feel, and live – and how you can change them*, Penguin, London

02

Be younger

Do you ever start dreaming of the weekend on the way to work on Monday morning? Do you find yourself nodding off on the couch in the evening before your kids are even in bed? Do you sometimes feel as though you've dragged yourself to the end of the week, but it still takes you all of Saturday to wind down? Do you find yourself falling asleep during the day at weekends and yet never feel fully rejuvenated by the 'rest'? Have you ever woken up feeling more tired than you did when you went to sleep? Do you still recognize yourself when you look in the mirror, or are you sometimes taken aback by how much you've aged? Are there days when you just feel utterly exhausted and emotionally and physically fried? If so, you're not alone.

Most of us struggle with the demands of modern life at some point or another. As human beings we only have a certain amount of energy and yet the demands on our energy reserves seem far from finite. No matter how hard we work or how productive we are there is always more to do, and this is especially true for busy professionals, senior executives or business leaders. Most leaders I meet are working harder now than ever before but most feel no more productive and sometimes feel less productive.

Collectively we fantasize about our two-week summer holiday, time to lie on the beach, soak up the sun and unwind. But when we get there, we are often so wound up it takes a week just to uncoil. If we are lucky, we then get to enjoy a couple of days of 'golden time' where we are genuinely relaxed, before wasting the remaining two or three days of the holiday thinking about all that needs to be done when we return to work!

Many executives feel increasingly burnt out, and most assume it just goes with the job. Often, our fatigue either goes unnoticed or it manifests as irritability, and more aggressive or autocratic behaviour. It can lead us to take excessive responsibility as we attempt to wrestle back control. Our perennial fatigue ultimately triggers poor commercial decision making.

It is estimated that we make 35,000 decisions every day, and this number increases the more responsible you are for others.[1] Also, as the world becomes more complicated, the number of decisions we need to make on a daily basis is significantly greater than our parents or grandparents ever had to make. The level of change and choice we have to deal with is increasing steadily as we seek to prosper in an uncertain, rapidly accelerating world. It's no wonder many feel 'in over their heads',[2] under intense pressure and living truly exhausting lives.

Time management vs energy management

In a desperate attempt to manage feelings of being overwhelmed, we have become obsessed with time. Most people feel 'time poor' and lament that they 'never have enough time' and there are 'not enough hours in the day'. They yearn for more 'time to think' or wistfully dream of 'time off'. As a result, many organizations run 'time management' courses in the mistaken belief that it is possible to 'manage time'. But time is not the problem.

The assumption is that if we could just learn to manage our time better, we would accomplish more in less time, so we wouldn't be so exhausted. It's a logical argument but it's not accurate. The truth is, if we look back to our twenties or thirties, time was never an issue. We would work hard all day, go out for dinner and a few drinks, and rock up to work the next day ready to do it all again. We didn't need to manage our time because we had enough energy to do everything we needed to do with plenty to spare.

Perhaps the reason we are so focused on time management as opposed to energy management is because it's easier to think about time than understand let alone manage our energy. Most of us do nothing about our energy levels other than think about sleep, maybe promise ourselves to exercise more or think that dietary changes are they key, although we rarely change our diet. What we don't think about is where our energy comes from or where it goes. We have no idea what our real energy source is, never mind how to manage it! We assume food is fuel and leave it at that. As a result, we attribute energy to youth and assume that it simply diminishes as we age. And whilst it's scientifically true that, from an energy perspective, most of us peak at 25 years old and, if left unchecked, our energy levels decline at roughly 3 per cent per year subsequently, there *are* ways to turn back the clock.

No one can hold back time, but in a stressful, demanding job it is energy management, not time management, that will transform results. If we learn how to manage our energy reserves properly, we can re-experience the energy and stamina of our youth.

What is energy and where does it come from?

When people talk about energy, they are really referring to their ability to make effort. Our ability to make effort requires a certain degree of physiological vitality. But how can we quantify our vitality in a way that is commercially relevant? The size of our muscles does not predict our ability to keep working on a strategic issue late into the night. Our raw physical fitness may give us a slight indication, but it is a very poor predictor of corporate capability or commercial vitality. Food may be a fuel, but most people eat a reasonable diet and you see as many tired vegans as you do exhausted carnivores and fatigued pescatarians.

Fortunately, it is now possible to scientifically quantify the exact amount of energy or power that is currently available to us in our system. We can also objectively measure how well or how appropriately we are using that available energy.

Energy is created automatically through the physiological processes that are occurring in our body all the time – whether we are consciously aware of them or not. If we want to make more effort, this is underpinned by our heart beating faster. An increased heart rate helps because it supplies more blood, and therefore more sugar, fat and protein, to our cells and muscles. There is a direct connection between the energy of our heart and our ability to make effort. The heart is literally at the heart of our performance. But how many leaders understand how the human heart works? This is ironic given that we often exhort our colleagues to 'put their heart into it'.

If we want to make more effort, do more with less, go further, faster, we must understand how our heart functions. If you watch any TV medical show, you will often see the patient hooked up to an ECG machine and their heart rate will blip its way across the green screen in a series of peaks and troughs. Figure 2.1 shows the different deflections in a single heartbeat. When you see your doctor and he reviews your ECG, he usually looks at four such beats and decides whether there is something untoward going on or whether your heart is healthy. But what is less well known is that it's not the shape of one or even four beats that really matters (unless you are having a heart attack right there in the doctor's office) – it's the space between the beats that counts. It's the heart rate variability, the pattern, the flexibility of our heart rate that can provide a massive amount of information about our health.

The flickering up and down spikes of an ECG, as indicated in Figure 2.1, simply reveal how the electrical current navigates its way through the conducting tissue within the heart itself. As the upper chambers of the heart contract, the electrical current initially moves towards the recording electrode on the front of the chest (giving rise to the P wave), as the lower chambers of the heart contract the electrical current moves away from the recording electrode (the Q wave), and then towards it (R wave) and away again (the S wave). The shape of the QRS complex can reveal information about the health of the main pumping chambers of the heart.

FIGURE 2.1   The different deflections in a single heartbeat

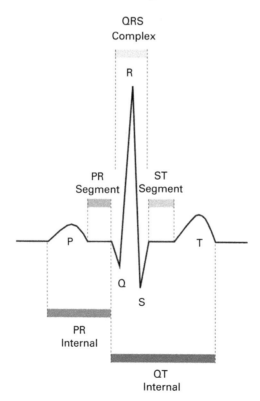

After the heart contracts, it relaxes to allow time for the chambers to fill back up with blood before the next contraction. As the chemical balance in every heart cell resets during this relaxation, or 'repolarization', it causes a deflection of the ECG needle, giving rise to the 'T' wave.

The gap between the 'S' and 'T' waves, called the 'ST segment', is used to determine whether there are any blockages in the arteries supplying the heart muscle with oxygen. If the ST segment is elevated, this suggests the patient may be having a heart attack. If the ST segment is depressed, this suggests that there is insufficient blood getting to the heart muscle and the coronary arteries may be partially blocked, which could lead to angina or chest pain.

From a medical perspective, the amplitude (height and depth) of the component parts of the single heartbeat each tell a story about the health of the heart. Since our heart creates a lot of our raw energy, if we want to increase our energy reserves or regain the energy we had ten years ago, we must understand how the heart functions. In business, the way our heart rate varies over times is extremely relevant for several reasons, as we shall see.

At Complete we have been studying the heart's variability in leaders for more than 25 years. We have now measured over 2,000 leaders through the course of a normal working day to assess the relationship between their heart rate variability (HRV) and their energy levels, their ability to get going, keep going, make effort, recuperate and be resilient.

Heart rate variability

When we ask leaders to estimate their energy levels, most are relatively inaccurate, overestimating and underestimating in equal measure.[3] So how do we know if our energy levels are above average or below average? How do we know if our fuel tanks are full or if we're running on fumes? We may have a vague subjective sense of our own energy levels and vitality, but how can we really know?

It's now possible to accurately determine how much energy a leader has by measuring their HRV.[4] Although most of us are not aware of it, our heart rate is changing all the time, which means that the distance between one beat and the next is constantly changing. Measuring HRV patterns during a normal working day reveals various underlying biological phenomena in the human system, which in turn can illuminate some, often disturbingly accurate, insights into an individual's performance without them uttering a single word.

For example, I was working with a former England footballer and the first thing I did was measure his HRV. We arranged a meeting so we could discuss his results and I proceeded to explain to him what his HRV assessment had highlighted. In conclusion I said, 'Your main problem is you find it difficult to motivate yourself – you can't get started. But once you've decided to do something and you get into action, you are totally relentless – like a dog with a bone.' He was speechless, and more than a little spooked because, although my statement was spot on, we had not discussed anything, never mind any performance issues he might have. He couldn't understand how I could possibly know what I knew. I knew because of his HRV patterns.

In a business setting, we are also able to pinpoint some critical areas of concern regarding productivity and performance. Just by looking at the results obtained over a 24-hour period, we can tell whether a leader's main problem is motivation or endurance, how much energy they have, whether they are wasting energy and feel exhausted or whether they are using their energy efficiently. We can tell if their system is breaking down or whether their body is recuperating properly. And we can even tell how much international travel they are doing and how well they are coping with it.

It's important to understand that measuring HRV is not the same as getting our heart checked in a standard corporate medical examination. When a doctor takes your pulse rate or does an ECG it's usually to determine your heart rate. But quantifying your average heart rate ignores the fact that it changes repeatedly, even though the difference is much too subtle to detect just by feeling your pulse.

Even if we have a full corporate medical, including a treadmill exercise test, this only measures around 1,000 heartbeats. Most of the time such tests conclude that everything is 'normal'. In contrast, when leaders complete a 24-hour HRV recording, we assess around 100,000 heartbeats per day, and we often record their data for three days.

The executive tachogram

The recording of the live changes in someone's heart rate is called a 'tachogram', which means 'speed picture'. A tachogram is therefore literally a picture of how the heart rate speeds up and slows down over time.

Figure 2.2 is an example of the information generated from a simple tachogram of a busy executive. Notice that while the executive was in

FIGURE 2.2   Example of executive tachogram

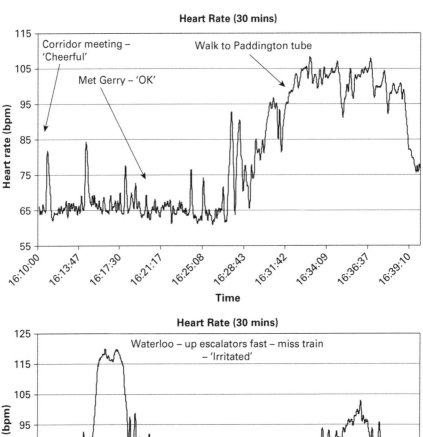

Heart Rate (30 mins)

Corridor meeting –
'Cheerful'

Met Gerry – 'OK'

Walk to Paddington tube

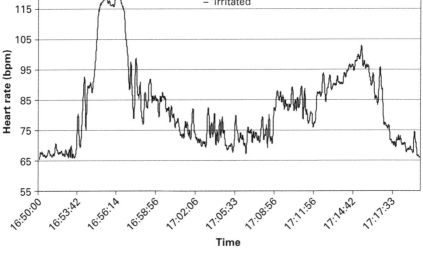

Heart Rate (30 mins)

Waterloo – up escalators fast – miss train
– 'Irritated'

meetings his heart rate was fluctuating around 65 bpm. When he left work his heart rate leapt almost immediately as he walked quickly to the tube station, reaching 105 bpm, falling slightly as he reached the station.

In the second tachogram, we can see what happens when the executive runs up an escalator. Again, his heart rate nearly doubles from a steady

65 bpm to 120 bpm before dropping back to a higher resting level of 75 bpm. But then something interesting happens – he realizes he's missed his train! He's not walking fast or running up escalators and yet for the next 10 minutes his heart rate remains elevated, reaching up to 100 bpm. Being frustrated at missing his train clearly has a direct effect on his physiology, causing him to burn energy at a much higher rate than necessary for at least 10 minutes. This not only explains why people who have endured a very frustrating day come home feeling exhausted, but also illustrates the critical importance of physiological and emotional coherence in energy management.

Watching an individual's tachogram during a normal working day reveals that, for most people, the 'normal' pattern of HRV is far from a state of equilibrium. In fact, most individuals' heart rates vary throughout the day in a pretty erratic way. Nearly every meeting or activity we engage in has an almost instantaneous effect on our HRV. These internal changes in HRV and other physiological signals, most of which we are unaware of, change the way we feel. This changes the way we think, which in turn changes what we do and the results we achieve.

Thus, there is a bi-directional interaction between our physiology and our working environment – both affect each other. If we want to feel younger and improve results, we must know how much energy or fuel we have in our tanks and how better to use this fuel. We must also learn to control our physiology so we can turn our erratic or chaotic HRV signals into more high-performance coherent signal. This is why measuring HRV in leaders is so important.

Why HRV is so important

There has been an explosion in interest regarding measuring HRV. A search of 'Heart Rate Variability' on pubmed.gov returns over 50,000 published scientific papers that explore the different aspects of HRV. But why is it important for a leader to know about HRV? There are four critical commercial reasons:

- HRV can predict employee health risk of death and illness as well as determine recovery rates.[5]
- HRV can be used to quantify an employee's energy levels and ability to respond to a threat.[6]

- HRV can be used to predict brain function and quality of thinking, and therefore quality of decisions that can drive growth and success[7].

- HRV influences identity and therefore the ability to be authentic as a leader and deliver results.[8]

HRV can predict employee health, risk of death and illness

Researchers around the world continue to publish papers on the ability of HRV to predict sudden death, including from over-work.[9] This association has been known for years, and occasionally makes the mainstream press. For example, in 1996 the famous Hollywood film producer Don Simpson went to visit a colleague of mine, Dr Bill Stuppy. Simpson was at the time the business partner of Jerry Bruckheimer. The pair produced some truly memorable TV series such as *Crime Scene Investigation (CSI)* and films like *Dangerous Minds*, *Beverley Hills Cop*, *The Rock* and *Top Gun*. It was Simpson who coined the phrase 'You'll never work in this town again.' Simpson's doctor, John O'Dea, was seriously concerned about Simpson's health and sent him to see Bill, who measured his HRV over the course of 24 hours. It was the worst he'd ever seen so he sent a letter to John O'Dea telling him that he needed to get Simpson into hospital immediately otherwise he'd be dead within six weeks – probably on the toilet or eating a meal.

Dr O'Dea was so concerned about these findings that he sent Bill's letter on to Don Simpson with a handwritten note on the letter asking him to come in right away. Don, being the work-hard-play-hard, take-no-prisoners kind of guy that he was, refused to accept the initial analysis and instead sought out a second opinion from another doctor. That doctor, however, only gave him a standard medical, monitoring his heart for a few minutes rather than 24 hours; it all sounded 'normal' so Simpson was sent home and told not to worry.

Six weeks after the initial HRV assessment, Don Simpson died on the toilet exactly as predicted. In an ironic twist of fate, reminiscent from a scene in CSI, the police found him in his bathroom. He'd been reading Oliver Stone's autobiography and his bookmark was the letter that Bill Stuppy had written, saying he was going to be dead in six weeks. Bill was subsequently brought in for questioning. But, he explained to the police, 'Of course, I didn't kill him; I just told him he was going to die if he didn't get medical help.'

That's the power of HRV.

Prior to that, in 1978 Dr Graeme Sloman was one of the first physician to report that HRV could predict adult mortality after a heart attack.[10] He noticed that some heart attack victims had a degree of variability while others' hearts ticked like a metronome. Those with a metronomic heart beat whose heart rate didn't vary never made it home to their family; they died right there on the ward. And yet none of the traditional risk factors such as age, cholesterol levels or smoking predicted the outcome. Since then, there have been thousands of studies that show the powerful ability of HRV to predict death from heart disease.[11]

In 1997 Jacqueline Dekker and her colleagues discovered that HRV was capable of predicting 'all-cause mortality'.[12] In other words, HRV could predict the demise of anyone from any cause.[13] Strangely, HRV, which is a measure of cardiovascular flexibility, can also predict death from diseases that are not cardiovascular, because HRV is a measure of our overall system flexibility.[14] A loss of flexibility means a brittle system that is unable to adapt to physiological stress. And a brittle system is likely to snap. HRV's ability to predict mortality is incredibly robust, as evidenced by over twenty years of research. For example, more recently HRV has been shown to predict all-cause mortality regardless of age.[15]

In the corporate world this is incredibly important for the health and well-being of executives, not to mention succession planning. Clearly, the sudden collapse or even death of a senior executive is tragic for the executive and their loved ones,[16] but it also presents a serious risk to the business. The implosion of a leader's health is more common than you might think. In Japan it's so widespread that there is even a term for such tragedies – karoshi, or death from overwork. In 2017 Japan's Ministry of Health reported that 190 people died from overwork.[17] More than half of them had worked more than 100 of overtime a month – something called the 'karoshi line'. The problem is not confined to Japan. Professor Jeffry Pfeffer argues in his book *Dying for a Paycheck* that 150,000 deaths in the USA and as many as 1 million in China can be attributed to overwork.[18] In 2010 Professor Michael Marmot and his team reported, in their Whitehall II study of more than 6,000 civil servants, that British employees who worked more than 10 hours per day were 60 per cent more likely to have heart problems than their peers who worked 7 hours per day. The findings were again independent of the usual cardiovascular risk factors or sleep deprivation.[19]

And the risk of excessive work leading to exhaustion and collapse has been exacerbated by the gig economy and the global pandemic enabling working from home.[20] For example, a recent *Harvard Business Review* article reported that half of all Millennials and 75 per cent of Gen Z voluntarily left roles for mental health reasons.[21] Such job burnout is now considered so widespread that the World Health Organization has classified it as an occupational hazard. This burnout is characterized by feelings of energy depletion, negative or cynical feelings about the job and reduced professional efficiency.[22]

Such energy depletion is not a new phenomenon; it has been impacting organizational performance and reputation for years. For example, ten years ago when Lloyds Banking Group CEO António Horta-Osório announced he would take six weeks' sick leave on the advice of his doctors after being diagnosed with extreme fatigue and stress, his decision wiped 4.4 per cent, or a whopping £930 million, off the value of Lloyds Banking Group shares.[23] He would have been acutely aware that his decision would cause such a reaction, and it is perhaps an indication of just how close to total collapse he really was. The sad part was that this could have been avoided. Had Horta-Osório had his HRV measured, the warning signs would probably have been clear to see months before any real physical symptoms emerged, giving him enough time to recalibrate his physiological system and learn how to effectively manage his energy levels and recuperate properly.

Poor HRV can't be fixed with a tablet, but it can be improved by embracing many of the skills outlined in this book, which we'll explore in the next chapter.

HRV AND BIOLOGICAL AGE

In addition to preventing death and predicting illness, both extremely useful in and outside business, the amount of HRV can also tell us a lot about our 'biological age', as opposed to our actual chronological age.[24] Without conscious intervention, our HRV declines by approximately 3 per cent per year, deteriorating from our mid-twenties[25] until we lose all variability and die. This decline is true for all populations.[26] This means that if our HRV is assessed it is possible to tell roughly how old we are to within about one year, based on the decline in our heart rate variability and your risk of burnout.[27] Figure 2.3 illustrate the difference in HRV amplitude in two individuals with a 20-year age difference. The 60-year-old has much smaller HRV amplitude than the 40-year-old.

Obviously, a birth certificate or pointed question could elicit someone's age, but biological age and chronological age don't always tally. Depending on how well someone has managed their energy, their true biological age as

FIGURE 2.3   HRV amplitude in a 60-year-old (top chart) vs a 40-year-old (bottom chart)

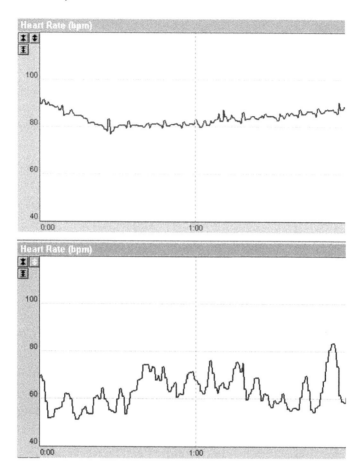

revealed by their physiology (HRV) may be considerably older than the actual number of birthdays they have had. This partly explains why prime ministers and presidents seem to age rapidly when they are in power. And their risk of death is significantly increased.[28] For example, it has been suggested that US presidents age twice as fast as normal.[29]

Although we can't change our chronological age, we can change our biological age and increase HRV with the right kind of lifestyle adjustments. It is therefore possible to improve HRV and turn back the clock through exercise, emotional self-management, omega-3 supplements and yoga.[30] The easiest and quickest way to roll back the clock and regain the energy levels you had ten years ago is to start to control your physiology and develop cardiac coherence through the breathing skills that will be explained a little later in this chapter.

HRV quantifies energy levels and levels of dynamism

Despite the huge energy demands of modern business, few executives ever consider their own energy levels and how to manage them appropriately. It's difficult to feel younger when you're exhausted all the time. In fact, it's pretty much impossible.

Most senior executives and business leaders that have made it to the C-suite have done so as a result of developing a specific expertise in a specific field or industry. They have put in hours of work and this effort has produced results, giving them qualifications, sellable knowledge and exploitable capabilities. It is therefore natural that they would assume that if they want to go further and perform to an even higher standard, they must continue to apply the same recipe that got them to the C-suite in the first place. This idea is incorrect for several reasons. What gets a leader to the C-suite is not the same as what makes them a great leader. Being a good leader is less about technical capability, in the 'IT' domain, and more about developing leadership capability in the 'I' and 'WE' domain. When we are promoted (and this principle applies not just to a promotion to the C-suite) it is necessary to start letting go of our expertise and broaden our abilities so we can handle the increased level of complexity at the new level we are operating it. This means we need more thinking time and we need to be less hands-on. Such a notion is encapsulated in the old adage of 'working smarter not harder'.

So many leaders are susceptible to a double whammy as far as energy reduction is concerned. Not only are they losing 3 per cent every year from their mid-twenties onwards but, under the relentless pressure to constantly improve performance and deliver shareholder value, they often work harder the more senior they become. With age, they have less fuel in the tank each year, particularly if they are not managing their energy levels and the much greater energy demands that comes with increased complexity and responsibility as they are promoted. No wonder that we witness accelerated aging in leaders and high levels of exhaustion.[31]

In the early stages of exhaustion there is often an excessive increase in adrenaline levels and an increased activation of the sympathetic nervous system (SNS). This can go hand-in-hand with agitation and hyper-vigilance, a picture often seen in individuals with chronic fatigue.[32] This type of excessive arousal can ultimately lead to sympathetic exhaustion. Senior executives and leaders who are under excessive pressure are constantly pumping adrenaline into their system and will often exhaust their adrenal glands' ability to produce sufficient adrenaline to cope with the demand. The amount of adrenaline produced by the sympathetic nervous system and the adrenal gland can also be quantified using HRV analysis. Thus, HRV can be used as a marker of excessive SNS activation and ultimately the degree of physiological exhaustion[33] and inability to think clearly.[34]

Furthermore, HRV analysis can be used to determine whether a low level of energy in the SNS is matched by a similarly low level of energy or vitality in the counterbalancing parasympathetic nervous system (PNS). Exhaustion of the PNS as well as the SNS/adrenals is more concerning than just SNS exhaustion, because it depletes our ability to make effort (SNS) and our ability to recover (PNS). The good news is that both can be improved, and we can restore our energy level to the one we had ten years ago.

CROCODILES AND WILDEBEESTS

One of the most poignant examples of the importance of HRV for energy levels and dynamism is seen when we compare mammals and reptiles, and their ability to respond to a threat or rise to a challenge. Reptiles, because they are cold-blooded, do not have much HRV. They can alter their heart rate, but they can't do it quickly. In comparison, all warm-blooded mammals, including humans, have a lot of heart rate variability and burn 5–10 times more energy than reptiles.[35] In fact, it is the high variability that makes mammals responsive and dynamic.

Imagine a situation where the world of mammals and reptiles collide – a watering hole in Africa. At the waterside is a warm-blooded wildebeest quenching its thirst. It's cautious because there are cold-blooded crocodiles in the water waiting for dinner. The wildebeest does, however, have a significant advantage – high HRV, which means that should a crocodile attack it can increase its heart rate very quickly, generate power and rapidly get out the way. A crocodile can also vary its heart rate, but not quickly. So, the crocodile only has one shot at its prey because it uses all its energy reserves making the initial attack and doesn't have the ability to change its heart rate quickly enough to chase the wildebeest.

Mammals have access to more energy because they have a much greater capacity to change their heart rate (HRV). Specifically, mammals can change their adrenaline levels (the accelerator hormone) and their acetylcholine levels (the brake hormone) more quickly than reptiles. This enables the wildebeest to rapidly mobilize the energy needed to escape a crocodile attack by releasing the brakes and applying the accelerator. Mammals can move from low energy to high energy repeatedly, but reptiles can't, because they don't have the HRV.

Think of it like a drag race. At the start of a race the driver has his feet on the accelerator and the brake. When the starting light turns green, he removes the brake and the car bursts forward as he applies the accelerator. In the same way that taking your foot off the brake in your car will make the car surge forward, the body can remove acetylcholine to achieve the same result. Luckily for the wildebeest and all other mammals, including us, the heart muscles metabolize acetylcholine much faster than adrenaline, and this can provide life-saving energy until adrenaline can kick in and provide a more sustained surge in energy. These hormonal brakes and accelerators are crucial to energy reserves and efficiency. How much energy we create is one thing; how appropriately we utilize that energy is something else.

HRV determines our ability to respond to the challenges life throws at us. This flexibility to adapt to our environment is part of what it means to be alive and dynamic. It is therefore possible to use the 'variability' of the heart's electrical signal to quantify the 'vitality' of the human system. HRV could be considered a way to measure 'aliveness'.

It is clearly imperative that leaders learn how to effectively manage their energy so that they can deal with the increasing demands of modern business and maintain their flexibility, yet most leaders never question why they are energetic one day and exhausted the next. Very few leaders know where their energy comes from, where it goes and why they feel utterly drained at the end of the week. Often the pressure is relentless, and unless we can harness our most critical resource it's impossible to sustain the kind of high-intensity effort that most leaders think is required to deliver results for very long.

The good news is that we can learn to increase our HRV, which will in turn improve our energy levels and effectively 'turn back time'. With tailored coaching, we've been able to demonstrate an average 30 per cent increase in all HRV parameters within six months for executives in multinational corporations.

HRV alters brain function

In addition to predicting death and ill health, quantifying biological age and defining energy levels (both amount and dynamism), HRV also influences brain function.[36]

HRV can have a profound influence on your ability to think clearly, and therefore plays a critical role in business. For example, it has been shown that resting HRV is linked to emotional sensitivity and the ability to map others' facial expressions.[37] In addition, HRV has been shown to increase when cognitive demands increase,[38] correlate with cognitive adaptability[39] and predict the ability to deliver results[40].

The skills described in this book integrate all this scientific research to enable leaders to manage their emotion, improve their HRV and step-change the quality of their cognitive performance. This is what ultimately makes them more commercially successful, regardless of market forces or external pressures. We'll describe these skills more in Chapter 4, 'Be smarter'.

How to be younger

In order to sustain performance at the very highest levels, it is necessary to balance intense effort with appropriate recuperation – it's simply not possible to keep going indefinitely. Ironically, most people accept the need for recovery time when it comes to sport, yet business executives are expected to keep going day after day, year after year. Clearly, business is different from sport, but learning how to manage our energy levels for maximum efficiency and recuperation can revolutionize performance in both business and sport. The first step toward consistently brilliant performance is developing physiological coherence, and that means mastering the physical skills of Exceptional Leadership.

In order to turn back time, have more energy and feel 10 years younger, we must become aware of and control our own physiological signals, especially our HRV. First, this is achieved through developing greater awareness of our physiological state, which is called 'interoception' in scientific circles. You can do this using the biofeedback module on our Complete app. The app is available from the App Store and Google Play. The Complete app enables you to see your HRV live in any meeting. It can help you improve your awareness of your physiology through the heartbeat detection task and the E-bank skill (see below). The energy bank (E-bank) skill can give you a much greater appreciation of what is currently boosting or draining your energy levels. Once you have cultivated a greater level of physical awareness, you can develop greater control of your physiology using the BREATHE skill (see below). You can then quantify the overall development of your physical intelligence (PQ) using the Complete app. Specifically, you can track the improvement in your physiological awareness using Dr Wolf Mehling's Multidimensional Assessment of Interoceptive Awareness (MAIA)[41] and the improvement in your physiological control by tracking the step change in your HRV parameters.

Boosting energy levels: the E-bank skill

The E-bank skill can help us to become more aware of where we are currently using our most important resource – our energy. This is achieved by tracking the events, situation and people that drain and boost our energy, and it can reveal areas of our life where we can make a significant difference, feel younger and preserve energy for only a small investment of time.

Take a moment to write down all the things, situations, events and people that increase your energy (deposits) and everything that robs you of energy (withdrawals). Don't worry about the timeframe or when these energy transactions occurred; just make a note of everything that positively or negatively impacts your energy account. Make sure you:

- re-live the deposits as you write them down;
- leave the withdrawals behind as you write them down.

The key benefit of this exercise is that it will give you awareness of your current energy levels and what affects those levels – either for better or for worse. Maybe you realize that the only energy boost or credit you've received in the last few days was the cuddle from your four-year-old daughter. Perhaps you realize just how debilitating your office manager, Marjorie, is to your energy levels.

Once you've created the lists, take a moment to really consider the insights that they present to you. Are there any conclusions that you can draw from these lists that will help you to better manage your energy levels? Can you spot any patterns in the timings, the people or the type of work that rob you of energy and vitality? Is there a common denominator between the experiences or events that add to your energy levels? If there are plenty of deposits and only a few withdrawals, perhaps the withdrawals are so significant that they cancel out the deposits. For example, a pending divorce can be a significant and consistent energy drain, and will not be easily alleviated by a good meeting with colleagues from work, even if you are not dealing with the divorce on a daily basis.

Go through the list and highlight the top three energy accumulators and the top three energy drains. Write down what action you can take to increase the accumulators and minimize the drains on your energy reserves.

Perhaps you realize that Marjorie is really wearing you down. Has she always been like that, or has the drain that flows from your interaction with her become more intense over the last couple of months? Maybe she's upset about the new database installation? If her negativity is related to a specific situation, do what you can to change the situation. If she just rubs you up the wrong way but is good at her job, change her reporting lines so she no longer reports to you. Find a way to either resolve her negativity or reduce your exposure to her so she does not rob you of energy. If you are struggling to come up with a solution, the SHIFT skill explored in Chapter 4 will also help.

Perhaps creating your E-bank allowed you to see a pattern? A director of a credit card company we worked with discovered a very toxic pattern when she documented her energy account in this way. What she discovered was that she was always thinking about the past. She wasted huge amounts of time and energy worrying about whether or not she made the correct decision and what she could or should have done differently. So much so that she didn't have any energy left for thinking about the present or the future. Reflection is an important quality for all senior executives and business leaders, but she needed to extract the lesson and move on quickly. Almost all ancient spiritual wisdom and some recent[42] reminds us that there is only one moment that really matters – right now. When we spend time in the past or the future, we rob ourselves of life.

When we interviewed Mike Iddon, the CFO of Pets at Home, about working with us he specifically mentioned the energy bank and how it helped him through a significant period of change:

> There are things in your life that make deposits and other things that make withdrawals. Over time, you need to ensure there are more deposits than withdrawals. It's a very helpful technique for thinking about your whole life, including work and home. Alan encouraged me to keep an energy bank account of my deposits and withdrawals. It drives me to do more things that lead to deposits. You beat yourself up over things that go wrong, but you rarely give yourself or your team credit when things go right. The E-bank helps to redress that, and it certainly helped me think differently.

When protecting your energy levels, watch out for self-criticism and self-judgement, as they are particularly powerful energy drains on your system. They act like direct debits going straight out of your account on a daily basis.

Also be aware that you can put deposits in other people's E-banks just with a simple act of kindness or an encouraging word. When you review your list of deposits, re-live the positives as you write them down; this can have the same effect as compound interest. Not only did you get a boost when that event happened but reflecting on it gives you a further boost when you write it in your E-bank.

Boosting energy levels: the BREATHE skill

One of the primary ways that we lose our energy is through incoherent or erratic breathing. In the same way that we use more fuel driving in the city than we do driving on the motorway, when our breathing is chaotic, we use up much more energy. Coherent breathing is like motorway driving – we travel further using less fuel, and there is less wear and tear on our system, so we not only feel younger but we also conserve energy and can actually restore the energy levels that we had when we were younger.

When we are reactive, we will, by default, have a chaotic and erratic HRV signal, in large part because our breathing is erratic. Our job is to create a coherent HRV signal so that we become dynamically responsive instead of reactive. This can be achieved by controlling our breathing in a very specific way. If we want to impact performance, we must stabilize our physiology. The quickest and easiest way to stabilize our physiology is to stabilize our breathing.

Just think about this for a moment… When you are surprised or shocked – what happens? When you get angry or upset – what happens? When you are relaxed – what happens? Your breathing is immediately and constantly affected by whatever is going on around you. In order to experience many negative emotional states, it is necessary to lose control of your breath. For example, 'panic' requires an individual to breathe in a rapid, erratic and shallow way. The first thing to 'go' in a difficult situation is our ability to breathe properly. As a result, what happens is that our breathing becomes chaotic, scrambling everything from how we feel to how we think, to what we do and ultimately our behaviour and our results.

Generating a rhythmic breathing pattern creates cardiac coherence. The rhythmic changes in intrathoracic pressure caused by rhythmic breathing cause the heart rate to vary in a dynamic stable way. As our cardiac physiology becomes coherent, the power output of the heart increases, and this drives other biological systems to synchronize with the heart, causing physiological 'entrainment'.

The easiest way to understand this is to imagine that the body is an orchestra. The heart is the string section of that orchestra. Within the string section there is a violin, viola, cello, double bass etc. This is the equivalent of the electrical signal, the electromagnetic, the chemical, the pressure waves, the heat waves and the sound waves. The electrical signal (HRV) that the heart generates is like the lead violin. Rhythmic breathing is our way of taking control of the biological equivalent of the lead violin. When we do that, the electrical signal the heart generates creates the equivalent of a harmonious note (Figure 2.4) instead of an erratic, chaotic 'white noise' signal (Figure 2.5). This strong coherent note from the heart in turn begins to entrain all the other physiological signals, which releases a lot more power. Cardiac coherence basically means a stable, rhythmic heart rate variation. This can occur at various frequencies – while beating quickly in a heightened state of awareness, say during a presentation or while beating more slowly as you sit at your desk. Both are easily visible when we measure our HRV.

FIGURE 2.4 'Coherence' seen in anabolic states

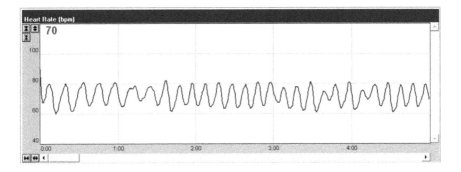

FIGURE 2.5 'Chaos' seen in catabolic states

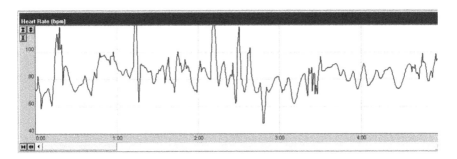

Because of entrainment, once we achieve cardiac coherence via our breathing it's much easier for the other members of the orchestra (lungs, kidneys, brain etc) to play their own coherent notes so that the whole system plays a series of coherent notes, which creates a more balanced and harmonious 'tune' and this physiological coherence facilitates 'emotional coherence'.

THE BREATHE SKILL

The conscious control of our breath is not a new concept; many disciplines such as public speaking, playing a musical instrument, sport, yoga, martial arts and meditation all teach people the importance of correct breathing. Although there are several aspects of our breathing that we can learn to control when it comes to facilitating coherence, only three matter:

1 Rhythmicity – a fixed ratio of in-breath to out breath.

2 Smoothness – a fixed flow rate per second on both in and out breath.

3 Location of attention – where is our attention when we are breathing?

The single most important priority is rhythm. First, we need to make our breathing rhythmic so that there is a fixed ratio between the in-breath and the out-breath. For example, you may decide to breathe in for the count of four seconds and breathe out for the count of six seconds. All that matters is that whatever ratio you choose you maintain that ratio consistently – three in three out, or four in six out, or five in five out.

There is a great deal of inherent power in rhythm – a fact not lost on sports like rowing, which is all about rhythm. I had the good fortune to work directly with the GB rowing squad going into the 2012 London Olympics and again in the 2016 Rio Olympics. Three months before the London Olympics Dr Ann Redgrave, the GB squad's medical advisor, asked me to talk to all the squad coaches to explain what else was needed to win a medal above and beyond what they were already doing. As Ann explains:

> When rowers go out to race, they leave the coaches and the support team at
> the landing stage around 30 to 40 minutes before the race. They go through
> a prepared warm-up routine and then they are required to sit on the start line
> for up to five minutes. Once they're on the start line what happens – self-doubt
> can creep in. I know because it happened to me when I was competing. You
> sit there, you find yourself wondering what you're doing there! It's the last
> place you want to be. It's exciting but also a bit frightening. Crazy thoughts

go through your head. Over the last few years, I've noticed this having a detrimental effect on the performance of our rowers as they leave the start line. What was needed was something to focus the attention and emotions of the rowers at the very time when they needed to do the job they had trained years for. Alan provided that.

After the initial presentation I worked closely with eight coaches and crews in the run-up to the Games. The first thing I taught them was the importance of the BREATHE skill. For them it was particularly helpful when they were waiting nervously before the start of the race and for some rowers it made a massive difference. Of the eight crews I worked with in 2012 six of them won medals (three gold, two silvers and a bronze), and of the seven crews I didn't work with only three medalled.

If someone learns to row, once they are in the boat, the cox shouts 'in–out–in–out', to help them establish a rhythm. If one person is trying to put the blades in the water when someone else is taking them out, the boat won't move very well. The first step toward coherent breathing is also rhythm.

Once you have established rhythmic breathing the second step is to create a smooth breath. It's is possible to breathe rhythmically but in a staccato 'jumpy' fashion. Coherence requires a smooth rhythm. This means we need to ensure a fixed volume of air is going in and out of our lungs per second.

Again, smoothness is also critical in rowing. Once the team has been taught to get the oars in the water at the same time in a rhythmic stroke, they must row smoothly through the water. If they put their blades in the water and pull really hard then let the oars drift a bit and then pull really hard again, the boat will spurt forward and then stop. What's needed is a smooth consistent stroke all the way through.

If you watch the GB rowers, you can see that they use the same amount of power at the start of the stroke as they do at the end of the stroke. It's the same in cycling. An amateur cyclist will kick off with a really big push and rely on momentum to bring the pedal back around so they can push down again and repeat. If you were to watch a professional such as Chris Froome, there is a smooth, consistent effort all the way round the cycle, even when they are lifting their foot up. And that generates a massive amount of force, pulling them away from less able cyclists.

And finally, the third important aspect of our breathing is our location of attention while we are breathing. We suggest rather than abdominal breathing it's important to focus on our heart or the centre of our chest. We say this for three reasons:

1 The heart is the main power station in the human system and generates considerably more energy than any other human organ or system.

2 When we feel most chaotic and our breathing and mind are scrambled, there is usually a great deal of 'noise' in our head as we wrestle to regain control. The very act of moving our attention away from all the noise and dropping it into our body is beneficial. By consciously moving our focus away from our head and into our body, we facilitate faster coherence.

3 When we focus on our heart or the middle of our chest, we are more likely to experience a positive emotional state because the heart is where most human beings experience their positive emotion. We say 'I love you with all my heart'; we don't say 'I love you with all my amygdala' or 'all my knee'. I don't love my sons with 'my anterior cingulate cortex' even though that's probably where the information registers. We feel the sensation of love in the centre of our chest. Thus, when someone has a positive emotional experience it's usually felt in the centre of the chest, so consciously shifting our attention to that area can facilitate positive emotion, which in turn moves us to the positive side of the Universe of Emotions. Figure 2.6 demonstrates the impact of rhythmic and smooth, heart-focused breathing by getting us to the midpoint of the universe. Ultimately the only way to get over to the left, positive side and stay there is by engaging positive emotions (which is the topic of the next chapter), but breathing creates the platform on which everything else – health, happiness, cognitive ability and elevated performance, success and influence – is built.

FIGURE 2.6   The impact of correct breathing

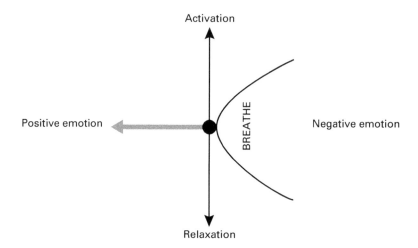

When we breathe rhythmically and smoothly, we create a coherent HRV signal. This then stabilizes our physiology and creates cardiac coherence – turning our HRV pattern from chaos to coherence, as illustrated in Figures 2.4 and 2.5. This allows us to maintain our self-control in highly charged situations, prevents our brain from shutting down and enables us to think clearly and become more perceptive. Plus, it gives us a better chance to change the way we feel, and prevents the unconscious expenditure of our most precious energy reserves.

The easiest way to remember this breathing technique is through the BREATHE acronym:

Breathe

Rhythmically

Evenly

And

Through the

Heart

Every day

If you control your breathing, you are in charge of your physiology. Events, situations and other people won't be able to scramble your thinking and make you reactive, which can often be disastrous for business. Michael Drake, the CEO of Cognita and previous MD of TNT Express for Asia Pacific, explains how he uses the BREATHE skill all the time to improve performance:

> I use the coherent BREATHE technique I've learnt on a regular basis, even outside of work. I play golf and I will do the rhythmic breathing a lot. It gets my heart rate to a level that will provide clarity of thought and help execution. It's the same before a big speech. I think about my breathing and what I'm going to do. I get my heart under control. Just the notion of taking two minutes to think about how I am feeling is beneficial... it builds confidence, and for whatever reason, I see the results in my performance. I feel calmer, more confident and focused, and all those things can only be beneficial in terms of performance.

THE COMPLETE APP

The Complete app is a health and well-being app with some biofeedback software embedded. Using a Kyto sensor that clips on the ear and a Polar chest strap or a Mio wrist strap that sends a Bluetooth signal to the app, you can see what is happening to your heart rate variability. The Complete app has a programmable breath pacer that you can follow to enable you to shift your heart rate from a chaotic signal into a coherent signal. These devices are designed to help you train your breathing pattern to generate greater levels of coherence and they are especially useful at the start of your leadership journey because they provide a visual guide to what your heart is doing right now.

The Complete app also allows you to experience just how much control you have over your heartbeat and how different it can feel when you achieve coherence.

Although we've been measuring HRV since 1996 it never ceases to amaze me how dramatic this information can be for executives. I've literally seen grown men cry when they realize that they can control their own response to stress and pressure. And they can see and feel the immediate effect rhythmic breathing can have on their system and how easy it is to generate coherence when they know how to do it. Suddenly, they have access to a skill that can change something they didn't think they could change.

HIERARCHY OF PRACTICE

The starting point for getting your system under control is to get your breathing under control. Don't underestimate its power or how quickly the skill can desert you when you need it most. It is important therefore to practise the BREATHE skill. You need to gradually build up your ability to create and maintain physiological coherence in increasingly difficult situations.

Start by practising alone with your eyes closed and work up the hierarchy of practice (Figure 2.7) until you can use the technique successfully in open conflict.

FIGURE 2.7   The hierarchy of breathing practice

10	Open conflict
9	Someone is really annoying you
8	Someone is annoying you
7	Someone is niggling you
6	You are talking back
5	You are listening
4	Someone is talking to you
3	In company eyes open
2	Alone eyes open
1	Alone eyes closed

Using the Complete app, you should be able to generate a coherent pattern within a couple of minutes. We have used this with children as young as three years old and people as old as 80 years with equal success. People often ask: how much should I practise? My answer is that you cannot over-dose on rhythmic breathing but do not obsess about it because the obsession will make your breathing chaotic again! Instead, simply practise whenever you remember. Use any down time you have, such as waiting for a meeting to start or when travelling. If you find just 10 minutes a day to practise this BREATHE skill, soon rhythmic breathing and physiological coherence will become your default pattern. When it does, you will discover that you are much less reactive than you were before. And you'll have much more energy. Plus, once you have your breathing under control you can start to develop your emotional coherence and get the whole orchestra playing in tune.

Physiological coherence facilitates emotional coherence

The reason many of our coaching programmes focus on physiology in the first 'season' of sessions is very simple – if we don't have enough energy it won't matter how good our strategy is, or how innovative our 'go to market' plan is; they won't be deliverable because we'll run out of steam. If we can recover the energy levels we enjoyed 10 years ago then we have more of a chance! When we manage our energy levels well, it's possible for us to end the day with as much energy as we had when we started the day and improve our performance as a result. But in order to unlock our potential we must first stabilize our physiology, and that is primarily achieved through rhyth-mic breathing and paying attention to what adds to and drains our energy reserves.

At Complete we work with some of the top CEOs and senior executives in the world. We measure their raw energy and energy efficiency using our Complete Energy Audit (CEA), which consists of a 72-hour analysis of their HRV plus an online assessment of emotional and social intelligence. This type of profiling is very powerful in generating highly specific insights into leadership and performance. The HRV assessment quantifies how much energy a business leader has in their tank and how efficiently they are using the fuel they have.

The other reason we start most coaching programmes by assessing phys-iology is that there are countless conversations it's possible to have with a leader but it is necessary to identify which ones would deliver the greatest benefit. The physiological profiling helps us to identify the specific conversations to have with each leader, so they get the biggest wins in the quickest time. Certainly, when energy is flagged as an issue, the executives we work with experience an average improvement of 25–30 per cent within just six months. Considering we lose 3 per cent per year from 25 years old onward, that is equivalent to giving these leaders the energy levels they had 8–10 years ago!

By increasing our physical intelligence, we move vertically up the first line of adult development. Physiological coherence is the platform on which health, happiness, smart thinking, improved performance, better relationships and greater influence is built. Learning to be aware of our energy reserves and how to breathe properly to protect them, harness them and recuperate our energy is therefore the critical first step to becoming an exceptional leader. Physiological coherence facilitates emotional coherence, which we will explore next.

Summary of key points

If you don't remember everything in this chapter, remember this:

- Energy management is much more important than time management.
- Energy is created automatically in the body, mainly by the heart, which is the body's primary power station.
- As part of Complete's unique approach to leadership and executive development we have been quantifying the energy levels of leaders and executives in many market sectors since 1996.
- The best way to ascertain how much 'fuel' someone has in their tank and how efficiently they are using that fuel is to measure their heart rate variability (HRV) over the course of 72 hours.
- This HRV assessment, which measures the distance between each heartbeat, not the beat itself, allows us to pinpoint critical areas of business

performance and productivity such as endurance, motivation, recuperation, effort, balance, optimism and vitality.

- HRV is an incredibly insightful metric, which can quantify the risk of death and illness, biological age, quantify energy levels and dynamism and illuminate brain function.

- It is possible to improve HRV and create cardiac coherence through the simple BREATHE technique.

- When we train our heart using this rhythmic breathing technique, we generate a coherent signal instead of a chaotic one, which in turn increases energy levels, reduces energy wastage, improves health and enhances brain function.

- Coherent breathing is like motorway driving – we travel further, using less fuel, and there is less wear and tear on our system, so we turn the clock back to gain the energy levels we had 10 years ago and feel much younger.

Notes

1   Hoomans, J (2015) 35,000 Decisions: The great choices of strategic leaders, The Leading Edge, https://go.roberts.edu/leadingedge/the-great-choices-of-strategic-leaders (archived at https://perma.cc/B6WY-76AT)

2   Kegan, R and Lahey, L (2009) *Immunity to Change: How to overcome it and unlock the potential in yourself and your organisation*, Harvard Business School Press Boston, MA

3   Lanaj, K, Foulk, T A and Erez A (2019) Energizing leaders via self-reflection: A within-person field experiment, *Journal of Applied Psychology*, 104 (1), pp 1–18

4   Laborde, S, Mosley, E and Thayer J F (2017) Heart rate variability and cardiac vagal tone in psychophysiological research: Recommendations for experiment planning, data analysis, and data reporting, *Frontiers in Psychology*, 8, p 213

5   Wulsin, L R, Horn, P S, Perry, J L, Massaro, J M and D'Agostino, R B (2015) Autonomic imbalance as a predictor of metabolic risks, cardiovascular disease, diabetes, and mortality, *The Journal of Clinical Endocrinology and Metabolism*, 100 (6), pp 2443–48

6   Shaffer, F and Ginsberg, J P (2017) An overview of heart rate variability metrics and norms, *Frontiers in Public Health*, 5, p 258

7   Thayer, J F, Hansen, A L, Saus-Rose, E and Johnsen, B H (2009) Heart rate
    variability, prefrontal neural function, and cognitive performance: The
    neurovisceral integration perspective on self-regulation, adaptation, and
    health, *Annals of Behavioral Medicine*, 37(2), pp 141–53; Park, G and Thayer,
    J F (2014) From the heart to the mind: cardiac vagal tone modulates top-down
    and bottom-up visual perception and attention to emotional stimuli, *Frontiers
    in Psychology*, 5 (May), pp 1–8; Roelofs, K (2017) Freeze for action:
    Neurobiological mechanisms in animal and human freezing, *Philosophical
    Transactions of the Royal Society B: Biological Sciences*, 372 (1718),
    20160206; Mather, M and Thayer, J F (2018) How heart rate variability
    affects emotion regulation brain networks, *Current Opinion in Behavioral
    Sciences*, 19, pp 98–104; Ottaviani, C (2018) Brain–heart interaction in
    perseverative cognition, *Psychophysiology*, 55 (7)

8   Critchley, H D, Mathias, C J and Dolan, R J (2001) Neuroanatomical basis for
    first- and second-order representations of bodily states, *Nature Neuroscience*,
    4 (2), pp 207–12; Critchley, H D (2005) Neural mechanisms of autonomic,
    affective, and cognitive integration, *Journal of Comparative Neurology*, 493
    (1), pp 154–66; Jerath, R, Barnes, V A and Crawford, M W (2014) Mind-body
    response and neurophysiological changes during stress and meditation:
    Central role of homeostasis, *Journal of Biological Regulators and Homeostatic
    Agents*, 28, pp 545–54; Owens, B P, Baker, W E, Sumpter, D M and Cameron,
    K S (2016) Relational energy at work: Implications for job engagement and
    job performance, *Journal of Applied Psychology*, 101 (1), pp 35–49

9   Lo, E V, Wei, Y H and Hwang, B F (2020) Association between occupational
    burnout and heart rate variability: A pilot study in a high-tech company in
    Taiwan, *Medicine (Baltimore)*, Jan, 99 (2)

10 Wolf, M M, Varigos, G A, Hunt, D and Sloman, J G (1978) Sinus arrhythmia
    in acute myocardial infarction, *Medical Journal of Australia*, 2 (2), pp 52–3

11 Sessa, F, Anna, V *et al* (2017) Heart rate variability as predictive factor for
    sudden cardiac death, *Aging (Albany NY)*, 210 (2), pp 166–77

12 Dekker, J M, Schouten, E G, Klootwijk, P, Pool, J, Swenne, C A and Kromhout,
    D (1997) Heart rate variability from short electrocardiographic recordings
    predicts mortality from all causes in middle-aged and elderly men: The
    Zutphen study, *American Journal of Epidemiology*, 145 (10), pp 899–908

13 Mayor, D F and Micozzi, M S (eds) (2011) *Energy Medicine East and West: A
    natural history of Qi*, Churchill Livingstone Elsevier, London

14 Gerritsen, J, Dekker, J M, TenVoorde, B J, Kostense, P J, Heine, R J, Bouter, L
    M, Heethaar, R M and Stehouwer, C D (2001) Impaired autonomic function is
    associated with increased mortality, especially in subjects with diabetes,
    hypertension, or a history of cardiovascular disease: The Hoorn Study,
    Diabetes Care, 24 (10), pp 1793–98

15 Hernández-Vicente, A, Hernando, D, Santos-Lozano, A, Rodríguez-Romo, G, Vicente-Rodríguez, G, Pueyo, E, Bailón, R and Garatachea, N (2020) Heart rate variability and exceptional longevity, *Frontiers in Physiology*, 17 Sep, 11, 566399

16 Benson, K (2015) Supporting employees after the sudden death of a CEO, *Industry Week*

17 Inoue, K and Hashioka, S (2019) The risk of overwork death (karoshi) in the wake of natural disasters, *BMJ Opinion*

18 Pfeffer, J (2018) *Dying for a Paycheck*, HarperBusiness, New York

19 Virtanen, M, Ferrie, J E, Singh-Manoux, A, Shipley, M J, Vahtera, J, Marmot, M G and Kivimäki, M (2010) Overtime work and incident coronary heart disease: The Whitehall II prospective cohort study, *European Heart Journal*, Jul, 31 (14), pp 1737–44

20 Davis, M F and Green, J (2020) Three hours longer, the pandemic workday has obliterated work–life balance, Bloomberg Business, www.bloomberg.com/news/articles/2020-04-23/working-from-home-in-covid-era-means-three-more-hours-on-the-job (archived at https://perma.cc/7C8N-H4SW)

21 Greenwood, K, Bapet, V and Maughan, M (2019) Research: People want their employers to talk about mental health, *Harvard Business Review*, https://hbr.org/2019/10/research-people-want-their-employers-to-talk-about-mental-health (archived at https://perma.cc/YY6F-U3ZJ)

22 Slager, S (2019) Burnout and the gig economy: What employers need to know, HR Technologist, www.hrtechnologist.com/articles/employee-engagement/burnout-and-the-gig-economy-what-employers-need-to-know (archived at https://perma.cc/8NZZ-U8GR)

23 Seamark, M (2011) Lloyds boss goes sick with 'stress': Shock departure eight months into job, *Daily Mail*

24 Umetani, K, Singer, D H, McCraty, R and Atkinson, M (1998) Twenty-four hour time domain heart rate variability and heart rate: Relations to age and gender over nine decades, *Journal of the American College of Cardiology*, 31 (3), pp 593–601

25 de Zambotti, M, Javitz, H, Franzen, P L, Brumback, T, Clark, D B, Colrain, I M and Baker, F C (2018) Sex- and age-dependent differences in autonomic nervous system functioning in adolescents, *Journal of Adolescent Health*, Feb, 62 (2), pp 184–90

26 Choi, J, Cha, W and Park, M G (2020) Declining trends of heart rate variability according to aging in healthy Asian adults, *Frontiers in Aging Neuroscience*, Nov, 26 (12), 610626

27 Wekenborg, M K, Hill, L K, Thayer, J F, Penz, M, Wittling, R A and Kirschbaum, C (2019) The longitudinal association of reduced vagal tone with burnout, *Psychosomatic Medicine*, Nov/Dec, 81 (9), pp 791–98

28 Olenski, A R, Abola, M V and Jena, A B (2015) Do heads of government age more quickly? Observational study comparing mortality between elected leaders and runners-up in national elections of 17 countries, *BMJ*, Dec, 14 (351), h6424

29 Dominguez, T (2016) Do presidents age faster than the rest of us? YouTube, www.youtube.com/watch?v=IH3d-qR25v4 (archived at https://perma.cc/P7DP-2GU3)

30 Watkins, A D (2011) The electrical heart: Energy in cardiac health and disease, in *Energy Medicine East and West: A natural history of Qi*, ed D F Mayor and M S Micozzi, Churchill Livingstone Elsevier, London

31 Lo, E V, Wei, Y H and Hwang, B F (2020) Association between occupational burnout and heart rate variability: A pilot study in a high-tech company in Taiwan, *Medicine (Baltimore)*, Jan, 99 (2), e18630

32 Boneva, R S, Decker, M J, Maloney, E M, Lin, J M, Jones, J F, Helgason, H G, Heim, C M, Rye, D B and Reeves, W C (2007) Higher heart rate and reduced heart rate variability persist during sleep in chronic fatigue syndrome: A population-based study, *Autonomic Neuroscience: Basic and clinical*, 137 (1–2), pp 94–101

33 Okawa, N, Kuratsune, D, Koizumi, J, Mizuno, K, Kataoka, Y and Kuratsune, H (2019) Application of autonomic nervous function evaluation to job stress screening, *Heliyon*, Feb, 5 (2)

34 Robinson, L J, Gallagher, P, Watson, S, Pearce, R, Finkelmeyer, A, Maclachlan, L and Newton J L (2019) Impairments in cognitive performance in chronic fatigue syndrome are common, not related to co-morbid depression but do associate with autonomic dysfunction, *PLoS One*, Feb, 14 (2)

35 Coates, J (2013) *The Hour Between Dog and Wolf: Risk taking, gut feelings and the biology of boom and bust*, Fourth Estate, London

36 Tonhajzerova, I, Mestanik, M, Mestanikova, A and Jurko, A (2016) Respiratory sinus arrhythmia as a non-invasive index of 'brain-heart' interaction in stress, *Indian Journal of Medical Research*, Dec, 144 (6), pp 815–22; Blons, E, Arsac, L M, Gilfriche, P, McLeod, H, Lespinet-Najib, V, Grivel, E and Deschodt-Arsac, V (2019) Alterations in heart–brain interactions under mild stress during a cognitive task are reflected in entropy of heart rate dynamics, *Scientific Reports*, Dec, 9 (1), 18190

37 Miller, J G, Xia, G and Hastings, P D (2019) Resting heart rate variability is negatively associated with mirror neuron and limbic response to emotional faces, *Biological Psychology*, Sep, 146, 107717

38 Fuentes-García, J P, Villafaina, S, Collado-Mateo, D, de la Vega, R, Olivares, P R and Clemente-Suárez, V J (2019) Differences between high vs low performance chess players in heart rate variability during chess problems, *Frontiers in Psychology*, Feb, 10, 409

39 Lin, F V, Tao, Y, Chen, Q, Anthony, M, Zhang, Z, Tadin, D and Heffner, K L (2020) Processing speed and attention training modifies autonomic flexibility: A mechanistic intervention study, *Neuroimage*, Jun, 213, 116730

40 Wei, L, Chen, H and Wu, G R (2018) Structural covariance of the prefrontal-amygdala pathways associated with heart rate variability, *Frontiers in Human Neuroscience*, Jan, 12, 2

41 Mehling, W E, Acree, M, Stewart, A, Silas, J and Jones, A (2018) The multidimensional assessment of interoceptive awareness, version 2 (MAIA-2), *PLOS One*, 4 December

42 Tolle, E (2005) *The Power of Now*, Hodder & Stoughton, London

03

Be healthier and happier

Do you find it weird that health and happiness is even being discussed in a leadership book? Perhaps you never think about your own physical well-being unless you are feeling ill or especially run down? Even if you are aware of your health, do you struggle to find the time, energy or motivation to do anything about it? Has your weight crept up over the years? Do you hear stories of CEO collapse, exhaustion and heart attacks, thinking it will never happen to you? Do you still enjoy your work or is it just a grind? Is the big salary really worth the pain? Do you even have time to enjoy that salary? Do you ever wake up in the middle of the night worrying about work and unable to get back to sleep? Do you feel permanently under pressure, undervalued and stressed but simply accept it as the price you have to pay for your position? If so, you're not alone.

In business, two things happen when it comes to health and well-being – either we completely ignore it, assuming it's irrelevant to business success and performance, or we know it's important but don't have the time or inclination to do anything significant about it.

The result is, however, often the same. António Horta-Osório, the new Chairman of Credit Suisse and the ex-CEO Lloyds Banking Group is not the only senior leader forced to step down, albeit temporarily, on health grounds.[1] The founder of JD Wetherspoon, Tim Martin, took a sudden six-month sabbatical before returning to the pub chain as non-executive chairman, working three days a week. Former Barclays Chief Executive John Varley left Barclays for one year because he was 'feeling quite worn out' and 'needed to do something different', and Jeff Kindler of Pfizer resigned as Chief Executive of the US pharmaceutical giant to 'recharge [his] batteries'.[2] C-suite burnout is now such a common phenomenon it has become an area or academic study with over 6,000 books, chapters and articles on the subject.[3]

Apart from the health, social and emotional cost to the individual, this can also be extremely detrimental to the business. If a key member of the team dies or needs to take time off to recuperate following a serious illness, clearly there are succession issues, and the loss will be felt by the team, and financially via the company's share price, its ability to raise capital and its balance sheet. Conversely, when individuals at any level are healthy and happy at work, they are much more likely to unlock discretionary effort that can significantly impact results.

If we are not paying attention to our health, we are almost certainly eroding it. We may all think we know what to do to improve our health, but it never seems quite enough to push us into consistent action. Instead, our lives are characterized by coffee-fuelled mornings and boozy evenings. Often, we don't even want to speak to anyone until we've had our double espresso or macchiato hit. And at the end of the day, we choose to unwind with a glass of whisky or a stiff gin and tonic. A few years ago, it was 'just the one' but these days it's always two and sometimes more.

We still dream of our two weeks in the sun – if only to put the guilt on hold and convince ourselves that we'll get serious about the changes we know we need to make when we get home. Only, the changes we need to make never happen. Life just keeps getting in the way. Besides, happiness has no real place in modern business – right? And yet how we feel on a daily basis is not just some touchy-feely idea; it is probably one of the most important factors that determine our most prized asset – our health.

So, if we want to improve our health and happiness, despite punishing schedules and immense pressure, how do we actually do that? There are three 'Big Es' that we need to attend to. Most of us know two of them and ignore the third. Thus, we understand the importance of what we eat (first 'E') and having a balanced diet. We also understand the importance of regular exercise (second 'E') in relation to health. But the third 'E' – emotion – is almost completely ignored, despite being, potentially, the most important.

The reason emotion is so crucial is because if we exercise at all, it's usually only a couple of times a week. If we eat it's a couple of times a day. However, our emotions are affecting us every single second of every single day. They also largely determine whether we can be bothered to exercise, and what, when and how much we eat. As psychiatrist and pioneer in the field of psychosomatic medicine Dr Franz Alexander said, 'Many chronic disturbances are not caused by external, mechanical, chemical factors, or by microorganisms, but by the continual functional stress arising from the everyday life of the organism in its struggle for existence'.[4]

Despite considerable scientific research documenting the connection between health and emotions, few business leaders take it seriously. If it's not immediately dismissed as 'new age' fiction, the 'health piece' is delegated to their chief medical officer or their occupational health department. Some businesses may seek to 'tick the health box' by installing a gym or pool, and occasionally physiotherapists or gym instructors are employed, but the health and fitness of leaders and employees are largely seen as a private matter of individual choice.

Health and happiness are simply not considered commercially relevant. This is a mistake. Why? Because there is now an overwhelming amount of scientific data showing that mismanaged emotion is the 'superhighway' to disease and distress. Your emotions not only determine whether you are likely to become ill, but they also determine your resilience and your ability to recover from a setback, whether that setback is physical or professional. Obviously if someone is ill, whether that is physically or mentally unwell, they won't perform at their best. Health is not an organizational nicety; it is a commercial imperative.

Health: the facts and the fiction

Most executives see health and happiness as a matter of personal choice or a conversation between them and their doctor. But are doctors the right people to turn to for guidance on health and happiness? As a medical doctor myself, I can assure you that doctors are not trained in illness prevention or happiness; they are trained to treat illness and disease once it has become well established. If we want to be healthy and happy well into old age, we need to appreciate how medical thinking has changed over the years so we can separate the facts from the fiction.

Up until the mid-1940s there was little in the way of effective medicine. If someone got toothache, pneumonia, meningitis or an STD, they probably died from it because there were no antibiotics. As a result, the biggest killer of both men and women was infectious disease. Although Alexander Fleming discovered penicillin in 1928, it wasn't purified and used as a mass-produced antibiotic until 1944 – during the Second World War. Antibiotics were phenomenally successful, and most of what was killing us prematurely was eradicated almost overnight. The philosophy of 'the magic bullet' was born, and scientific medicine started to hunt for single treatments that could erad-icate complex multi-factorial diseases.[5]

For the first time in history, we believed that we finally had the upper hand over disease, and the 'magic bullet' approach changed the nature of medical thinking. If we could discover a pill that could cure all these infec-tious diseases, surely it was just a matter of time before we found a magic bullet for the other big killers such as heart disease and cancer. Health researchers moved, en masse, to find those magic bullets. Initially attention turned to heart disease, which, following the advent of readily available penicillin, had been promoted from the number two killer to the number one killer – a position it's maintained ever since.[6] In the developed world today, at least a third of all premature deaths, male and female, are caused by cardiovascular disease, which includes heart disease, hypertension and stroke.[7] Traditionally, women are often more concerned with breast cancer, but heart disease kills twice as many women as breast cancer.[8]

The first sign of heart disease in 50 per cent of men is death.[9] This stark statistic says much about men's inability to notice an imminent disaster. Most men press on, unaware of the impending doom. Doctors themselves are not necessarily any better at spotting the warning signs because they've been trained to spot symptoms, not warning signs. Traditional medical teaching rarely focuses on the anticipation of a crisis. Rather, it tends to wait until the crisis has occurred and attempt heroic intervention. Consequently, those who suffer a heart attack often say, mistakenly, their heart attack 'came out of the blue'. Often, their physician may say the same thing. Illness rarely arrives out the blue – most medical conditions have been brewing for months if not years. The problem is, we just don't see the signs or heed the signals.

In an attempt to change this, and hopefully reduce mortality rates, in the 1940s the US government, specifically US health policy-makers, joined forces with the medical community to solve the mystery of heart disease by conducting a long-term research project into the causes of heart disease in an 'average' American. To do this, they needed to identify 'anytown USA' that was representative of the US population.[10] The town they chose was Framingham.

Heart disease: the Framingham Heart Study

At the time, Framingham was a small, beautiful, leafy town of 28,000 work-ing people, 20 miles from Boston. It was extremely stable socially – if someone was born in Framingham they usually lived and died there, too.

This was essential for the research, because the study was going to monitor the health of 5,209 volunteers every two years for the next 50 years! It would have been extremely difficult to conduct this research if the subjects moved away and were scattered across America. In 1948 a small army of medical scientists descended on the town, and research data into the causes of heart disease has been pouring out of the Framingham Heart Study ever since. The longevity of the study and the depth of the data collected means that the findings at Framingham have influenced medical thinking in this area more than anything else – by far.

But, as it turns out, Framingham was not 'anytown USA'. Because the researchers didn't know what they were looking for or what they would find, it didn't occur to them that Framingham wasn't actually representative of America. It was a small, mostly white, mostly middle-class town that enjoyed almost total employment. There was very little poverty; the divorce rate of 2 per cent was considerably lower than the national average at the time of 10 per cent. It was also incredibly socially cohesive – everyone knew everyone else in the town and there was strong social support. Framingham was – socially at least – nothing like inner city Detroit, Las Vegas or New York. And, frankly, even if the researchers had realized this fact, there was absolutely no evidence to suggest these issues had any bearing on heart disease.

Ironically, the researchers had chosen a town that just happened to be naturally insulated from heart disease in the first place. As a result, the causes of heart disease in Framingham were never going to be the same as the causes of heart disease in just about any other large town or city in America. The researchers had inadvertently discounted a vast array of contributing factors that have struggled to become recognized as contributing factors ever since. Issues such as poverty,[11] social inequality,[12] low educational attainment,[13] stress,[14] social isolation, depression,[15] anxiety[16] and hostility[17] are now known to be highly predictive of heart disease. The hostility demonstrated on Twitter, for example, predicts heart disease mortality! These factors didn't really exist in Framingham and hostile social media feeds certainly didn't, so the researchers didn't consider them as contributing factors.

It follows, therefore, that if many of the real driving forces for heart disease were not even looked for in the research group, what was left was the 'other', possibly less important, contributing factors for heart disease – high blood pressure, cholesterol, age, diabetes, smoking, obesity/lack of exercise, other medical conditions and family history. And it is these other 'causes' that have since been written into medical law as the 'traditional risk factors' for heart disease. The truth, however, is that over half of all the incidence of heart disease can't be explained by the standard physical risk factors.[18] Doctors all over the world are scratching their heads because people are dying of heart disease every day even though they exhibit none of the traditional risk factors. The real reason they are dying is, largely, because of mismanaged emotions such as depression, anxiety, anger, hostility and cynicism brought on by poverty, social inequality, low educational attainment, stress and social isolation. Some of the confusion arises because these factors may then increase the risk of traditional factors such as high blood pressure, obesity, diabetes and high cholesterol.

It wasn't that Framingham was some utopian nirvana where nothing went wrong and everyone was happy, it was just that when the inevitable knocks and bumps of life occurred the inhabitants of Framingham had strong social networks to help them through. Those types of networks are not always present in large, transient cities and these real risk factors are hugely important. Ironically, Framingham inadvertently demonstrated the antidote for heart disease – healthy emotional management that is manifest through strong social bonds and social cohesion.[19] Don't get me wrong, the traditional risk factors are important, but we must urgently reconsider the social, educational, interpersonal or physiological factors that were almost entirely absent from Framingham if we are serious about preventing heart disease.

To raise awareness of these critical but largely ignored causes of heart disease, Dr James Lynch went back and re-analysed all the data from Framingham. What he discovered was that when those original 5,209 volunteers aged between 30 and 62 were initially interviewed, the only information that was gathered was medical – height, weight, blood pressure and a host of other physical factors. The researchers neglected to record any social, educational, interpersonal or physiological data at all, and yet those are the things that probably account for most of the 'inexplicable' cases of heart disease where no risk factors are present.

Whilst the Framingham Heart Study has produced incredible insights into heart disease, it has also inadvertently caused the general public and medical professionals the world over to minimize or ignore one of the most important risk factors in heart disease – mismanaged emotions.

Depression

Everyone knows that smoking is bad for you, and we are rightly bombarded with adverts telling us to stop smoking. Everyone also knows that they should stop smoking if they have suffered a heart attack. People are twice as likely to be dead within a year of their heart attack if they smoke. What is less well known, however, is that if a person is depressed after their heart attack, they are four times as likely to be dead within one year.[20] But we don't see adverts telling us to 'Cheer up! Stop being so miserable – it's killing you!'

Some doctors, aware of the significant link between depression and heart attack, have sought to treat heart attack patients with antidepressants.[21] Whilst sensible and often brave, this hasn't always worked because the current treatment options of cognitive behavioural therapy (CBT) or drugs only make a difference to some patients.[22] As a result, the medical profession has often wrongly concluded that depression is not a big deal when it comes to heart disease. It is just that the current treatments don't address the root cause of depression, which is mismanaged emotions.

Mismanaged emotions such as worry, loneliness, anxiety and depression are seriously toxic. The Harvard School of Public Health conducted a 20-year study on the effects of worry on 1,750 men. Researchers found that worrying about typical issues such as social conditions, health and personal finances – something most of us are familiar with – all significantly increased the risk of developing coronary heart disease.[23] Hopelessness in middle-aged men is as detrimental to cardiovascular health as smoking a pack of cigarettes a day.[24] Anxiety, loneliness and panic have also been associated with either increased risk of cardiovascular disease[25] or diminished heart rate variability (HRV), which is a potent predictor for heart disease[26] and sudden cardiac death, as well as 'all-cause mortality'.[27]

But these negative emotions are not just toxic for our physical health; they are having a considerable impact on our ability to be happy, content and fulfilled. Anxiety, loneliness, worry, panic and even many cases of depression are caused primarily by our inability to regulate our own emotions. Individuals who become stuck in these emotional states for too long may start to identify with these states. We often hear people say 'I am depressed' or 'I am anxious'. Whereas they are merely stuck in a state of depression or anxiety – it is not who they are. This inability to effectively manage our emotions is a developmental problem and we should stop medicalizing it and making it a disease.

The real problem is that, collectively, we have not been taught about emotion, how to differentiate between various emotions and how to manage them effectively. As children, when we were upset many of us were told to calm down, 'get a grip' or stop crying. Even if we were bursting with excitement or some other positive emotion, we may have been told to calm down! We were never taught how to distinguish between anger and annoyance, or anger and frustration, or boredom and apathy. And even if we could tell the difference, we were almost certainly not taught how to manage those emotions, take appropriate action or change the emotion.

As a result, most people believe that emotion is something to be avoided or hidden. It's as though emotion is considered part of our childhood that must be shed like a beloved comfort blanket or favourite toy as part of the inevitable metamorphosis from emotional child to fully functioning non-emotional adult. We learn to ignore and suppress emotion and proceed into adulthood with a degree of emotional literacy that can differentiate between 'feeling good' and 'feeling bad' but little else. For many people, all our negative emotions congeal into a single emotional state called 'bad' and all our positive emotions congeal into a single emotional state, which, depending on which part of the world you are in, is either called 'not-bad', 'fine' or, in more upbeat cultures, 'good'.

If we experience more 'bad' emotion than 'good' emotion, then the 'bad' emotion can elongate into a bad mood. Over time, this bad mood can cut a groove in our life, like an overplayed LP record. A person may play the same negative tune over and over again until it becomes an ingrained habit. The vast majority of people who are diagnosed with depression or anxiety disorders don't have a medical condition (yet); their record player has just got stuck playing the emotional record of anxiety or sadness and they don't know how to cut the power or change the record to something more upbeat and positive. And this is having a huge impact on individual health and happiness.

What's more, emotional and stress-related disorders significantly impair productivity. In one study depression was identified as the most common mental health condition, responsible for 79 per cent of all time lost at work – significantly more costly to the employer than physical disease.[28] Depression is a driving force for sickness absence,[29] and the longer the period of depression the longer the sickness absence.[30] This association is worse in people from lower income families.[31]

Cancer

Cancer is currently the second biggest killer, responsible for about a fifth of all deaths globally.[32] That means that heart disease and cancer collectively account for around 50 per cent of all premature deaths! And negative emotion has been proven to drive both.[33] Way back in 1870, Queen Victoria's physician and surgeon, Sir James Paget, stated, 'The cases are so frequent in which deep anxiety, deferred hope and disappointment are quickly followed by the growth and increase of cancer that we can hardly doubt that mental depression is a weighty addition to the other influences favouring the development of a cancerous constitution'.[34]

Since then, the volume of evidence linking emotional dysregulation and the development of cancer, tumour recurrence and cancer-specific mortality is overwhelming.[35] So much so that it has been said that 'the data are now so strong that [they] can no longer be ignored by those wishing to sustain a scientific attitude towards the cancer field'.[36] There is now zero doubt that the superhighway to disease, including cancer, is mismanaged emotions.

The big questions regarding cancer have been: 'Can we predict who gets cancer?' And, 'Can we predict who is going to survive cancer?' This a highly controversial subject and the scientific community is deeply divided on the issues.[37] Most scientists suggest that there is no link between personality and cancer – although this suggestion is way too imprecise and generic to be of any help. The controversy is compounded by people jumping to the conclusion that if a 'cancer-prone' personality were identified then it would be a small step to being able to blame individuals for the development of their tumour. This is obviously nonsense. Unfortunately, such an over-simplistic assumption leads people to erroneously conclude that 'nothing can be predicted from our lifestyle choices', which are largely driven by how we feel. This leads us then to conclude that the aetiology of cancer is unfathomable, random and has nothing to do with us personally. This can lead people to absolve themselves from taking better care of themselves. When we ask much more specific questions, it is obvious that our lifestyle choices are absolutely crucial. We must still eat well, take regular exercise and most importantly develop the ability to manage our emotions if we want to reduce our risk of ill health. Persistently mismanaged emotions will increase our lifetime burden of cortisol, and impair our immune system, which is one of the reasons why cancer is more common as we age.[38]

Psychologist and the 'Father of Positive Psychology' Dr Martin Seligman and two colleagues studied members of the Harvard graduating classes of 1939 to 1944.[39] Following their return from the Second World War, the men were interviewed about their war experiences and physically examined every five years. Where the post-war interviews indicated that individuals had been optimistic in college, their emotional disposition directly correlated to better health in later life. Seligman stated that, 'The men's explanatory style at age 25 predicted their health at 65,' adding 'around age 45 the health of the pessimists started to deteriorate more quickly'. People's explanatory style impacts how they explain the inevitable ups and downs of life to themselves, which in turn influences their behaviour and performance. For example, pessimists interpret a failed exam or missed promotion as though it were a permanent reflection of their own personal failings that will infect all areas of their life. Optimists, who have greater emotional intelligence, will look at the same event or situation and see it as temporary, fixable and only confined to the area it originally affected. A more recent study found that post-traumatic stress disorder doubled the risk of ovarian cancer and an increased risk of cardiovascular disease in a 26-year follow-up study of 54,000 nurses.[40]

If we are negative, if we feel that we can't control our destiny, if we feel put upon and internalize our frustrations instead of talking about them and finding solutions, to quote Woody Allen, we 'will grow a tumour'. Emotional distress can influence the incidence and progression of cancer.[41]

How this works biologically is that if someone is negative or feels as though they have limited control over their life, their body creates more cortisol and cortisol suppresses the immune system.[42] We all, for example, generate cancer cells in our body every day but if someone is cheerful, positive and emotionally coherent most of the time, their immune system will simply flush out those potentially problematic cancer cells as part of its normal function. This doesn't happen if someone is perpetually miserable or emotionally incoherent. Once cortisol levels have suppressed the immune system over a long period of time, the cancer cells are not adequately disposed of by the poorly functioning immune system and instead they can take hold and develop into cancer.

Happiness: the facts and the fiction

Whilst conceptually health and happiness may mean very different things, especially to busy executives who don't consider either relevant to quarterly results, in daily life it's virtually impossible to separate health from happiness – the two are inextricably linked. When someone has the 'giving-up–given-up complex'[43] or experiences 'the emotional eclipse of the heart',[44] their gloomy expectation and negativity will facilitate a host of negative consequences – physically and mentally. Those that are more optimistic or are at least able to manage their emotions and use their feelings to initiate constructive action to solve their problems are almost always healthier and live longer, happier, more contented lives.

Interestingly, the scientific literature on the negative consequences of emotions is about 10 times larger than the evidence on the beneficial effects of positive emotions. Psychology and psychiatry, for example, are almost exclusively focused on dysfunction, studying it and treating it respectively. For decades, it was widely considered 'a career-limiting move' or academically inappropriate to research happiness or elevated performance from an emotional perspective.

Thankfully the tide has turned, and it's no longer career suicide to study positive psychology, positive affect, emotional regulation and its health benefits. We now realize that we can actively alter our emotional outlook, which in turn can enhance our immune system and increase our protection and resilience against disease and illness.[45] We now realize that positive emotions, that make us feel happy, contented and confident, can be learnt, practised and purposefully incorporated into our daily lives. And such positive affect can reduce the ten-year incidence of heart disease.[46]

For years we were told that happiness and positivity were largely genetic – we were either born optimistic or pessimistic. But this is not true. Optimists may have won the 'cortical lottery'[47] because they habitually look on the bright side and more easily find the silver linings, but this ability is open to all of us. Thanks to research giants such as Abraham Maslow, Aaron Antonovsky, James W Pennebaker, Suzanna Kobasa, Tal Ben-Shahar, Dean Ornish, Martin Seligman and Mihaly Csikszentmihalyi amongst others, we now understand that our emotional outlook is not fixed as a permanent set point but rather that we each have a range. Whether we view the glass as half-empty or half-full can be significantly altered through emotional coherence and self-management so that we habitually operate at the top end of our emotional range.

When crisis strikes – and it does for everyone – most people will deal with crisis in one of three main ways. They will get into action and fix the problem (active coping), reappraise the situation (engage in inner emotional and cognitive work to find the silver lining) or avoid the problem (engage in distraction tactics such as alcohol or drugs so they can forget or blunt the emotional reaction).[48]

Many years ago, Holmes and Rahe developed a stress scale of traumatic 'life events' to help us better understand the effects of these events on health and happiness. Of course, it was also hoped that these insights would lead to a way to help people find the right coping strategy for crisis.

Holmes and Rahe found that if someone experienced several life events such as divorce, death of a loved one, redundancy or moving house they would be more susceptible to physical illness, disease or depression. Research proving such correlations continues to this day 50 years after the original research was published.[49] But over the years something else interesting emerged from the data. There were some individuals who experienced a great many of these major life events and yet didn't get ill. Social psychologist Jamie Pennebaker's work suggested that the event may not be the issue; he suggested that what matters is what happens after the event and what meaning the individual attributes to the event and their future life.[50]

After Holmes and Rahe published their life event research Aaron Antonovksy suggested that some people had 'resistance resources' which buffered them against the vicissitudes of life.[51] Suzanne Kobasa defined a concept called 'hardiness', or what today we call 'resilience'. She described the 'three Cs' where people saw problems as positive challenge, felt they could potentially control the outcome and were committed to trying.[52] And, subsequent research studies have validated her idea.[53]

Today, in addition to a wealth of research on resilience a new concept that picks up the original work of Pennebaker has focused on what has become known as post-traumatic growth (PTG) – the ability to find something positive and beneficial out of even the most difficult experiences.[54] This is not optimism or pessimism per se, but the ability to manage emotion and create meaning. When people were able to express themselves emotionally and talk about what happened within social networks or strong relationships, they were largely spared the damaging effects of trauma to physical and mental well-being. (Remember this when we explore the potent impact of positive relationships for personal and professional success in Chapter 6.) Those with greater emotional coherence were also better able to put a cognitive frame around the event that allowed them to make sense of what happened and move on.[55]

How we view the world is not set in stone. We may not always have control over situations or events, but we always have control over how we interpret them, what we do about them and what we make them mean.

From a business perspective it has also been found that those who are mentally healthy and happy have a higher degree of 'vertical coherence' among their goals and aspirations.[56] In other words, they have dovetailed their short-term goals into their medium-term and long-term goals so that everything they do fits together and pulls them toward a future they want. I would go so far as to extend this definition of 'vertical coherence' to include coherence within all the areas of vertical development – especially, in this context, emotions.

Vicious cycles caused by mismanaged emotions

Clearly, it's not the event or situation that impacts the outcome; it's what happens emotionally as a result of those events and situations that really makes the difference between life and death, success and failure, happiness and misery. This is the distinction that is so often missing in modern medicine.

Earlier I said that the real risks of heart disease were not so much the widely publicized traditional risks of blood pressure, cholesterol, diabetes, etc but the relatively less well-known social, educational, interpersonal or physiological risks such as poverty, social inequality, low educational attainment, stress, social isolation, depression, anxiety and anger. These things, in and of themselves, won't necessarily kill us, but what these things do to our biology can.

Low educational attainment doesn't cause heart disease, but it usually leads to poverty because the individual doesn't have the knowledge, skills or self-confidence to earn a decent living, and that creates poverty. But, even then, it's still not the poverty that is creating the heart disease; it's the fact that poverty usually creates emotional distress, worry and pressure – especially if that person has a family to support. If the poverty creates emotional incoherence in the physiology it's probably experienced as worry, panic, anxiety and depression. The person may feel worthless, helpless and socially isolated, which further suppresses the immune system and increases cortisol levels still further, thus laying the body open to a host of diseases, of which heart disease and cancer are just two.

One of the commonest feelings that people live with is that they are 'not enough': that they are deficient in some way or there is something lacking in their world. These feelings of deficiency or inadequacy may be personalized into 'I am not a good enough husband/wife, father/mother or friend.' Women often specialize in feeling bad about their physicality: 'I am too fat' or 'My [insert appropriate body part] is too big/too small.' Men's specialist inadequacy is often centred on their ability to make money, their perceived success or their physicality such as whether they are tall enough. Too many people don't feel good about themselves and lead lives of quiet desperation. Whether their backside looks big in those jeans or not is largely irrelevant; it's what that observation does to the person's physiology that damages their health and happiness.

Remember, what we eat and how often we exercise are relevant to optimal health, but they are nowhere near as relevant as we've been led to believe. Emotion is the elephant in the room. When we understand emotion and create emotional coherence, so we can differentiate between the various emotional tunes our body is playing and behave appropriately, our health and happiness will improve dramatically.

The simple, unequivocal fact about health and happiness is that emotion is the active ingredient, and developing emotional coherence will not only make you more productive but just might save your life.

Emotions and feelings: what's the difference?

Most people, including medical professionals, use the words 'emotion' and 'feeling' as interchangeable terms, believing they are essentially the same thing. They're not.

Going back to the integrated performance model (Figure 1.1), physiology is just the raw data or the biological 'notes' that our body is playing. Emotion is the integration of all the various physiological signals or 'notes' into a tune. In contrast, a feeling is the awareness and recognition, in our mind, of the tune that is being played by our body. Or, as neuroscientist Joseph LeDoux suggests, feelings are merely the 'observation' of the emotion.[57]

The physiological 'notes' are literally our energy (E) in motion (e-motion). The human system is a multi-layered integrated hierarchy in a state of constant flux, with each system – heart, lungs, kidneys, liver, brain – playing a tune that contributes to the overall score of the orchestra. Our body is always playing a tune, whether we are aware of that tune or can recognize it or not. When we become aware of the tune that all our bodily systems are playing, we are 'feeling' the e-motion. Emotion is, therefore, the link between biology and behaviour – a fact not lost on Henry Maxey, CEO of Ruffer Investment Hedge Fund. Ruffer is an independent and privately owned investment management firm employing over 160 people, with offices in London, Edinburgh and Hong Kong. When we interviewed Henry on his experiences of working with us, he said:

> The whole financial market is about perceptions... Because it's about
> perceptions, human behaviour plays a huge part, hence the importance of
> understanding the real drivers of behaviour, namely emotions. Since emotions
> play such a huge part in this job it's very helpful to have some understanding
> of them, your emotional state and how that's influencing your behaviour when
> you're interacting with markets.

Learning how to create greater emotional coherence has therefore been extremely valuable. Henry was one of the very few financial analysts to predict the credit market collapse of 2007, successfully moving his clients' investments ahead of the turmoil and massively enhancing his firm's reputation and profile as a result.

Making the distinction between emotions and feelings may seem like semantics, but it's a crucial differentiation because it suddenly resolves so much of people's misunderstanding about how we function. If we want to develop as human beings, we must improve our ability to differentiate between different emotions, between emotions and feelings, and between feeling and thoughts.

For us to develop as business leaders we need to improve our ability to differentiate things that are not traditionally thought of as related to business – human biology and human nature – most of which isn't even given a cursory nod in business schools. And yet the benefits of this knowledge are profound. When leaders, senior executives and employees understand that emotions and feelings are completely different phenomena, it enables them to learn how to control both and ultimately build better relationships with customers and colleagues alike.

There is little doubt that some individuals have already learnt a degree of emotional 'self-control', or at least they think they have. However, such self-regulation often only extends to the control of the more obvious manifestations of body language rather than the emotional energy itself. For example, an executive may be able to conceal the fact that they are feeling angry or are desperately unhappy. They may be able to stop themselves flying into a rage at a colleague or cover up frustration in a meeting, but this is usually no more than gross control of body language. It might look like they've 'got their act together' but inside their body they are still experiencing the negative consequences of those negative emotional signals whether they actually feel the feeling or express those feelings or not. In other words, it might look like they are listening to Beethoven, and they may even be able to kid themselves that their body is playing Beethoven, but their physiology is still reacting to what's really going on and is playing thrash metal at full volume.

Going back to our orchestra metaphor again, underneath the external façade of 'controlled emotions' is a vast number of individual musicians, each playing different 'notes' or sending subtle (and not so subtle) signals around the body. An examination of these uncontrolled signals can be a very revealing window on the underlying emotional state that is currently impacting the individual. Few people recognize, let alone control, the fine emotional nuances of their physiological orchestra. And sophisticated control does not mean simply throwing a blanket over the whole orchestra; it means knowing how and when to allow the expression of each musician within the orchestra and how to bring coherence to the tune being played to create something genuinely astonishing. When we develop genuine control over our emotional repertoire, we alter our physiology and this can literally protect us from the illness and disease caused by mismanaged emotions. It can also protect us from poor decision making.

The business impact of conditioning

Shifts in our emotion can be triggered by the perception of anything external to us or by internal thoughts or memories. Most of what we perceive with our senses does not reach conscious awareness. We already know, for example, that the central nervous system is only capable of processing a tiny fraction of what it could be aware of via our senses. The retina transmits data at 10 million bits per second, our other senses process one million bits per second and only 40 (not 40 million) bits per second reach consciousness.[58] Our subconscious mind, ie the mind that is busy doing stuff so we don't have to think about things like pumping blood or digesting food, is capable of processing 20 million environmental stimuli per second versus the rather puny 40 environmental stimuli that our conscious mind is processing.[59]

So not only are we privy to a vast amount of data we are never consciously aware of but, because of a process called conditioning, any one of those millions of external cues could trigger an emotion that alters our behaviour or decision making without us knowing why. Conditioning is an automatic survival and learning mechanism that starts shortly after we are born and long before we are able to speak. The purpose of this automatic response is to evaluate threats to our survival and trigger a response that keeps us alive. And it's made possible by the body's emotional early-warning system – the amygdala.

Neuroscientist Joseph LeDoux from the Center for Neural Science at New York University was one of the first academics to highlight the key role – and shortcomings – of the amygdala in decision making. It is the amygdala that is often to blame when, feeling threatened, we blurt out something stupid in a meeting or get caught off guard by a journalist. In certain situations, the old maxim 'think before you act' is actually a biological impossibility.

Before LeDoux's research, it was widely believed that the sensory signals received via our senses travelled first to the thalamus, where they were translated into the language of the brain. Most of the message then travelled to the neocortex so an appropriate response could be initiated. If there was an emotional component to those signals, a further signal was passed from the neocortex to the amygdala for emotional perspective but the neocortex was considered to be the boss. But this isn't what happens.

Instead, there is a neural emergency exit connecting the thalamus to the amygdala, which means that a smaller portion of the original message goes directly across a single synapse to the amygdala – bypassing the thinking brain altogether and initiating action before the rational brain even knows what's going on. This allows for a faster response when our survival may be threatened. And all this happens in a fraction of a second below conscious awareness, and what becomes an emotional trigger largely comes down to individual conditioning.

Human beings are born with only two fears – falling and loud noises. Everything else, whether that is fear of failure, fear of success, fear of death, clowns, heights or spiders, we've learnt from someone else or from experience. As we grow up, we absorb a massive amount of information largely through conditioning and there are two types of conditioned learning. If we burn our hand on a hotplate, we don't repeat the mistake because the experience is sufficiently painful that the conditioning is immediate. Such experiences are called single-trial conditioning and, as the name would suggest, they teach us very quickly via a single exposure to the event or situation.

However, most learning is not that intense and involves 'multiple-trial learning' where we must repeat the experience over and over again until it becomes embedded in our mind and we have learnt an appropriate response. Conditioning was first described by the great physiologist Ivan Pavlov who investigated the whole phenomena of unconscious learning and how it drove our biological responses. Working with dogs, Pavlov noticed that if he gave his dogs food while also making a sound such as blowing a whistle or ringing a bell then over time the dogs would associate being fed with the sound. With repetition it was therefore possible to get the dogs to salivate just by ringing the bell. Clearly there is no logical connection between salivating and the sound of a bell, and this highlights the often inaccurate and unsophisticated nature of the conditioning process. It matches stimuli that don't necessarily belong together and the subsequent presence of one or more of those stimuli can trigger an emotional response that doesn't match the situation.

Part of the reason conditioning is so inaccurate is that the system is designed around survival, not sophistication. A conditioned response is often blunt and can mean that we occasionally use a sledgehammer to crack a nut. Say someone ate a poisonous mushroom as a child and was violently ill for 24 hours; the conditioned response to that event would have been single exposure and the child's brain would have immediately scanned the situation to establish the characteristic of the event so as to ensure it never happened again. Even after the child grows up and learns that there are many different types of mushrooms that are tasty, they probably won't ever eat mushrooms again, even if they don't remember the mushroom incident that created the conditioning in the first place. Their rational, intelligent adult brain will not be able to override the 'Danger! Danger!' siren that is set off by the amygdala to save them from eating a 'dangerous' mushroom. The amygdala's mission is to detect danger. Precision decision making is the domain of the frontal cortex, but the amygdala engages far faster than the frontal cortex. Plus, when we are making all these early associations through the process of conditioning, our frontal lobes are not fully developed, which further reinforces the inaccuracy of the conditioning process.

The amygdala has a comparative function. That means it's constantly comparing current reality with all previous experience from the day we were born. Every new incident, event or situation is unconsciously compared to all the data we possess to ascertain if there is any danger. Every new client we meet, or every executive we interview for a position, will be compared to everyone in our amygdala's vast rolodex of names and events to see if there are any correlations that could signal danger. And if it finds a match the amygdala will trigger a biological response that will cause us to get nervous, irritated or uncomfortable in some way.

If we don't have a sophisticated understanding and awareness of the emotional signals created by our body, we can miss these messages or completely misinterpret them. Neither is great. With greater emotional awareness, literacy and self-management, we are better able to avoid poor decisions based on imprecise interpretation of a conditioned response we don't remember, a response that has absolutely no real bearing on current reality. Conditioning acts like the strings on a puppet and emotion pulls the strings. The trouble is, we think we are pulling the strings based on rational, verifiable data – we're not. Without conscious intervention, a huge number of our so-called 'decisions' are unconscious, amygdala-based knee-jerk reactions to long-forgotten events, designed to protect us from things we are scared of or have been trained to be scared of. And it's all happening without involving reason or rationality.

Imagine four-month-old William has colic and doesn't sleep for more than 20 minutes at a time. This goes on for weeks on end and his parents are at the end of their tether. Exhausted and bewildered, William's mother finally loses her temper one evening and screams at William, 'For goodness sake go to sleep!' Of course, that makes William cry even louder because he feels threatened – his primary carer is angry, and he senses danger to his survival. William's amygdala springs into action and goes into 'situation assessment mode' so that it can log all the features and characteristics of the moment for future reference so he can avoid this type of threat in the future. For example, his amygdala might log that his mum is wearing a yellow shirt, that his favourite blanket is on the floor, not in his cot and that the bedside light is on. William's amygdala stores upset = yellow shirt = dropped blanket = light. It's pre-verbal so this isn't conscious or stored as words, but that's essentially the message.

Fast-forward 50 years, and William's interviewing candidates for a new commercial director position. William is the CEO. It's late afternoon in winter, and as William's secretary shows the last candidate into his office she flicks on the light and a man in a yellow shirt walks in. William immediately feels uncomfortable. What he doesn't appreciate is that his amygdala has matched 'light' and 'yellow shirt' and triggered an emotional response even though he has no conscious memory of the colic episode. Assuming William is not exceptionally emotionally literate, he will take an instant dislike to the candidate and dismiss him immediately or simply go through the motions of the interview. He will misinterpret his discomfort as something else and justify and rationalize that initial conditioned response as 'gut instinct', 'intuition' or 'business experience'. Either way, his 'decision' is not based on real data and due interview process of a viable candidate; it is based on an erroneous survival-based conditioned response created when he was four months old and feeling a bit poorly!

As bizarre as this may sound, it is happening all the time – inside and outside business. And the only thing that could rein this conditioning in and facilitate consistently better decision making is emotional awareness and emotional regulation. Unfortunately, we are so disconnected from our emotions, especially at work, that we're often not even aware of the shifts in our energy-in-motion. We certainly can't articulate what that emotion is, which means that we almost certainly don't have the cognitive ability to ask ourselves whether the conclusion we've just jumped to is based on anything solid or not.

This is why the emotional line of development is so important for developing leadership. It allows us to wrestle back power from the hyper-vigilant, over-protective amygdala and not have historical ghosts determine our choices in the here and now. That way, perfectly capable candidates in yellow shirts don't get thrown out without due consideration.

In addition, it has been demonstrated that what we 'think' we are capable of is often nothing more than a conditioned response or habit.[60] In other words, we need to learn how to tap into our innate emotional signals so we can stop jumping to erroneous conclusions based on long-forgotten events and misperceived threats. When we do, we can tap into our true potential instead of an outdated idea of that potential. We need to become more 'response-able' rather than reactive. We can't stop the e-motion happening (at least, not without a lot of practice) but we can learn to intervene and manage the response.

The *real* E-myths

According to Michael Gerber's *E-myth*, if you wanted to be a successful entrepreneur you had to systemize your business.[61] What I'm suggesting is that the real E-myths that are holding businesses back are the universal dismissal of E-motion as a business tool and the fact that intellect is viewed as considerably more important.

Business is often perceived as the cool, rational pursuit of profit. In the history of commerce, it's been largely a male-dominated sport and even today if you look at the statistics for women in senior roles the percentage is woefully small.[62] The vast majority of businesses are still run by men. Most cultures still condition their sons to be strong, show little or no emotion, be the protectors who provide for the family. What we instinctively assume about business is therefore mainly dominated by our outdated and inaccurate assumptions about men. Emotion is seen as a demonstration of weakness preserved for the 'weaker sex' and is often the whispered, outdated, invalid misogynistic justification for why women are unsuitable to lead businesses. Men are rational, socialized from a very early age to dismiss emotion and feelings almost entirely – or so the story goes.

This is so ingrained into our collective psyche that if we ask a man what he feels, he will tell us what he thinks. If we ask a male CEO how he is feeling after the dismissal of a colleague for example, he will tell us how the decision was necessary and how the business is going to move forward. He may not even understand the question. If he does, he is often conditioned to ignore or suppressing his feelings or he has no lexicon to answer the question. The challenge for men is their low level of emotional awareness.

For women, it's slightly different because they tend to be more aware of their emotions in the first place. This awareness is facilitated by their direct experience of their physical and emotional tides on a monthly basis. The challenge for women is therefore less about a lack of awareness and more about the ability to manage their emotions. Women may sometimes be overwhelmed as they sense the energy bubbling to the surface more readily. The risk of being overwhelmed by your emotions is widely perceived as a 'female' issue, especially in business. As a result, men and women struggle in this endless dance where a woman's struggle to regulate her emotions can reinforce the male belief that emotions are unhelpful. And a man's lack of awareness can reinforce a woman's belief that men lack empathy and have limited emotional bandwidth. The truth is that it's emotional mismanagement that's unhelpful, not emotions themselves, and this is true for both sexes.

Emotional suppression is every bit as toxic and unhelpful as emotional excess and over-expression. Unfortunately, this misdiagnosis of emotions as the problem rather than emotional mismanagement creates a vicious cycle where men justify their lack of awareness, fearing that if they paid attention to emotions, they could become overwhelmed, lose control and make poor decisions. They dismiss the whole topic of emotions, which makes women even more irritated, triggering even more upset that further solidifies the unhelpful stereotypes and maintains the endless dance.

This blanket dismissal or underplaying of emotion is further compounded by the fact that we prize cognition significantly more than emotion. For many centuries it's been intelligence, creativity and thought that have been valued above all else. Consider the intellectual transformation brought about during the Renaissance between the 14th and the 17th centuries, the Age of Enlightenment in the 17th and 18th centuries, or the New Thought Movement of the early 19th century. Thought has been king for a very long time. In business strategy, analysis, customer insight, like-for-like sales figures, process reengineering and a whole manner of other rational pursuits are highly prized. Relationship dynamics, sensitivity, trust, cultural nuance, emotion and feelings are less explored and at times seem almost taboo.

In the workplace we often hear how a certain individual is 'highly intelligent' or 'super smart'. That's a compliment. When someone is described as 'emotional', however, it is never a compliment, and such a statement is most often directed toward a female executive. Ironically, if a male executive does occasionally express emotion it is more often regarded in a positive light such as 'assertive' or 'passionate'.

This supposed difference between men and women is simply not true. Every human being – male or female – has emotion. Everyone has physiology that is in a constant state of flux, and this energy in motion creates signals that are being sent continuously and simultaneously around the body across multiple biological systems. The fundamentals of the physiological reaction to the world are therefore no different between the sexes; the triggers and intensity of emotions and the degree of self-regulation vary by person. The fact that emotions occur every second of every day is true of both men and women. The only thing that is different is the weight of thousands of years of gender-based expectations that can manifest as unhealthy biases inside and outside business. This in turn has created a mistaken belief that emotions are commercially irrelevant and do not belong in a modern business context.

Nothing could be further from the truth.

Why emotions are important in business

In 1776 Adam Smith wrote *The Wealth of Nations*, a treatise on economics and business that is still considered a classic today. In it, Smith talks about the division of labour. Everyone in a business was to have a particular job and they did only that job. People were rewarded for doing the tasks they were assigned and punished if they didn't. Simple – and, during the Industrial Revolution, it was very effective. But getting people to do what you want them to do is not just about reward and punishment.

Social science has conclusively proven that reward and punishment only works for very specific types of tasks – known as algorithmic tasks. These are tasks that follow a set path to a set outcome, and as such are often monotonous and boring. For everything else, known as heuristic tasks or those that require creativity, innovation and trial and error to perfect, reward and punishment don't work and can often elicit the very behaviour you are trying to stop.[63] A hundred years ago most people spent most of their time doing algorithmic tasks; today technology and innovation have replaced many of those jobs and that trend is gathering pace.[64]

For the roles left in the wake of automation, people are people and not machines, so treating them like machines is no longer effective. People have emotions, so asking them to leave their emotions at the door is like asking them to stop their heart beating while they are in the office because the noise is a little distracting. Besides, dismissing emotion in the workplace is not commercially smart because it renders employees incapable of making good decisions, and unable to work hard, unlock their discretionary effort or feel a sense of fulfilment. Plus, it facilitates terrible customer service. If we are serious about securing a commercial edge over our competitors, we really must understand how central emotions are to human functioning and the development of potential.

It was MIT management professor Douglas McGregor who really started to question this 'leave emotion at the door' approach to business back in 1960. Drawing on the work of motivation luminaries such as Harry Harlow and Abraham Maslow, McGregor refuted the notion that people, men included, were basically walking machines that needed to be programmed to do a job and kept in line. McGregor believed that the productivity and performance problems that plague business – then and now – are caused by a fundamental error in our understanding of human behaviour. He described two very different types of management – Theory X and Theory Y.[65] Theory X assumes people are lazy, and to make them conform you need a command-and-control approach. Emotion has no place in Theory X, and if anything is considered a show of weakness. Theory Y, on the other hand, assumes that work is as universal and necessary as rest and play, and when you bring people together toward a shared vision that everyone is emotionally connected to, truly amazing things are possible. McGregor's insights, made all the more palatable because he had real leadership experience as well as a Harvard PhD in psychology, did help to shift work practices a little, but for many organizations Theory X is still the dominant management style. We still seem reluctant to embrace the very thing that makes us human in the first place – emotions.

The biggest reason we cling on to Theory X in some form or another is because the alternative is terrifying. Theory Y requires that we break down the barriers and start really communicating with each other. And by this I don't mean the surface diplomacy or professional politeness. I mean a deeper understanding of who we are, and who our colleagues really are. The proactive desire to understand each other's past, present and hopes for the future. A passion to build trust and cultivate acceptance. To do this means facing the messy and unpredictable side of humanity – emotions. And if we don't even appreciate our own emotions and how we feel on a daily basis, 'feelings' can seem like an alien and unfathomable concept. So, instead, we try to ignore the fact that business is first and foremost a collection of emotional human beings. It's like owning a Formula One team but refusing to hire mechanics to look under the shiny red exterior!

We discussed this with Orlagh Hunt, the Chief People Officer at Yorkshire Building Society. She reflected on her time as Group HR Director for RSA and talked about the critical importance of embracing the human element of business – and that means emotion. With a 300-year heritage, RSA is one of the world's leading multinational insurance groups, employing around 14,000 people, serving 9 million customers in around 100 countries. Talking about her time with RSA, Orlagh said:

> In theory, we worked together, but our old way of operating had been all about driving individual performance. That was how our performance management and people management processes were set up. But to think bigger you need to have more collaboration and innovation, and that requires different ways of working... Individually, for members of the executive team, it was very much about being open. We needed to stop the sense that you have to have all the answers just because you're in a senior position. That means being open to including more people in decision making... Moving our leadership style on in that way was very important.

And the effort paid off. By looking under the hood of the team dynamic and really seeking to understand human behaviour in a more sophisticated way, RSA achieved significant wins:

> We moved to a more human and engaging leadership style that supported the organic growth phase and teed up opportunities for us to think differently about how ambitious our strategy could be... The outcome has been that the organization moved from failing to being well respected on the FTSE. Not only that, but the organization has seen benefits in terms of significant levels of

organic growth despite a difficult economic environment; and world-class levels of employee engagement (as measured by Gallup).

Emotions must be understood if the leadership journey is to be successfully navigated. Of course, it is still possible to be a powerful business figure with low levels of emotional and social intelligence (ESQ). But this type of leadership is considered outdated and counterproductive in most modern organizations. Leaders who have the courage to embrace emotions and become more emotionally and socially intelligent will significantly improve results. They will improve their working relationships, improve their leadership presence, health and well-being, increase enjoyment and quality of life, ignite meaning, significance and purpose, improve motivation and expand their sense of self. But, perhaps more importantly in a business context, emotional mastery can:

- improve clarity of thought and the ability to learn;
- improve the quality of decision making;
- facilitate effective management of change.

Improve clarity of thought and the ability to learn

We've all found ourselves in the middle of a heated argument saying something stupid, only to think of the most brilliant comeback five minutes after the other person has stormed out of the room. Unfortunately, it's impossible to think of smart comebacks or great ideas when our internal emotional signals are going haywire – even if we appear the picture of calm on the outside. Whether we feel the emotion or not doesn't alter the fact that the emotion is present. And it's already impacting our clarity of thought and the outcome.

We will explore this idea in more detail in the next chapter, but ultimately chaotic physiology and turbulent emotions cause the frontal lobes to shut down. The clear thinking that we believe we have in that moment is actually just the amygdala's triggered reactivity, not the quality cortical precision we need. Our emotions are constantly modulating our clarity and our ability to learn; the only real question is whether that influence is unconscious and potentially negative, or whether we consciously manage it and make it positive.

There are millions of bits of information from the internal and external world that are competing to get into our conscious awareness. Unless we develop emotional mastery and self-management so we can take conscious control of that filtering process, what we become aware of will largely be determined by long-forgotten conditioning and the hyper-vigilant and over-protective amygdala. Plus, it takes at least 500 milliseconds longer for information to reach our frontal cortex and for a thought to emerge than it does for the amygdala to trigger a more defensive, faulty thought based on a historical misinterpretation. That's why we say stupid things in an argu-ment – our amygdala reacts before our rational frontal cortex realizes what is happening.

This 'process emotion before thinking' loop is incredibly fast. If the amyg-dala detects danger, real or perceived, it will send a signal to our heart and cause it to speed up. The heart rate can jump from 70 to 150 beats per minute – within one beat. This change in the energy of the heart (e-motion) is sent back into our amygdala, the anterior cingulate cortex, hippocampus and the motor cortex. In that half a second our physiology has already changed; the emotion has emerged and, whether we were aware of that emotion or not, it's already initiated a potentially inappropriate response.

This biological phenomenon means that we are all living our lives about half a second behind reality, and it also explains why feelings dominate thinking and not the other way around. Feelings are faster than thoughts, and set the context in which all thoughts even occur. Thoughts are slower, and they are emergent phenomena that don't occur independently of the constant changes in our emotion. The specific thought we have at any moment often wouldn't have emerged had our physiology and emotion not changed first.

This mechanism can be useful in alerting us to danger, but without greater emotional intelligence our 'trigger happy' amygdala can undermine our abil-ity to think clearly, and that's not useful in business. If we are aware of only a tiny fraction of what we could potentially be aware of, it makes sense to develop a much greater awareness of our internal data. If we do this, then we can make better decisions and accurately determine what's really commercially relevant instead of making knee-jerk emotional reactions that can pollute our thinking and hamper performance.

Developing the ability to activate an appropriate emotional state is also key if we want to optimize our ability to learn from our experiences. In the training and development industry this is called 'learner readiness', but it's little more than common sense. If we are spending a fortune on internal training that isn't working, at least part of the reason is down to emotion. If trainees are in a negative emotional state, if they are hostile or resentful at having to be in the training in the first place or they think the course is a waste of time, they won't learn and they certainly won't implement. When their physiology is chaotic, they are generating much higher levels of the stress hormone cortisol. Cortisol is well known to inhibit learning and memory.

If we become a more mature, more exceptional leader we can help to shift the emotional response of the people around us, which can improve their ability to learn and enhance their performance.

Improve the quality of decision making

In the mid-19th century, a man called Phineas Gage had an accident that would change our understanding of decision making forever. Gage was a railway construction foreman in the United States in the 1840s.[66] Rather than weave the railway around a rock formation, it was easier to blast through the rock. Gage, an explosives expert, was employed for that task. The process involved drilling a hole in the rock, half-filling it with gunpowder, inserting a fuse and filling the rest of the hole with sand. The sand would be 'tamped in' very carefully with a 'tamping rod' to pack the sand and explosive in place, before finally lighting the fuse. Unfortunately, on 13 September 1848 25-year-old Gage started tamping before the sand was packed in and a spark from the tamping rod ignited the gunpowder, sending the six-foot-long iron tamping rod straight through his brain to land 80 feet away. Amazingly Gage survived – conscious and talking just a few minutes after the accident.[67]

Antonio Damasio has written extensively on the consequences of Gage's injury and its implications for decision making. Based on medical records at the time and brain reconstructions, Damasio suggests that the iron pole cut through his brain and disconnected the logic centres located in his frontal cortex from the emotional centres located further back, including his amygdala. Prior to the accident, the railway company that employed Gage considered him to be one of the most capable men in their business. However, after the accident his character changed, and although he could answer basic logic problems, he was unable to make decisions, or he would make decisions and abandon them almost immediately.

Gage's inability to make effective decisions led neuroscientists to realize that decision making requires emotion. In order to decide anything, we have a 'feeling' first and then we simply look for rational data to support that initial feeling. All the decisions we ever make are really just feelings justified by logic. It is impossible to exclude feelings from the decision-making process. Even the most hard-bitten neuroscientist will tell you that the emotional system and logical system are inseparable.[68] Emotions, specifically the electrical and chemical context in which all decisions are made, have been shown to explain a great deal of the variance in decision making.[69]

If you put this book down and find yourself saying 'That's rubbish' it is likely that you are having an emotional reaction to the information that is causing you to 'feel' like rejecting what is written here. Chances are, you pride yourself on your logic and the mere idea that your decision-making is anything other than supremely rational is offensive to you. But the fact remains, emotion is driving your decisions whether you like it or not. Many executives, unable to concede that their decisions are emotionally driven, may prefer to embrace the idea that their decisions are based on their 'commercial experience'. Which is ironic, considering 'commercial experience' is really just emotionally laden data that is unconscious or 'preconscious',[70] stored in parts of their brain they don't know about, resurfacing when they are asked to make a decision today. They may not call it emotion but that is exactly what it is.

Facilitate effective management of change

When we look back over recent years, from the 2008 global economic meltdown, to the chaos of Brexit, to the global 'Extinction Rebellion', 'Me Too' or 'Black Lives Matter' protests and the global pandemic, it is clear that today's leaders need to be much better at predicting and proactively managing change. There is no such thing as 'business as usual' in the 21st century. The idea of a 'new normal' is an unrealistic romantic desire for regression. The pace of change is increasing, and it won't slow down any time soon. We live in highly volatile, accelerating world. Most leaders know this, but few have studied the principles and dynamics of change in any great detail and many don't know how to consistently manage complex and dynamic change effectively.[71]

No business stays the same for very long and survives. But the process of change is an emotional roller-coaster. Ever since Swiss-American psychiatrist Elisabeth Kübler-Ross proposed the five stages of grief that someone goes through when they learn of their own or a loved one's impending death, we have understood that change is a challenge. Kübler-Ross described those

FIGURE 3.1   The change curve

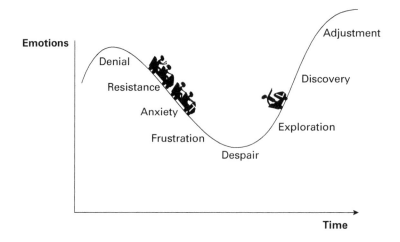

key emotional stages as denial, anger, bargaining, depression and accept-ance. Her model has since been expanded and is widely used in business to explain the emotional transition that occurs around any type of change, from new IT implementation to new management to strategic direction to new product line (Figure 3.1). Everyone goes through an emotional roller-coaster when they encounter change of any type. It follows, therefore, that if you want to manage change properly, you need to properly manage human emotion.

When CEOs or senior executives lead their people through change, they are usually further ahead on the change curve than their colleagues. Leaders need a greater understanding of what's ahead, what needs to be done and why if they want to lead effectively. The leader may have fully explored the suggested change and feel certain that it will result in significant positive benefits for the people in the business and the bottom line. But the work-force, who have not been privy to all the information, are probably still not convinced about the merit or need for the change. The leader is effectively saying, 'Come on in; the water is lovely' while their colleagues may be stand-ing at the side, clutching their towels, not sure they even want to get their feet wet! If leaders don't understand that emotionally their colleagues are in a different place, they risk being seen as unrealistically optimistic or delu-sional. They will then struggle to get their followers to embrace change with an open mind. Threatening them or bribing them is not the answer. Instead, leaders need enough emotional flexibility to be able to retrace their steps back along the change curve to an emotional position that is not so far ahead of everyone else so they can encourage their colleagues, address their fears and help them to take the necessary forward steps.

When people are in a state of anxiety looking at the implications of change, they need strong leadership and encouragement to reassure them it's going to be OK. But once they dive in, they can often feel even worse about the change and are now angry about trusting the leader in the first place. The leader needs to provide even stronger support, to work alongside their colleagues so they can hopefully continue to inspire them to keep going until they reach the discovery, adjustment and implementation stages. The most mature, coherent leaders will therefore not only recognize that their colleagues are in an emotionally different place from them, which is itself a skill, but will have sufficient emotional flexibility to offer different emotional input depending on where the team is on the roller-coaster of change. And the best leaders will change their emotional state rather than expect others to change their emotional state. The wise leader knows that if they don't go back and emotionally connect with their colleagues then the people will not follow, or the best they can hope for is compliance rather than acceptance and integration.

How to be healthier and happier

We believe that it's the emotion line of development that holds most senior executives and leaders back, at least initially. It is, however, important to understand that emotional coherence is much more than the basics of 'emotional intelligence' that many managers and leaders are already familiar with. The reason people don't effectively manage their emotions is that they don't know how to. Changing neurocircuitry and 'patterned responses' requires an individual to lay down new emotional circuits, patterns and experiences, and that's called 'practice'.

In Chapter 2 we covered the physical skills. Now it's time to explore some of the personal skills that leaders need to develop to become exceptional leaders. Specifically, the E-diary enhances emotional intelligence or awareness and MASTERY develops greater emotional literacy, while PEP and Landscaping facilitate emotional self-management. Each of these skills builds upon the other. Emotional intelligence transcends and includes physical intelligence, and that's why breathing is such an important platform on which everything else is built.

The BREATHE skill, described in the last chapter is specifically designed to stabilize our physiology and create a coherent electrical signal from our heart. If we are on the right-hand side of the Universe of Emotions experiencing apathy, anger or frustration, just taking some time to engage in smooth, rhythmic breathing while focusing on our heart will move us to the midpoint of the Universe of Emotions (Figure 1.4, Figure 2.6).

The real benefits, however, are experienced when we move to the left side of the Universe of Emotions and stay there. And that's what the next few skills are designed to facilitate.

Emotional coherence – emotional intelligence: the E-diary

If we want to live our life on the positive left side of the Universe of Emotions and stay there, we first need to develop our emotional intelligence. In its most basic form, intelligence is just awareness. Emotional intelligence is really just the process of cultivating awareness of our emotions. After all, we can't use emotions or change our emotions if we don't know what emotions we are experiencing.

The scientific community is divided on how many emotions it's possible for us to experience and how to categorize them. Some authors have suggested that there are only two opposing emotions, love and fear, and all other states are variations and modifications of these two.[72] Other scientists have argued that there are eight primary emotions.[73] In the same way that we can mix primary colours together to get all the other colours of the rainbow, these primary emotions mix together to give rise to all the other secondary emotions.

Having spent the last 25 years studying the literature and working with leaders every day discussing their emotional life, we believe that human beings can experience up to 34,000 different emotions.[74] Most individuals, of course, don't have anywhere near that level of sophistication and can only identify, at best, a dozen 'planets' in the 'Universe of Emotions'.[75] Most people cluster different emotional states in the same way they cluster or categorize music. Where some people would only ever listen to classical music, others prefer show tunes or opera while still others enjoy a wide eclectic mix. The most important aspect for health, happiness and performance is not the individual emotion but whether we tend to live our lives on the positive or negative side of the Universe of Emotions. Unfortunately, most of us don't really know what emotions we feel at any specific moment, so emotional intelligence is the critical first step in changing that.

One way of developing our emotional awareness is to keep track of exactly what emotions we feel over the course of several weeks. This can be achieved by keeping an E-diary or using our Complete app.

- When you are in a meeting or during the course of your day, simply jot down any emotional state you notice and make a note of what you believe you are feeling at that moment.
- At the end of the day reflect on how many different emotions you noticed or felt.
- How many are positive?
- How many are negative?

When I work with executives and encourage them to keep an E-diary, I often get them started by asking them to make a note of the emotions they have been aware of in the last 24 hours. What's always interesting is what they focus on and how many they identify.

Once they get over their initial resistance ('Why are we doing this? It's silly.'), most executives or leaders will start to note the emotions they have been aware of at work. The commonest emotion experienced at work is frustration. It is experienced four times more often than any other emotion. Overall, people's E-diary tends to be stacked with negative feelings, with perhaps one 'token' positive emotion thrown in so as not to appear too miserable.

With an impoverished emotional palette, we simply don't have the emotional vocabulary to describe most of the emotions we feel, and we don't appreciate the important nuances between similar emotional states. For example, I remember coaching a young golfer a few years ago and I started to explain to him the importance of sustained positive emotion. He replied, 'But I play some of my best golf when I'm angry.' I suggested that this was almost certainly not the case. He was probably 'extremely deter-mined' rather than angry and just couldn't tell the difference. I suggested to him that if he were really angry, he would probably want to hit someone with his club rather than take his determination out on the ball, which is what he'd been doing. Helping him to understand the difference between these two highly activated states helped him get into the correct perfor-mance state when he was in competitive situations.

Being able to identify just a dozen emotions is the equivalent of barely being able to tell the difference between red wine and coffee. Learning to distinguish more emotions can therefore massively increase our emotional literacy and enable us to connect much more effectively with those around us.

The first step is to take the time to make a note of the emotions we currently feel so that we can bring them into conscious awareness. After all, we can't change or utilize something that we don't know we have. Use the E-diary or the Complete app to familiarize yourself with your current repertoire and notice if they are largely positive or negative.

Emotional coherence – emotional literacy: MASTERY

Once we have started to notice the number and variety of emotions we experience, using the E-diary or the Complete app, the next step is to cultivate emotional literacy or the ability to distinguish between different (and similar) emotions and accurately label each one.

The skill for emotional literacy is MASTERY.

Most people are unable to discriminate similar emotions. This is simply because they haven't spent any time reflecting on what emotional states they are experiencing. Therefore, the first step to developing better emotional literacy is to start objectifying what is normally a subjective, inner experience. This 'subject-to-object' (S2O) manoeuvre facilitates a much greater understanding of any phenomena. Think about MASTERY like a wine-tasting course. Expert wine tasters with a highly sensitive palette have used the S2O approach to distinguish between a Chardonnay and a Chablis, and can even differentiate different types of Chardonnay, noting which country a wine came from, what year it was made, what grape was used and sometimes even the type of soil the grape was grown in. Wine experts are not born with this knowledge; they train their palette to objectify sensations so that they can distinguish one wine from another with an ever-increasing degree of sophistication. And it's possible to do the same thing with our emotions.

It is important to be able to discriminate our emotions for two reasons:

- Access. If we know the exact 'features' of a particular feeling that we are trying to recreate and know exactly how we experience it in our body, we can have conscious access to that emotion. And if we have conscious access to it instead of just haphazard, unpredictable unconscious access to it, we can turn that emotion 'on' when we need it. For example, confidence is a potent emotion that impacts performance negatively or positively. If we don't know what confidence is as an experience and have no appreciation for how it feels in our body, we don't have access to it. If on the other hand we have developed emotional literacy and have prac- tised the emotional MASTERY skill, we will understand how to actually recreate a state of confidence whenever we need it, whether in a tennis final or in front of the shareholders.

- Action. The purpose of emotion is to provoke action, and every emotion is designed to provoke a different action. As such, emotions have distinct survival advantages. If, however, we are unable to differentiate which emotion we are feeling, it is highly likely that we will select the wrong action for the situation we're faced with. For example, when we see a grizzly bear, it triggers an emotion (our heart rate becomes erratic, our palms become sweaty, etc) and we feel fear. The fear is designed to provoke an action, ie running away, which will hopefully save our life. That's the purpose of the fear. If we don't feel the fear or if we misinter- pret the emotional signal as confusion we are likely to remain immobi- lized for too long and risk attack.

Similarly, in a meeting, if we can't tell the difference between frustration and disappointment, we are much more likely to take the wrong action. The purpose of disappointment is to provoke us to step back so we can evaluate the situation more closely. The purpose of frustration is to step forward and overcome the stumbling blocks. If we can't tell the difference, sometimes we will step forward when we should have stepped back and become reflective, and vice versa.

Most of us don't have a clue how we are really feeling at any moment, and even if we do we are unable to accurately tell the difference between those emotions – especially those that are similar to each other. If we can't distinguish between emotions, we have no emotional literacy and our health, happiness and performance may suffer as a result. The MASTERY skill is therefore a technique to build our emotional repertoire so we can tell the differences between the emotional data we are privy to. You may, for exam- ple, know the intellectual difference between frustration and disappointment, but MASTERY teaches us how to recognize the difference in our body so we can differentiate between the emotional states as an experience.

THE MASTERY SKILL
When someone attends a wine-tasting course, they are given a glass of wine and asked to describe it. At first, assuming the learners didn't know much

about wine, they probably wouldn't know what to say other than 'It's white' or 'It's red'. Their teacher would lead them through a process to deepen their observation and appreciation of the wine by asking pertinent questions to elicit more detailed descriptions. With practice, the budding wine aficionados would soon begin to surprise themselves as they describe the wine in increasingly sophisticated terms. Before long, they would be able to accurately describe the colour of the wine, how it smells and how it tastes. Developing emotional literacy follows the same process by providing a structure to describe our emotions in greater and greater detail.

THE MASTERY PROCESS

1   Sit in a comfortable position, close your eyes and BREATHE.

2   Simply notice what emotion exists in your body right now.

3   If you're not feeling a distinct emotion, try triggering an emotion through the use of music, a memory or a picture/vision.

4   Once you have identified the emotion, give it a label or word that you think best captures it. Write that word down.

5   It actually doesn't matter if the label you choose is accurate or not at this stage. What matters is that you familiarize yourself with the experience of that emotion.

6   Explore the features of the emotion within your body. How does the energy feel? What is the location of the emotion in your body? What is the size of the emotion? What colour is the emotion? What sound does the emotion make? What is the emotion's temperature? What is its intensity?

7   Moving on to the movement features. Take a moment to describe how the emotion moves through your body. Does it stop at your skin or does it radiate off your body?

8   Does the emotion have any special features?

9   Make a note of any insights that may have surfaced during the process.

When people first hear about this process, it always sounds weird, especially to seasoned business leaders and senior executives. No one thinks that their emotions have a colour or a temperature or a location, and yet once people get over their initial scepticism and run through the MASTERY process outlined above, they are usually very surprised to realize that the emotion does have a colour and a size, etc.

Consistent practice of this MASTERY skill has also been shown to produce significant and sustained biological improvements over time. By learning how to convert something that is normally an entirely subjective inner experience into an objective, observable and repeatable one, we can build resilience, improve energy levels, happiness and fulfilment, and enhance effectiveness. The more we understand the subtlety of our inner experience, the more we will be able to control the very thing that drives our own and other people's behaviour.

MASTERY IN ACTION

I remember coaching a real 'alpha male' executive who wanted to master 'contentment'. His explanation of how it felt stayed with me: 'Contentment is a small, glowing ember at the base of my heart. It's red-golden, and it's oozing through my chest and my arms and into my legs and I glow like the Ready Brek Kid, and it purrs like a Cheshire cat.' His description was so beautiful and vivid that I actually started to feel his contentment; he had infected me with it! (And in case you don't already know, Ready Brek is a sort of porridge-like breakfast cereal that, according to their advertisers, gives the consumer a full body halo of heat all day.)

Whenever this executive was frustrated or irritated in a meeting or with one of his staff, he was able to turn on contentment as an antidote because he had practised the MASTERY skill.

MASTERY allows us to build up a database of the emotions we experience the most, work out the distinctions between similar emotions, and consciously build up an expanded repertoire of positive emotions we would like to feel more often. In Chapter 4 we'll explore the SHIFT skill, which allows us to consciously move from a negative emotion to a positive emotion at will. This is also an extremely powerful skill, made even more powerful once we've mastered some positive states to move into.

Emotional coherence – emotional self-management: positive energy practice and landscaping

I've lost count of the number of times I've taught the MASTERY skill to business executives, reminded them that it can transform their life, and picked up our conversation a month later only to hear they didn't find time to practise. The people I work with are leaders of large global companies and they are usually beyond busy, so I fully appreciate that the idea of developing new skills that require practice is not terribly appealing. Clearly, what was needed was a way to help executives practise without it feeling like practice. The positive energy practice (PEP) skill is a way to help them 'practice without actually practising'.

POSITIVE ENERGY PRACTICE (PEP)

We may not always realize it, but we don't actually make that many conscious decisions in a working day. If we look at our life, we are largely repeating a series of daily habits or rituals. These rituals populate our day, from our 'breakfast ritual' to our 'commute to work ritual' to our 'meeting ritual' to our 'winding down ritual'. Most of our day is highly structured and these rituals tend to occur in what I call the 'transition points' – the space between activities where we are transitioning from one activity to another.

For example, the first ritual that nearly all of us have is the 'getting up ritual' that signals the transition from being horizontal to being vertical. Everyone has a morning ritual although few are really that aware of it. Some people wake up to the alarm and some don't. Some of the people who wake up to the alarm will get up as soon as it goes off, others will hit the snooze – some will hit it once, some twice or more. Some leap out of bed, some swing their legs over and sit up in the bed, stretch and push their feet into their slippers before padding to the bathroom. Some go to the bathroom and others go straight to the kitchen to put the kettle on and then go back to the bathroom. When we start to think about it, most people can identify between three and ten steps in their 'getting up ritual'. The idea behind PEP is to identify the rituals that we already engage in and enhance them with positive energy practice.

For example, in our 'getting up ritual' we would do what we always do but include an additional step that involves feeling a positive emotion, such as appreciation. PEP therefore encourages us to insert a few seconds of positive emotion into an existing ritual.[76] Instead of hitting snooze and going back to sleep we might choose to take a few moments in bed to feel warm appreciation for the fact that we are alive or that our partner is next to us or that we have our health or it's a sunny day outside. For just 30 seconds we feel appreciation, and get on with the rest of our ritual as normal. Psychologist Sonja Lyubomirsky from the University of California studied 'happiness boosters' and found that those who found the time to consciously count their blessing – even just once a week – significantly increased their overall satisfaction with life over a six-week period.[77]

When my wife Sarah and I were in India for three months in our 20s I distinctly remember getting to Kathmandu and experiencing a warm shower for the first time in three months. I can't tell you the joy I experienced from the warm water. It was a real golden nugget of positivity and I remember thinking at the time: 'I must save this experience; it can help me in the future.' Today part of my 'getting up ritual' is to spend 30 seconds to a minute in the shower reliving that amazing moment of sheer joy. Every day of my life starts with 30 seconds of appreciation and a minute of sheer joy. It's a great way to start the day.

Similarly, I remember coaching an executive to identify his 'car ritual'. Initially he didn't have a clue what I was talking about but as I asked him questions it soon emerged that he did actually have quite a detailed car ritual: open the car with the beeper – open the door with right hand – get in, sit down – put the key in the ignition – turn the engine on – put his seat belt on – turn on Radio 4 – drive to work. Once the ritual was identified I got him to do exactly the same but for the first five minutes of his 30-minute journey he was to listen to his favourite CD instead of Radio 4. While listening to his favourite music he was to rehearse the feeling of exhilaration and sing at the top of his voice! He noted that five minutes into his journey there was a physical landmark that would remind him to stop his PEP and tune into Radio 4, turn on his phone and carry on driving to work as normal. This executive was dubious, to put it mildly, but he did it, nonetheless. For five minutes every morning he rehearsed exhilaration. What surprised him was that this little and simple practice meant that he began to arrive at work feeling energized and optimistic, which in turn had a positive impact on his day and the people around him.

The best way to incorporate PEPs into your day is to identify your rituals around transition points and enhance them by rehearsing an emotion for 30 seconds to a few minutes. This way, life just becomes practice.

LANDSCAPING

In addition to experiencing more positive emotions throughout our day with a PEP plan, it can also help to engage in formal times of practice in order to embed the positive emotion into our life. The best way to do this is to 'landscape' our week. Landscaping is about identifying where we can get the most 'bang' for our practice 'buck'.

Imagine your diary is like a half-full bucket of water and we are going to add rocks, pebbles and sand to the bucket. The rocks are 15-minute blocks of time where you practise emotional self-regulation, the pebbles are 2–5 minutes of practice and the sand is <2 minutes of practice in any week. The best way to landscape your week is to put in the big chunks of practice (rocks) where you really need them, say just before a really tough meeting.

That way you will be in the best possible emotional state prior to the meeting so your practice immediately provides a practical real-world benefit to your day. Depending on the space you have left in your bucket, you would then landscape in the pebbles around events that were not so critical, and finally trickle in a few handfuls of sand where you were practising for under two minutes as and when you can.

For example, you might have a board meeting on Friday – that's a really important meeting so you might want to spend 10 minutes before that meeting getting into the right frame of mind and the right emotional state. You might have a weekly meeting with your department heads that's important but nowhere near as important as the board meeting, so it might only need a few minutes of emotional preparation. By landscaping your week, you factor in a little extra time before each activity, depending on the importance or significance of that activity, and it can really help if you make your executive assistant complicit in this plan.

Landscaping is a tool that acknowledges that you are already busy while encouraging you to incorporate the practice into your normal business day rather than some hypothetical situation. That way, you can experience the benefits of emotional self-regulation in situations that really matter. This approach also allows us to recuperate and refresh ourselves as we go through the week rather than having to rely on weekends or holidays to recover. Practice thereby becomes part of the way we operate. Unconscious competence is established and the benefits accumulate.

Emotional coherence facilitates cognitive coherence

In business, the emotional line of development is often ignored or considered irrelevant. This is a mistake, and robs us of a massive amount of data, energy and cognitive ability. It is, however, easy to understand the reluctance of senior leaders to embrace emotion. For a start, many of the diagnostic tools available to measure emotion are cumbersome. They rarely provide information that can be acted upon at a managerial level. To overcome these limitations, we developed the emotional and social intelligence (ESQ) profile. The ESQ profile gives a leader a sense of the emotional state of the employee base. For example, if a leader can establish that 72 per cent of his senior or managerial team feel tired or exhausted often or most of the time, clearly that is impacting results and needs to be addressed.

The ESQ assessment provides leaders with meaningful data about the level of energy, emotional negativity and positivity in the workforce. It was built after we reviewed more than 200 existing assessment instruments in the market and over 1,000 questions. Most of the existing instruments suggest there are three or a maximum of six dimensions to emotional and social intelligence, and many of these instruments are contaminated with constructs that have little to do with emotional intelligence. We believe there are 12 separate dimensions to ESQ. We also think to assess ESQ accurately you need a mixed methodology. All the other instruments are self-assessment instruments. This is an error. Thus, everyone is likely to rate themselves as empathic, but the only way to accurately assess your empathy levels is to ask others rather than yourself. Similarly, most people are likely to overrate their emotional literacy levels, but if we track what emotions you actually experience over time, we can much more accurately determine your real level of differentiation based on real data. Our Complete app assesses all 12 dimensions of ESQ, and we believe, therefore, it's the most precise assessment of ESQ currently available, anywhere in the world.

We may not be able to change the difficult situations we find ourselves in, but we can change how we process them, and that's largely done through emotional self-regulation. How we feel is a choice; we can choose to rehearse happiness, gratitude and appreciation or we can choose to practise upset, anger and frustration. Such an insight is not new; happiness is essentially a habit.[78] The skills in this chapter allow us to become much more familiar with our emotions and the skills of MASTERY, PEP and Landscaping provide a methodology for turning happiness and health into a habit.

Health and happiness are only possible when we learn to appreciate our emotions, differentiate between them and ultimately manage them. The second step towards Exceptional Leadership is therefore emotional coherence, which is facilitated by emotional intelligence, emotional literacy and emotional self-management. And this in turn facilitates cognitive coherence, which we will explore next.

Summary of key points

If you don't remember everything in this chapter, remember this:

- Health and happiness are relevant to business because they reduce absenteeism, increase employee engagement, diminish the risk of unexpected succession and improve productivity throughout the company.

- Mismanaged emotion is the superhighway to disease and distress. There is now a mountain of evidence linking prolonged negative emotion to heart disease, cancer, stroke and depression.

- Emotion is significantly more important to health and happiness than exercise or what you eat.

- Emotions are composite physiological signals. A feeling is the conscious awareness or observation of that composite data. Everyone has emotion: male, female, young and old.

- Even if people look calm on the outside and have learnt to ignore or suppress their feelings, that doesn't mean they are coherent on the inside. The emotional data may still be chaotic, and it's this emotional chaos that is so toxic for mental and physical health.

- The real E-myth that is holding business back is the universal dismissal of (E)motion as a business tool and the fact that intellect is mistakenly viewed as considerably more important in business.

- In business we think we are making rational logical choices based on verifiable data and intelligent thought. Without emotional management what's actually happening is that our emotionally driven amygdala is initiating a subliminal knee-jerk reaction based on long-forgotten conditioning designed to protect us from external threats.

- Emotional mastery is critical in business because it improves clarity of thought, ability to learn, decision making, relationships at work, effective management of change, leadership presence, health and well-being, enjoyment and quality of life, meaning, significance and purpose, motivation and resilience and facilitates an expanded sense of self.

- Emotional coherence is created by developing emotional intelligence or awareness (E-diary), greater emotional literacy (MASTERY) and emotional self-management (PEP and Landscaping). All available on the Complete app.

Notes

1   Makortoff, K (2020) Lloyds chief António Horta-Osório to chair Credit Suisse, *Guardian*, 1 December

2   Treanor, J (2011) Lloyds chief Horta-Osório takes time off with fatigue, *Guardian*, 2 November

3 Sirén, C, Patel, P C, Örtqvist, D and Wincent, J (2018) CEO burnout, managerial discretion, and firm performance: The role of CEO locus of control, structural power, and organizational factors, *Long Range Planning*, 51 (6), pp 953–71; Ochoa, P (2018) Impact of burnout on organizational outcomes, the influence of legal demands: The case of Ecuadorian physicians, *Frontiers in Psychology*, 4 May; Schaufeli, W B, Leiter, M P, and Maslach, C (2009) Burnout: 35 years of research and practice, *Career Development International*, 14, pp 204–20

4 Alexander, F (1939) Psychological aspects of medicine, *Psychosomatic Medicine*, 1 (1), pp 7–18

5 Le Fanu, J (1999) *The Rise and Fall of Modern Medicine*, Little, Brown and Company, London

6 Townsend, N, Wickramasinghe, K, Bhatnagar, P, Smolina, K, Nichols, M, Leal, J, Luengo-Fernandez, R and Rayner, M (2012) *Coronary Heart Disease Statistics*, British Heart Foundation, London

7 World Health Organization (2011) *Global Status Report on Noncommunicable Diseases 2010*, Geneva, World Health Organization

8 British Heart Foundation (2021) Twice as deadly as breast cancer, www.bhf. org.uk/informationsupport/heart-matters-magazine/medical/women/coronary-heart-disease-kills (archived at https://perma.cc/Q8ZK-9SE6)

9 Society for Heart Attack Prevention and Eradication (2021) What you should know, https://shapesociety.org/what-you-should-know (archived at https://perma.cc/HQ58-ZEFC); News Medical (2012) First sign of coronary heart disease in men could be death, www.news-medical.net/news/20120208/First-sign-of-coronary-heart-disease-in-men-could-be-death.aspx (archived at https://perma.cc/HX98-5FFA)

10 Lynch, J L (2000) *A Cry Unheard: New insights into the medical consequences of loneliness*, Bancroft Press, Baltimore, MD

11 Lönn, S L, Melander, O, Crump, C and Sundquist, K (2019) Accumulated neighbourhood deprivation and coronary heart disease: A nationwide cohort study from Sweden, *BMJ Open*, Sep, 9 (9); Akwo, E A, Kabagambe, E K, Harrell, F E Jr, Blot, W J, Bachmann, J M, Wang, T J, Gupta, D K and Lipworth, L (2018) Neighborhood deprivation predicts heart failure risk in a low-income population of blacks and whites in the southeastern United States, *Circulation: Cardiovascular Quality and Outcomes*, Jan, 11 (1); Kelli, H M, Hammadah, M, Ahmed, H, Ko, Y A, Topel, M, Samman-Tahhan, A, Awad, M, Patel, K, Mohammed, K, Sperling, L S, Pemu, P, Vaccarino, V, Lewis, T, Taylor, H, Martin, G, Gibbons, G H and Quyyumi, A A (2017) Association between living in food deserts and cardiovascular risk, *Circulation: Cardiovascular Quality and Outcomes*, Sep, 10 (9)

12 Schultz, W M, Kelli, H M, Lisko, J C, Varghese, T, Shen, J, Sandesara, P, Quyyumi, A A, Taylor, H A, Gulati, M, Harold, J G, Mieres, J H, Ferdinand, K C, Mensah, G A, and Sperling, L S (2018) Socioeconomic status and cardiovascular outcomes: Challenges and interventions, *Circulation*, May, 137 (20), pp 2166–78; Tawakol, A, Osborne, M T, Wang, Y, Hammed, B, Tung, B, Patrich, T, Oberfeld, B, Ishai, A, Shin, L M, Nahrendorf, M, Warner, E T, Wasfy, J, Fayad, Z A, Koenen, K, Ridker, P M, Pitman, R K and Armstrong, K A (2019) Stress-associated neurobiological pathway linking socioeconomic disparities to cardiovascular disease, *Journal of the American College of Cardiology*, Jul, 73 (25), pp 3243–55

13 Lynch, J L (2000) *A Cry Unheard: New insights into the medical consequences of loneliness*, Bancroft Press, Baltimore, MD

14 Vaccarino, V, Sullivan, S, Hammadah, M, Wilmot, K, Al Mheid, I, Ramadan, R, Elon, L, Pimple, P M, Garcia, E V, Nye, J, Shah, A J, Alkhoder, A, Levantsevych, O, Gay, H, Obideen, M, Huang, M, Lewis, T T, Bremner, J D, Quyyumi, A A and Raggi, P (2018) Mental stress-induced-myocardial ischemia in young patients with recent myocardial infarction: Sex differences and mechanisms, *Circulation*, Feb, 137 (8), pp 794–805

15 Hartmann, R, Schmidt, F M, Sander, C and Hegerl, U (2019) Heart rate variability as indicator of clinical state in depression, *Frontiers in Psychiatry*, Jan, 9, p 735; Case, S M, Sawhney, M and Stewart, J C (2018) Atypical depression and double depression predict new-onset cardiovascular disease in US adults, *Depression and Anxiety*, Jan, 35 (1), pp 10–17; Zhou, L, Ma, X and Wang, W (2020) Inflammation and coronary heart disease risk in patients with depression in China mainland: A cross-sectional study, *Neuropsychiatric Disease and Treatment*, Jan, 16, pp 81–86

16 Berge, T, Bull-Hansen, B, Solberg, E E, Heyerdahl, E R, Jørgensen, K N, Vinge, L E, Aarønæs, M, Øie, E and Hyldmo, I (2019) Screening for symptoms of depression and anxiety in a cardiology department, *Tidsskr Nor Laegeforen*, Oct, 139 (14)

17 Eichstaedt, J C, Schwartz, H A, Kern, M L, Park, G, Labarthe, D R, Merchant, R M, Jha, S, Agrawal, M, Dziurzynski, L A, Sap, M, Weeg, C, Larson, E E, Ungar, L H and Seligman, M E (2015) Psychological language on Twitter predicts county-level heart disease mortality, *Psychological Science*, Feb, 26 (2), pp 159–69; Newman, J D, Davidson, K W, Shaffer, J A, Schwartz, J E, Chaplin, W, Kirkland, S, and Shimbo, D (2011) Observed hostility and the risk of incident ischemic heart disease: A prospective population study from the 1995 Canadian Nova Scotia Health Survey, *Journal of the American College of Cardiology*, Sep, 58 (12), pp 1222–28; Stewart, J C, Fitzgerald, G J and Kamarck, T W (2010) Hostility now, depression later? Longitudinal associations among emotional risk factors for coronary artery disease, *Annals of Behavioral Medicine*, Jun, 39 (3), pp 258–66; Benson, E (2003) Hostility is among best predictors of heart disease in men, American Psychology Association, www.apa.org/monitor/jan03/hostility (archived at https://perma.cc/KD9S-2N72)

18 Rosenman, R H (1993) The independent roles of diet and serum lipids in the 20th-century rise and decline of coronary heart disease mortality, *Integrative Physiological and Behavioral Science*, 28 (1), pp 84–98; Anand, S S, Abonyi, S, Arbour, L Balasubramanian, K, Brook, J, Castleden, H, et al (2019) Explaining the variability in cardiovascular risk factors among First Nation communities in Canada: A population-based study, *The Lancet*, Dec, 3 (12)

19 Valtorta, N K, Kanaan, M, Gilbody, S and Hanratty, B (2018) Loneliness, social isolation and risk of cardiovascular disease in the English Longitudinal Study of Ageing, *European Journal of Preventive Cardiology*, Sep, 25 (13), pp 1387–96

20 Glassman, A H and Shapiro, P A (1998) Depression and the course of coronary artery disease, *American Journal of Psychiatry*, 155 (1), pp 4–11; Rahman, I, Humphreys, K, Bennet, A M, Ingelsson, E, Pedersen, N L and Magnusson, P K (2013) Clinical depression, antidepressant use and risk of future cardiovascular disease, *European Journal of Epidemiology*, Jul, 28 (7), pp 589–95; Murphy, B, Le Grande, M, Alvarenga, M, Worcester, M and Jackson, A (2020) Anxiety and depression after a cardiac event: Prevalence and predictors, *Frontiers in Psychology*, Jan, 10, 3010

21 Sweda, R, Siontis, G C M, Nikolakopoulou, A, Windecker, S and Pilgrim, T (2020) Antidepressant treatment in patients following acute coronary syndromes: A systematic review and Bayesian meta-analysis, *ESC Heart Failure*, Sep, 7 (6), pp 3610–20

22 Antonuccio, D O, Danton, W G and DeNelsky, G Y (1995) Psychotherapy versus medication for depression: Challenging the conventional wisdom with data, *Professional Psychology, Research and Practice*, 26 (6), pp 574–85; Douros, A, Dell'Aniello, S, Dehghan, G, Boivin, J F and Renoux, C (2019) Degree of serotonin reuptake inhibition of antidepressants and ischemic risk: A cohort study, *Neurology*, Sep, 93 (10)

23 Kubzansky, L D, Kawachi, I, Spiro, A I, Weiss, S T, Vokonas, P S and Sparrow, D (1997) Is worrying bad for your heart? A prospective study of worry and coronary heart disease in the Normative Aging Study, *Circulation*, 95 (4), pp 818–24; Li, J, Ji, F, Song, J, Gao, X, Jiang, D, Chen, G, Chen, S, Lin, X and Zhuo, C (2020) Anxiety and clinical outcomes of patients with acute coronary syndrome: A meta-analysis, *BMJ Open*, Jul, 10 (7)

24 Everson, S A, Kaplan, G A, Goldberg, D E, Salonen, R and Salonen, J T (1997) Hopelessness and four-year progression of carotid atherosclerosis: The Kuopio ischemic heart disease risk factor study, *Arteriosclerosis Thrombosis Vascular Biology*, 17 (8), pp 1490–95

25 Li, H, Zheng ,D, Li, Z, Wu, Z, Feng, W, Cao, X, Wang, J, Gao, Q, Li, X, Wang, W, Hall, B J, Xiang, Y T and Guo, X (2019) Association of depressive symptoms with incident cardiovascular diseases in middle-aged and older Chinese adults, *JAMA Network Open*, Dec, 2 (12)

26 Bu, F, Zaninotto, P and Fancourt, D (2020) Longitudinal associations between loneliness, social isolation and cardiovascular events, *Heart*, Sep, 106 (18), pp 1394–99

27 Dekker, J M, Schouten, E G, Klootwijk, P, Pool, J, Swenne, C A and Kromhout, D (1997) Heart rate variability from short electrocardiographic recordings predicts mortality from all causes in middle-aged and elderly men: The Zutphen study, *American Journal of Epidemiology*, 145 (10), pp 899–908

28 Burton, W N, Conti, D J, Chen, C Y, Schultz, A B and Edington, D W (1999) The role of health risk factors and disease on worker productivity, *Journal of Occupational and Environmental Medicine*, 41 (10), pp 863–77

29 Melkevik, O, Clausen, T, Pedersen, J, Garde, A H, Holtermann, A and Rugulies, R (2018) Comorbid symptoms of depression and musculoskeletal pain and risk of long term sickness absence, *BMC Public Health*, Aug, 18 (1), p 981

30 Endo, M, Haruyama, Y, Mitsui, K, Muto, G, Nishiura, C, Kuwahara, K, Wada, H and Tanigawa, T (2019) Durations of first and second periods of depression-induced sick leave among Japanese employees: The Japan sickness absence and return to work (J-SAR) study, *Industrial Health*, Feb, 57 (1), pp 22–28

31 Linder, A, Gerdtham, U G, Trygg, N, Fritzell, S and Saha, S (2020) Inequalities in the economic consequences of depression and anxiety in Europe: A systematic scoping review, *European Journal of Public Health*, Aug, 30 (4), pp 767–77

32 Whiting, K (2020) As the COVID-19 death toll passes 1 million, how does it compare to other major killers? World Economic Forum, www.weforum.org/agenda/2020/09/covid-19-deaths-global-killers-comparison (archived at https://perma.cc/MW72-9TGR)

33 Ciuluvica Neagu, C, Amerio, P and Grossu, I V (2020) Emotional dysregulation mechanisms in psychosomatic chronic diseases revealed by the instability coefficient, *Brain Science*, Sep, 10 (10), p 673

34 LeShan, L (1977) *You Can Fight for Your Life*, M Evans, New York

35 Grossarth-Maticek, R (1980) Psychosocial predictors of cancer and internal diseases: an overview, *Psychotherapy and Psychosomatics*, 33 (3), pp 122–28; Pettingale, K W, Philalithis, A, Tee, D E and Greer, H S (1981) The biological correlates of psychological responses to breast cancer, *Journal of Psychosomatic Research*, 25 (5), pp 453–58; Levy, S M, Lee, J, Bagley, C and Lippman, M (1988) Survival hazards analysis in first recurrent breast cancer patients: Seven-year follow-up, *Psychosomatic Medicine*, 50 (5), pp 520–28;

Wang, X, Wang, N, Zhong, L, Wang, S, Zheng, Y, Yang, B, Zhang, J, Lin, Y and Wang, Z (2020) Prognostic value of depression and anxiety on breast cancer recurrence and mortality: A systematic review and meta-analysis of 282,203 patients, *Molecular Psychiatry*, Dec, 25(12), pp 3186–97; Ding, T, Wang, X, Fu, A, Xu, L and Lin, J (2019) Anxiety and depression predict unfavorable survival in acute myeloid leukemia patients, *Medicine (Baltimore)*, Oct, 98 (43)

36 Bolletino, R and LeShan, L (1997) Cancer, in *Mind–Body Medicine*, ed A Watkins, pp 87–109, Churchill Livingstone, New York

37 Eskelinen, A and Ollonen, P (2011) Assessment of 'cancer-prone personality' characteristics in healthy study subjects and in patients with breast disease and breast cancer using the commitment questionnaire: A prospective case–control study in Finland, *Anticancer Research*, Nov, 31 (11), pp 4013–17; Neuroskeptic (2019) The cancer personality scandal (part 1), *Discover Magazine*, www.discovermagazine.com/the-sciences/the-cancer-personality-scandal-part-1 (archived at https://perma.cc/32MA-CHZ2); Nabi, H, Kivimäki, M, Marmot, M G, Ferrie, J, Zins, M, Ducimetière, P, Consoli, S M and Singh-Manoux, A (2008) Does personality explain social inequalities in mortality? The French GAZEL cohort study, *International Journal of Epidemiology*, Jun, 37 (3), pp 591–602

38 Butcher, S K and Lord, J M (2004) Stress responses and innate immunity: Aging as a contributory factor, *Aging Cell*, Aug, 3 (4), pp 151–60

39 Goleman, D (1987) Research affirms power of positive thinking, *New York Times*, 3 February

40 Roberts, A L, Huang, T, Koenen, K C, Kim, Y, Kubzansky, L D and Tworoger, S S (2019) Posttraumatic stress disorder is associated with increased risk of ovarian cancer: A prospective and retrospective longitudinal cohort study, *Cancer Research*, Oct, 79 (19), pp 5113–20; Agnew-Blais, J, Chen, Q, Cerdá, M, Rexrode, K M, Rich-Edwards, J W, Spiegelman, D, Suglia, S F, Rimm, E B, Koenen, K C, Sumner, J A, Kubzansky, L D, Elkind, M S and Roberts, A L (2015) Trauma exposure and posttraumatic stress disorder symptoms predict onset of cardiovascular events in women, *Circulation*, Jul, 132 (4), pp 251–59

41 Kiecolt-Glaser, J K, Stephens, R E, Lipetz, P D, Speicher, C E and Glaser, R (1985) Distress and DNA repair in human lymphocytes, *Journal of Behavioral Medicine*, 8 (4), pp 311–20

42 Kakoo Brioso, E, Ferreira, C S, Costa, L and Ouakinin, S (2020) Correlation between emotional regulation and peripheral lymphocyte counts in colorectal cancer patients, *PeerJ*, Jul, 8

43 Engel, G L (1968) A life setting conducive to illness: The giving-up–given-up complex, *Annals of Internal Medicine*, 69 (2), pp 239–300

44 Purcell, H and Mulcahy, D (1994) Emotional eclipse of the heart, *British Journal of Clinical Practice*, 48 (5), pp 228–29

45 Pressman, S D, Jenkins, B N and Moskowitz, J T (2019) Positive affect and health: What do we know and where next should we go? *Annual Review of Psychology*, Jan, 70, pp 627–50

46 Davidson, K W, Mostofsky, E and Whang, W (2010) Don't worry, be happy: Positive affect and reduced 10-year incident coronary heart disease: The Canadian Nova Scotia Health Survey, *European Heart Journal*, May, 31 (9), pp 1065–70

47 Haidt, J (2006) *The Happiness Hypothesis: Putting ancient wisdom and philosophy to the test of modern science*, Arrow Books, London

48 Carver, C S, Scheier, M F and Weintraub, J K (1989) Assessing coping strategies: A theoretically based approach, *Journal of Personality and Social Psychology*, 56 (2), pp 267–83; Lazarus, R S and Folkman, S (1984) *Stress, Appraisal, and Coping*, Springing Publishing Company, New York

49 Jafri, S H, Ali, F, Mollaeian, A, Mojiz Hasan, S, Hussain, R, Akkanti, B, Williams, J, Shoukier, M and El-Osta, H (2019) Major stressful life events and risk of developing lung cancer: A case-control study, *Clinical Medicine Insights: Oncology*, May, 13; Bagheri, B, Meshkini, F, Dinarvand, K, Alikhani, Z, Haysom, M and Rasouli, M (2016) Life psychosocial stresses and coronary artery disease, *International Journal of Preventive Medicine*, Sep, 7, p 106

50 Pennebaker, J W (1997) *Opening Up: The healing power of expressing emotions*, Guilford Press, New York

51 Eriksson, M (2017) The sense of coherence in the salutogenic model of health, in *The Handbook of Salutogenesis*, Springer, Cham

52 Kobasa, S C (1979) Stressful life events, personality, and health: An inquiry into hardiness, *Journal of Personality and Social Psychology*, Jan, 37 (1), pp 1–11

53 Karimi, S, Jaafari, A, Ghamari, M, Esfandiary, M, Salehi Mazandarani, F, Daneshvar, S and Ajami, M (2016) A comparison of type II diabetic patients with healthy people: Coping strategies, hardiness, and occupational life quality, *International Journal of High Risk Behaviors and Addiction*, Jan, 5 (1)

54 Slade, M, Rennick-Egglestone, S, Blackie, L, Llewellyn-Beardsley, J, Franklin, D, Hui, A, Thornicroft, G, McGranahan, R, Pollock, K, Priebe, S, Ramsay, A, Roe, D and Deakin, E (2019) Post-traumatic growth in mental health recovery: Qualitative study of narratives, *BMJ Open*, Jun, 9 (6); İnan, F Ş and Üstün, B (2019) Post-traumatic growth in the early survival phase: From Turkish breast cancer survivors' perspective, *European Journal of Breast Health*, Dec, 16 (1), pp 66–71; Cui, P P, Wang, P P, Wang, K, Ping, Z, Wang, P and Chen, C (2020) Post-traumatic growth and influencing factors among frontline nurses fighting against COVID-19, *Occupational and Environmental Medicine*, Oct

55 Ragger, K, Hiebler-Ragger, M, Herzog, G, Kapfhammer, H P and Unterrainer, H F (2019) Sense of coherence is linked to post-traumatic growth after critical incidents in Austrian ambulance personnel, *BMC Psychiatry*, Mar, 19 (1), pp 89

56 Sheldon, K M and Kasser, T (1995) Coherence and congruence: Two aspects of personality integration, *Journal of Personality and Social Psychology*, 68 (3), pp 531–43

57 Coates, J (2013) *The Hour Between Dog and Wolf: Risk taking, gut feelings and the biology of boom and bust*, Fourth Estate, London

58 Coates, J (2013) *The Hour Between Dog and Wolf: Risk taking, gut feelings and the biology of boom and bust*, Fourth Estate, London

59 Norretranders, T (1998) *The User Illusion: Cutting consciousness down to size*, Penguin, New York

60 Ikai, M and Steinhaus, A H (1961) Some factors modifying the expression of human strength, *Journal of Applied Physiology*, 16 (1), pp 157–63

61 Gerber, M E (1995) *The E-Myth Revisited*, HarperCollins, New York

62 Grant Thornton (2020) Women in business 2020: Putting the blueprint into action, www.grantthornton.global/globalassets/1.-member-firms/global/insights/women-in-business/2020/women-in-business-2020_report.pdf (archived at https://perma.cc/7Z8J-BLWR)

63 Pink, D H (2009) *Drive: The surprising truth about what motivates us*, Penguin, New York

64 Bughin, J, Woetzel, J and Manyika, J (2011) Jobs lost, jobs gained: Workforce transitions in a time of automation, McKinsey's Global Institute, www.mckinsey.com/~/media/mckinsey/industries/public%20and%20social%20sector/our%20insights/what%20the%20future%20of%20work%20will%20mean%20for%20jobs%20skills%20and%20wages/mgi%20jobs%20lost-jobs%20gained_report_december%202017.pdf (archived at https://perma.cc/33VN-DQ8P)

65 McGregor, D (1960) *The Human Side of Enterprise*, McGraw Hill, New York

66 Damasio, A (2000) *The Feeling of What Happens: Body, emotion and the making of consciousness*, Vintage, London

67 Damasio, A (2006) *Descartes' Error*, London, Vintage

68 El Othman, R, El Othman, R, Hallit, R, Obeid, S and Hallit, S (2020) Personality traits, emotional intelligence and decision-making styles in Lebanese universities medical students, *BMC Psychology*, May, 8 (1), p 46; Mazzocco, K, Masiero, M, Carriero, M C and Pravettoni, G (2019) The role of emotions in cancer patients' decision-making, *Ecancermedicalscience*, Mar, 13, p 914; Morawetz, C, Mohr, P N C, Heekeren, H R and Bode, S (2019) The effect of emotion regulation on risk-taking and decision-related activity in prefrontal cortex, *Social Cognitive and Affective Neuroscience*, Oct, 14(10), pp 1109–18

69 Berry, A S, Jagust, W J and Hsu, M (2019) Age-related variability in decision-making: Insights from neurochemistry, *Cognitive, Affective, and Behavioral Neuroscience*, Jun, 19(3), pp 415–34

70 Coates, J (2013) *The Hour Between Dog and Wolf: Risk taking, gut feelings and the biology of boom and bust*, Fourth Estate, London

71 Berman, S (2010) *Capitalizing on Complexity: Insights from the Global Chief Executive Officer Study*, IBM Global Business Services, Somers

72 Walsch, N D (1998) *Conversation with God, Book 3*, Hampton Road Publishing Company, Vancouver

73 Plutchik, R (1967) The affective differential: Emotion profiles implied by diagnostic concepts, *Psychological Reports*, 20 (1), pp 19–25

74 Goleman, D and Dalai Lama (2004) *Destructive Emotions: And how can we overcome them*, Bloomsbury, London

75 Universe of Emotions on the App Store (apple.com)

76 Rahm, T and Heise, E (2019) Teaching happiness to teachers: Development and evaluation of a training in subjective well-being, *Frontiers in Psychology*, Dec, 10, 2703

77 Wallis, C (2005) The new science of happiness: What makes the human heart sing? *Time Magazine*, 17 January

78 Maltz, M (1960) *Psycho-Cybernetics*, Simon and Schuster, New York

04

Be smarter

Have you ever had the experience of being in an important meeting when you suddenly go blank, forgetting everything you've rehearsed? Have you ever nipped out of the office to get something and been so distracted that you forgot what you had nipped out for? Have you ever needed to focus on a certain task and project but found it impossible to think? Do you find that some days you are 'on fire' and other days you couldn't come up with a good idea if your life depended on it? Are you tired of telling your people to 'think outside the box' even though you're not sure where the box is or what's outside it? Have you ever made decisions or barked out orders that you later regret? Do you ever wonder if your anger or volatility are negatively affecting your decision making but have no idea how to change it? If so, you're not alone.

Growing a business requires clarity of thought, or at least the ability to out-think the competition. But the content and the quality of our consciousness is determined by our physiology. This chapter explores what drives thinking, both the content (ie *what* we think) and the quality (ie *how well* we think it). We will discover that our physiology doesn't just impact on our energy levels, health and happiness but also our ability to think and clearly articulate our point of view – a fact not lost on G4S's former CEO Nick Buckles, who was able to use his mastery of many of the techniques in this book to deliver a much more coherent performance the second time he faced a Home Affairs Select Committee investigation. He notes that the techniques:

> helped me to project myself better and, as a result, I was better able to get the key points across... and to be more positive and to channel energy away from being apologetic. I focused on what we had done to rectify the problems,

without being arrogant. In this kind of situation, if you show any fear it is very easy to allow others to take control of the situation.

Companies need people who can think high-quality thoughts consistently. They need innovators able to generate great ideas, spot opportunities and define the things that provide a competitive advantage.[1] Without innovation and quality thinking, executives just come up with the same old ideas, same old strategies and same old products that either they or someone else has already thought of, often repackaged as though they were new. If we look at some of the companies that are growing very fast, like Tencent in China, or the German unicorn Celonis, we can see that they employ the best thinkers available, capable of disruptive innovation. The way to really get ahead and stay ahead is to become smarter than everyone else. And that starts with physiology.

The DIY lobotomy

People don't think straight under pressure. Everyone has experienced this at some point or another. Most of us can remember going through the pressure of exams, for example. Endless hours of revision can evaporate the moment we turn over the question paper and the stress causes our brain to shut down – we experience a 'do-it-yourself' (DIY) lobotomy.

Two hundred thousand years ago, when humans first stood upright, this sort of brain shutdown under pressure gave us a distinct survival advantage. When our ancestors were wandering across the savannah and they encountered a lion, they didn't need clever thinking. If they stood in front of the lion musing on whether the lion looked hungry, or was watching them, then they would probably have been killed. In an emergency, human beings evolved a mechanism for shutting down all the clever thinking parts of the brain to leave only two options: fight/flight (adrenaline driven) or play dead (acetylcholine driven). In the face of real danger, our brain goes binary to save our life.

The problem is that here we are 200,000 years later still using the same mechanism. We are using 200,000-year-old software and we've never had an upgrade. The only difference today is that very few of us meet lions on the savannah. We meet each other. We meet demanding bosses, difficult colleagues, agitated partners and disgruntled customers. They are the lions of today. Unfortunately, the difficult boss or colleague still causes the same DIY lobotomy, just as effectively as the lion ever did.

And, to make matters worse, once our brain has shut down, we often don't even realize it because we don't have enough remaining perceptual awareness to notice we've lobotomized ourselves. We think we are still functioning well, when in fact we have lost focus, drifted off the point, become confused or even started to babble. Because of the pressure of modern business, too many people are wandering around corporate offices with a partial, or in some cases almost complete, self-induced lobotomy that is massively impacting their cognitive ability and therefore their ability to deliver results.

Most leaders may think about the challenges they face, but what they never think about is their own thinking. They rarely wonder why they may be full of ideas one day and the next day they can't come up with a single useful insight. We simply don't understand the nature of human cognition and we don't realize that the thoughts we think don't happen in a vacuum. There isn't a series of bubbles coming out of our head like in the comic books. Our thoughts occur in the context of our physiology. When we think, our heart is always beating, our guts are always digesting, our muscles are always moving, and these physiological signals can have a profound effect on what we think and how well we think it.

This is why it's imperative to build coherence from the ground up, starting with physiology, because without physiological coherence emotional coherence is almost impossible and without emotional coherence consistent, high-quality thinking is also much more difficult.

When people make mistakes, be it in an exam, in a shareholder meeting or when being interviewed by a journalist, we usually shrug our shoulders and dismiss this phenomenon with a statement such as 'These things happen' or 'It was human error' as though such phenomena are inevitable or, worse, normal and acceptable. They may be common, but they are completely avoidable.

Many senior executives try to minimize the possibility of making stupid blunders by putting themselves under 'exam conditions' ahead of time in the mistaken belief that if they get used to the pressure this will stop the blunder from happening. It won't. Our biology is too powerful. Practising a speech is, of course, helpful, but it's not enough to stop us going blank when we get a tricky question from an analyst afterwards that we were not expecting. No matter how much we have practised we are still at risk of brain shut-down, binary thinking, gross over-simplification or what we may later need to try and excuse with that modern euphemism, a 'mis-step' or the claim that we 'mis-spoke'.

We have all made decisions or done something that, with hindsight, we find utterly bewildering. But it's not bewildering if we realize how cognition works and the fact that we are permanently on the edge of a lobotomy. Our brains are constantly getting signals from all the bodily systems, but particularly from the heart, via the vagus nerve. When we are under pressure our heart rate variability (HRV) becomes super-chaotic, which causes 'cortical inhibition', and our frontal lobe function evaporates.

I demonstrated this in a TEDx talk I did in 2012. My brave volunteer, Neil, came up on stage and I attached a small clip to his earlobe to measure his HRV, which was displayed on a big screen behind him. Initially Neil's heart rate was pretty normal at about 75 bpm. But then I asked him to perform a maths challenge. I gave him a number and all he had to do was subtract three from that number and give me the new answer and repeat the task. Pretty straightforward, especially as Neil assured me that he was 'quite good' at maths. Interestingly as soon as he said 'quite good' his heart rate spiked, which indicated he perhaps wasn't as confident as he suggested. I started him at 300 and immediately he set off well, '297', '294'. Then I started to feed him the wrong answers. This added to the pressure. He soon became flustered and his heart rate variability became super-erratic, as we could see on the screen behind him. Neil still looked calm and confident but his brain stopped working because of the pressure I had put him under. His erratic heart rate variability signal had caused a DIY lobotomy. In a matter of a few seconds, I had turned a normally smart person dumb.

Neil didn't want this to happen – it just happened. When you call an emergency crisis meeting to deal with a breaking news story or a faulty product don't be reassured by the fact that your senior team appear composed and rational on the surface. If you were to attach an HRV clip to their ear, their physiology would probably tell a very different story. Just because someone looks composed and calm on the outside does not mean they are composed and calm on the inside. And if their HRV is totally erratic, what's really happening is your people have probably lobotomized themselves under the pressure of the crisis and neither you nor they realize it.

When we cut off access to our frontal lobes with a chaotic HRV (Figure 4.1) we can experience the consequences of brain shut down – albeit temporarily. The frontal lobes are the 'executive part' of our brain where most of our smart thinking occurs. Losing frontal lobe function therefore takes us back to very primitive, minimal function and capability.

FIGURE 4.1   Schematic for the effect of physiology on brain function

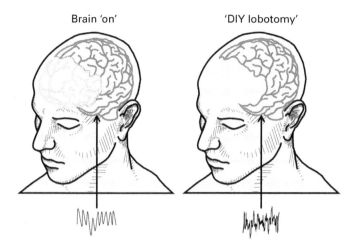

A chaotic signal from the heart:
- impairs perceptual awareness;
- reduces mental clarity;
- reduces creativity;
- impairs problem solving;
- reduces the ability to make effective decisions.

A coherent signal from the heart:
- enhances clarity;
- enhances creativity;
- enhances reaction speed;
- enhances thinking and decision making.

Physiological and emotional coherence will certainly facilitate a significant improvement in cognitive function and ability, but if we want to make a quantum leap, vertical development of adult maturity is the only way. If we are to prosper and genuinely thrive in a complex world, we need to expand our awareness and maturity to raise the calibre of leadership exponentially. The way that we think and lead an organization is fundamentally altered by our level of consciousness, our awareness and the level of maturity we operate from at any given time. These levels literally transform our ability to succeed.[2]

Let's explore a metaphor to convey the game-changing nature of such development. Everyone understands that all children go through the same specific stages of development physically, emotionally, cognitively and morally. These stages are often visible and obvious. Most of us, as parents, aunts or uncles, have witnessed this development first hand. When human beings reach the level of development of the average 14-year-old most have acquired the necessary skills and capabilities to function in an adult world. After 14 years of age there is no 'burning platform' or strong need for individuals to develop any further.

Subsequently they may leave school, get a job or go to university and climb a new 'learning curve'. But many individuals believe that once they reach about 22 or 23 years of age, they've essentially completed their education and their development. The truth, however, is that they've just completed child development, and most haven't even started the first stage of adult development, where the real magic happens. They may have reached physical maturity but the internal, invisible work that is critical to vertical adult development and holds the key to unlocking the vast reservoir of human potential in society has yet to begin.

Adult development is an invitation to become more than a 14-year-old. It's a massive new journey, not just physically but energetically, emotionally, mentally and morally. This vertical adult development facilitates a broader, deeper, more mature and sophisticated perspective. When we expand our awareness as a result of growing up as an adult it radically alters behaviour and results, not to mention health and well-being.

Most corporate training or leadership programmes are not even aware of adult development. Instead, they focus, almost exclusively, on horizontal skills acquisition. Of course, individuals need to improve their skill base but this isn't development. Corporate skill building is beefed up by adding knowledge building and ensuring a great user experience. But none of this is development. Development means we change as a human being. It is less about what we know and much more about the way that we know. Although worthwhile, horizontal skill acquisition creates incremental shifts, at best. It rarely, if ever, delivers expanded awareness or increased maturity.

Just because someone looks 'all grown up' on the outside doesn't mean they are on the inside. Remember the successful female executive from Chapter 1 who acquired some horizontal skills; because she hadn't woken up to the world around her and grown up as an adult human being, the additional skills just made her a more effective bully. She was the same person, just more knowledgeable about how to get her own way. That's not helpful.

The acquisition of skills, knowledge and experience gets us to the starting line not the finish line. It's vertical development that expands our capacity, capability, creativity and productivity. Despite the game changing nature of adult development, most organizations are blissfully unaware of the huge academic literature on the stages of adult development. Most companies have not yet realized that the future of their business depends on the vertical development of their leaders.

When it comes to understanding adult development and maturity, there have been many significant contributions, from the early days of Piaget,[3] Kohlberg[4] and Loevinger[5] to luminaries such as Ken Wilber, Susanne Cook-Greuter, Bill Torbert and Clare Graves. Each describes the vertical evolution of maturity and adult development from a slightly different perspective (Table 4.1). Wilber, who has written most extensively and has even done all the work contrasting the developmental models for us,[6] looks at the evolution of levels of consciousness. This is especially useful when considering how to be smarter and how to elevate our own personal levels of maturity. Cook-Greuter explores level of ego development, which is related to our ideas of identity and is unpacked in detail in my book *4D Leadership*.[7] Torbert's 'Action Logic' looks at how those stages play out in business; this can be especially insightful when looking at behaviour and will be explored in more detail in the next chapter. And finally, Graves' evolving values systems will be explored in more depth in Chapter 6. Graves' work is especially helpful in business when working to transform team dynamics and culture. See Table for 4.1 for comparisons.

These models offer us clear and elegant frameworks for understanding some profound truths and insights into how our life works. As Graves puts it, their purpose is to illustrate:

> that the psychology of the mature human being is [an] unfolding, emergent, oscillating, spiralling process marked by progressive subordination of older, lower-order behaviour systems to newer, higher-order systems as an individual's existential problems change. Each successive stage, wave, or level of existence is a stage through which people pass on their way to other states of being. When the human is centralized in one stage of existence, he or she has a psychology that is particular to that state. His or her feelings, motivations, ethics and values, biochemistry, degree of neurological activation, learning systems... conceptions of and preferences for management, education, economics and political theory and practice are all appropriate to that state.[8]

Regardless of which academic theorist we tap into, or which aspect of vertical development fires our imagination, there are various processes that will

TABLE 4.1 Comparison of key adult development frameworks

Wilber's Levels of Consciousness	Graves's Value systems	Cooke-Greuter's Ego development*	Torbert's Action Logic	World view
10. Non dual		Illuminated		
9. Pure awareness		Embodied		Post-post conventional (Cosmo-centric)
8. Unity in duality		Unitive	Ironist	
7. Pure being (*walk the walk*)	Planet, Turquoise	Alchemist	Alchemist	
6. Integrated self (*walk the talk*)	Paradox, Yellow	Integrator	Strategist	Post convertional (World-centric)
5. Transpersonal self (*talk the walk*)	Profit, Orange	Achiever	Achiever	
		Expert	Expert	Conventional (Ethno-centric)
	Process, Blue	Conformist	Diploma	
4. Concrete self (*talk the talk*)	Power, Red	Self-protective	Opportunist	Pre-conventional Egocentric
3. Conceptual self	Paternalistic, Purple	Ego-centric	Impulsive	
2. Emotional self	Survival, Beige	Impulsive		
1. Physical self				Pre-Egoic

NOTES
We adapted the labels from Graves' original to make it more comprehensible.[9]
* Cook-Greuter considers that there are six main stages of adult development and some of them are intermediary between more well-established stages. We have adapted the labels from Cook-Greuter original to make it more comprehensible.[10]

or can occur in the transition from one level to the next. As Goethe once said, 'Progress has not followed a straight ascending line, but a spiral with rhythms of progress and retrogression, of evolution and dissolution'.[11] Behavioural scientists have also confirmed Goethe's original insight. Progress is almost always followed by faltering, stagnation or regression.[12] As we enter each new level of development, we are somewhat unstable. The transition can feel uncomfortable and unfamiliar. It is important, when helping someone to jump up a level of development, that you are skilful at helping them deal with this discomfort so the new level delivers transformational development and regression is avoided.

The process of moving through the levels and any sub-levels (which we call stages) involves:

- Differentiation: Understanding how this level differs from the previous level.
- Integration: Internalizing the learning of this new level.
- Consolidation: Increasing comfort and identification with the new level.
- Realization: Realizing something's missing and becoming restless with the status quo.
- Transformation: Moving into the next level.
- Regression: Backslide to the previous level if proper consolidation doesn't occur.

To succeed in an accelerating and unstable world, leaders need to develop much more sophisticated, systematic thinking. They will need to master collaboration and effective change management, and these are all abilities that only start to become really sophisticated at Level 6 and above (see Table 4.2). Unfortunately, as Torbert reported in the *Harvard Business Review*, a whopping 85 per cent of leaders are currently operating below that level.[13] A little over half of all leaders (55 per cent) are currently operating at a level of sophistication that is insufficient if their business is to prosper in the future. Although this probably goes some way to explaining the levels of stress in modern business, it can all change with genuine vertical development.

Our level of maturity or awareness is therefore fundamental to our ability to be smarter because it effectively creates a lens through which we view and interact with the world. Most of us are completely unaware that we are looking at the world from a relatively constrained perspective that is determined by our individual level of maturity, our values and a whole host of other factors. Only once we 'wake up' to this fact can we truly 'grow up' and 'show up' differently.

Think of it like a fish swimming in water. The fish has no idea it's even in water and yet its entire life is determined and dictated by the water. Its very existence depends on the water. Human beings are the same, in that we are swimming around in our own particular pool of consciousness or maturity and we assume that everyone else is swimming in the same pool and seeing the same things, thinking the same things and viewing the world in exactly the same way. We're not.

What we experience and think about, and the depth and breadth of those thoughts, is very much dependent therefore on what pool we are swimming in. It can be extremely helpful to understand what pool we are in or what level of consciousness or maturity we are currently operating from, so we can truly understand where we are and appreciate the next step of our vertical development journey.

The 10 levels of consciousness

Living things may become consciously aware of their environment at the level of 20,000 neurons,[14] but as human beings we have 7 billion neurons in our head, not to mention the neural networks elsewhere in the body. The integrated neural network in our whole body is capable of extremely sophisticated consciousness. As we grow, most human beings unlock the first four levels of consciousness but never make it past the 'Concrete' of Level 4 and certainly don't reach Level 10 (Table 4.2).[15]

Leaders who have started to develop their self-awareness and have begun to reflect on the quality of their own thinking have often found new meaning in the movie *The Matrix*. While the film works as a basic boys' 'shoot 'em up' action movie, it's also an insightful commentary on human consciousness. Computer hacker Neo, played by Keanu Reeves, discovers a reference to the Matrix in computer code and seeks out the answers. By way of messages on his computer screen he is encouraged to 'Wake Up Neo' and follow a 'white rabbit', itself a reference to Lewis Carroll's *Alice in Wonderland*, a story on altered states of consciousness. Eventually Neo meets Morpheus, who offers him the choice between a red and a blue pill. Choosing the red pill, he becomes aware of a deeper 'unseen' reality – billions of people connected to a machine that is harvesting their energy while they experience a simulated virtual reality. Each of these individuals effectively chose the blue pill and they believe they are walking around, talking to friends and living a normal life. But it's all really an illusion and Neo, having chosen the red pill, is able to see the truth.

As human beings develop, they experience something similar, because at each stage of development we feel sure that we are experiencing reality as it really is. We're not; we're experiencing reality from that level of consciousness only. If we want to massively shift our thinking into a totally different dimension of depth, perception and insight, we must understand

TABLE 4.2 The 10 levels of consciousness

Level of awareness	Average age of first bloom	Key characteristics
10. Non-dual		Same as 9 but with an evolutionary spin; vast transcendent blissful emptiness, immediacy, pure presence.
9. Pure awareness		Pure awareness, direct experience where 'observer' has gone, transcends subject–object relationship, transcends time, space and concepts of such. 'Formless union'. Tinged with bliss.
8. Unity in duality		Experience of 'divine' union, 'oneness' with an object (God, golf ball, lover), but subject and object remain. Can foster an obsession with the focus of the 'union'. Duality as there is a witness observing the union.
7. Pure being (*walk the walk*)		More consistent 'being' state, with nourishing personal presence, phenomenal energy and powers of concentration, incredible selflessness. Experienced by others as a 'spiritual person'.
6. Integrated self (*walk the talk*)		Major development work completed, emotional baggage resolved and 'shadow' integrated.
5. Transpersonal self (*talk the walk*)	11–15 yrs and many adults	Interior world opens up properly for the first time. Thinking about thinking emerges, abstraction and algebra become possible.
4. Concrete self (*talk the talk*)	7–11 yrs and most adults	Clearly recognizable 'consciousness' or awareness. Engagement with the material world. Rules and roles drive behaviour (cf *The Matrix*).
3. Conceptual self	3–6 yrs	Three-dimensional representation of the world. Language is the main gain here and the ability to label the world.
2. Emotional self	2–3 yrs	Two-dimensional, emotions give depth to experience. Formal self-identity starts to emerge based in how 'I' feel. And 'I' may feel different things from 'you'.
1. Physical self	~1 yr	One-dimensional, experience dominated by physical needs and driven by physiology. Realization that 'I' am separate from 'you'.

consciousness and actively develop it so we expand our awareness beyond the ordinary. When we vertically develop our awareness, we're able to tap into an extreme competitive advantage. With each level we expand our perception still further, making us smarter and smarter and finally giving us access to the ideas and innovation outside that famous box everyone is talking about! As we develop, we see more of what's really going on, and with that knowledge comes power to change the game.

Below is a brief description of each of the 10 levels Wilber has described.

Level 1: the physical self

The first level of consciousness that emerges is the awareness of the physical self. This normally occurs within the first year of life when an infant realizes that biting his thumb hurts and biting his blanket doesn't! The first level of conscious awareness is therefore rooted in physical sensation. 'I am the thing that hurts when I bite it.' Prior to this there is no 'self' and there is little discrimination of an external world or other people. It is all just 'me'. Even at this first level of consciousness, the world is still pretty one-dimensional and awareness of anything other than physical needs and bodily functions is largely absent. This level is grounded in physiology.

Level 2: the emotional self

Once the physical self becomes stabilized and recognizes itself as separate from others, some time in the second year the emotional self starts to emerge, although these early levels may vary in when they blossom. At this level infants begin to realize that they are not only physically separate from others but that they may not be experiencing the same emotions as others. For example, a child may be very upset at having their needs thwarted by their parents and be completely baffled as to why their parents are not also upset.

Prior to this differentiation, children do not really make a distinction between their emotional needs and the emotional needs of others. This phase has often been referred to as the 'terrible twos' because of the tantrums that occur in an attempt to control the environment and have their needs met. However, it's really only a developmental level.

At this point, because of the lack of separation, infants are emotionally contagious. They easily spark each other into tears or laughter, and they are also easily influenced by the mood of the adults around them. They are incredibly egocentric as they want their emotional needs met.

Once this separation begins and the emotional self develops, suddenly the world has more depth; it has become two-dimensional. Entering this second dimension is a magical time for children. There is, as yet, no real responsibility and no great understanding of what makes the world work. Children at this point are physically and emotionally separate entities from the world around them but their thinking is still magical. To a child of this age, the clouds are following them.

Level 3: the conceptual self

Once a child is two to three years old, they will start to use language, images, symbols and concepts to represent the world, and this is the dominant level until the child is about six years old. Children acquire words at a phenomenal rate during these early years; roughly six new words a day are absorbed. They start to label everything, and this helps them navigate their world. They develop feelings as the emotions previously experienced are represented conceptually and start to be consciously appreciated as belonging to them. The world becomes three-dimensional and the thinking moves from magical to mythical – they know that they can't order the world around (magical) but someone can (mythical). This can be a little frightening as a child realizes that they are no longer in charge of the world; someone else is. Nightmares can start to occur. At this level feelings are central.

Level 4: the concrete self

At the fourth level of consciousness, both self-consciousness and consciousness of the self start to emerge. The three-dimensional world becomes much more concrete. There are rules and regulations that govern the world, and these must be followed. Children often become much more conformist and develop a belief in 'right' and 'wrong'. They start to rehearse various social scripts as a way of learning the social rules or ways of behaving. The constant stream of 'why mummy' questions testify to an incredible curiosity about the world but also a desire to understand the rules of the game. There is a strong need to belong and children succumb to peer pressure and herd mentality. Rationality and 'self-talk' begin as we become much more sophisticated in justifying our behaviour. This level normally starts to develop at five or six years old and continues to eight or nine years old initially.

The concrete level is the first level where there is some, albeit limited, sophistication in the thinking. It is also the level that Einstein refers to when he suggested that human beings are boxed in by the boundary conditions of their thinking. Level four consciousness is where the box that boxes us in is created, and unfortunately this is where the journey ends for many as they live out their days in this concrete three-dimensional world, with rules and regulations to be followed or ignored. There is a degree of consciousness of self at this level, but life is very concrete and materialistic. It's about working out the rules and following them, doing a good job; taking care of needs and 'getting through' is the primary objective. The recipe for life at this level of consciousness is:

HAVE

DO

BE

So, 'If I have enough money, I will be able to do what I want and then I will be happy.' Or 'If I have enough time, I will be able to do my job and I will be successful.' Or 'If I did not have parents on my case all the time, I would have the freedom to do the things I like doing and then I would be less trouble.' There are many versions of this recipe.

Most of us have encountered plenty of people in businesses who are still operating from this level of maturity. They are following the rules laid down by their industry, company or boss, and most of the time they conform to those rules without question or they deliberately 'break the rules' to operate 'out of the box', which ironically has itself become a rule for how to operate!

People may be 40 years old on the outside but on the inside, developmentally, they may be operating at a much younger level. Perhaps you've witnessed managers behaving like children in an attempt to assert their own egocentric needs. This is really a combination of a Level 3 desire to have needs met fuelled by an egocentric rule that 'I am the boss so I should be able to satisfy my needs.' Playground behaviour such as bullying can also occur when a manager has not grown beyond this level. This is the level of *The Matrix* where the manager has swallowed the blue pill. We think we know how the game is played and we are following the rules, largely unaware that we are following the rules. We may be breaking the rules but in a way that also still stays within the confines of the rules for rule-breaking. At this level leaders are not really awake or able to appreciate that there is something going on, a more sophisticated version of reality, although in almost every case, executives at this level already believe they *are* aware.

It's worth pointing out, however, that Einstein also said that you can't solve a problem from the same level of consciousness that created it. When people get stuck at Level 4 consciousness it's almost impossible to find new, creative and innovative solutions to challenges because they can't exit the level of consciousness that created the problem in the first place – they literally can't think outside the box.

At Level 4 individuals are said to 'talk the talk'. They are talking about stuff but it's not necessarily the right stuff or appropriate stuff and they are certainly not applying or doing anything about that stuff.

Level 5: the transpersonal self

Between the ages of 9 and 14 the individual starts to become aware that something else is going on beyond what they were told or had previously realized. Given Level 4 is where most adults live and breaking free of the concrete is the first real developmental task, it may be worth spending a little time unpacking the key sub-levels to the emergence of this level.

In the swampy foothills of the fifth level, the tribal, ethnocentric herd mentality of the third dimension collapses. There is a realization that it's no longer just about 'me'. Individual awareness becomes more 'transpersonal' and the ability to think about thinking emerges. The frontal lobes and nerve tracts have become fully myelinated, which allows high-speed 'broadband' connections within the frontal cortex and with other brain regions. This drives more sophisticated thinking and abstraction becomes possible. As a result, children can learn algebra.

If you ask an eight-year-old child '4B=16, what does 'B' equal?' they will look at you with baffled amusement. Ask the same question to a 12-year-old and they can hold the 'B' in abstraction while they resolve the relationship between '4' and '16'. Once they realize that the answer is 'x4', they retrieve the 'B' from abstraction to generate the answer 'B=x4'.

These new cognitive functions cause the interior world to open up for the first time. As a result, a fourth dimension is accessed for the first time. Self-reflection becomes possible, even desirable. This is a watershed moment because the physical world is no longer three-dimensional, as it at first appeared. There is a realization that it is possible to transcend the concrete rules and roles, that there is more to life than following the roles laid down by other people, generations or society. The ability to judge and criticize comes to the fore, so individuals at this level initially become critical, judgemental and intolerant of themselves and others.

This angst may remind you of another stage within this level – the teenage years! A surge in curiosity about how the world really works means that teenagers think more. No longer constrained by solely meeting their own egocentric needs, they start to question the rules and test the boundaries. This is often a source of significant parent–teenager conflict. A battle of wills often ensues as smart teenagers start to realize that the rule book given to them by their parents is almost exclusively fabricated and arbitrary. At this stage the teenager has bitten off a corner of the red pill and is beginning to see the world as it really is. The battles on rules, roles and teenage identity can rage on for years, particularly if neither side realizes that this is a normal developmental stage and not a game of 'chicken'.

Regardless of who wins that particular battle, when the young adult leaves home they encounter a much more powerful parent called 'society', which imposes its own rules: 'get a job', 'get a qualification', 'get married', 'earn money', 'have kids', 'be a good citizen'. The inability to break free of this omnipotent 'parent' often causes despondency and hopelessness that pushes the young adult back into Level 4 consciousness and the concrete world. Effectively they fail to fully consume the red pill and instead unwittingly choose the blue pill and the course of least resistance. They conform, follow the masses, assume safety in numbers and slavishly follow societal conventions and social norms. The alternative is often too scary, so they become unconscious again, 'forget' the glimpses of reality they were privy to and plug back into the Matrix.

For those who have dropped back down into the concrete self, life can become very stereotypical as the rules and roles take control once again. It is during the transpersonal stage that we are invited to pull back the veil and think about the nature of thought. What is it? Where do thoughts come from? What determines what we think and what determines how well we think it? The quality of our thoughts is not just dependent on our knowledge and experience and our access to that data; it is also dependent on the content of our consciousness or how aware we are.

WAKING UP – THE DISEASE OF MEANING
The conformity of Level 4 is, however, often interspersed by glimpses of transpersonal stage awareness. If our life is just not conforming to some set

of rules, be they societal, organizational or some alternative group, we may have entered the trials and tribulations of the lower fifth transpersonal level. The first sign that we have is that we feel uncomfortable. The world is no longer safe or secure or as stable as we thought it was. Something is wrong but we don't know what it is. Unfortunately, being slightly out of our comfort zone is insufficient to wake most people up.

If the individual is really lucky something disastrous happens to fully waken them or shock them from the slumber of their concrete world. Most often this is a personal crisis in the form of a loss, such as the loss of a job, a marriage, a loved one, the loss of purpose or the loss of self-esteem through a period of depression. This usually occurs in mid-life and the crisis marks the entry into a nihilistic crisis that is often called the 'disease of meaning'. Individuals start to realize that they have been following a set of rules and playing certain roles for decades on the implicit 'understanding' that it would yield a certain reward. Only, the health, wealth and happiness they were 'promised' didn't materialize!

When inflicted with the disease of meaning, people ask themselves, 'What's the point?' They feel despondent because they kept their side of the bargain. They believe they have been a dutiful husband/wife, father/mother, leader, worker, friend and colleague and it still didn't work out. They feel cheated. After all, they played their part – they followed the rules, but the reward never arrived or if it did it wasn't nearly as good as they were led to believe!

I have seen this sense of injustice so often in business. It often occurs during a merger or acquisition where one side feels they have been hard done by or when one side isn't 'playing by the rules'. It also occurs when someone is suddenly made redundant after 25 years of loyal service. They didn't quite make it to the board and were cast aside. It often comes as a terrible shock that they could be treated this way, because they never even considered that their organization would be so callous and inhumane. And yet we hear stories all the time of people being marched out of the building by security guards as soon as they become surplus to the new requirements, regardless of how long they have been working for the company.

Not everyone catches the disease of meaning through an acute crisis; for some it creeps up on them as a growing sense of dissatisfaction and a recognition that something's not working. At this level people feel as though their life has not turned out as they expected it would, that somehow they are missing out on something. Sometimes the pain of this realization can be very sharp indeed. In religious terms this sub-stage is often referred to as purgatory or 'hell on Earth'.

Many people spend their life stuck in this 'meaningless' swamp of early transpersonal awareness without realizing that it's just a developmental stage. Instead of moving on to higher levels of consciousness, they wrongly believe it's something they have to live with and set out on a quest to dull the pain. The two most popular strategies to dull the pain are:

- anaesthetic;
- distraction.

Anaesthetizing the pain usually takes the form of excessive alcohol or drug consumptions – prescription or otherwise. Alcohol is especially popular with busy executives, who frequently get by with a glass of wine or whisky every lunchtime or every evening.

The range of distraction strategies and games that people play to avoid facing the issue of meaning are numerous. The commonest example of the 'mid-life crisis' is having an affair. During the excitement of deception or the act of physical intimacy, individuals may be distracted from the perceived lack of real meaning in their life. Unfortunately, affairs end or the novelty wears off and the pain returns, only now it's amplified by remorse and guilt. And repeated or multiple simultaneous affairs don't solve the problem either.

Materialism is another common distraction strategy. When you are roaring around in a new Ferrari you are too exhilarated to consider the deeper meaning of life and why you are doing what you are doing. For a few weeks your life may actually take on new meaning as you tend to your beloved car, driving fast and showing off to colleagues, family and friends. But, again, it soon wears off, the car is dented or scratched and you get used to the speed and envious looks. Before long it's just another car and the disease of meaning has flared up again. Spending money on any major purchase or shopping until you literally can't carry another bag is another common distraction strategy that delivers nothing more than a temporary balm and an inflated credit card bill.

Obsessive exercise is another common distraction strategy, where executives turn into 'gym bunnies' obsessed with the 'body beautiful'. When they are 'feeling the burn' on the stair-master they do not have to think about meaning. Although a healthier distraction than alcohol or drugs, the preoccupation with exercise usually wears off too and the disease of meaning returns.

All these strategies are seeking to find meaning using the Have, Do, Be recipe and it doesn't work. The only real solution is to fully wake up and start growing up the levels of consciousness. At some point, the pain of the mid-life crisis becomes very intense. Often this intensity is the only way to achieve a breakthrough. People hit 'rock bottom' and enter a very dark phase; they appreciate that their life isn't working and, perhaps most importantly, that nobody is coming to help. There is no white knight charging in on a majestic steed to save the day. No one is coming to save them.

This is the most important moment in any life. When we finally realize that our parents aren't going to fix it, our boss isn't going to fix it, society or the government aren't going to fix it and that it's down to us to fix it we finally take ownership, we evolve and we expand our awareness and our potential exponentially. At this level, individuals are forced to turn their attention from the outside to the inside. They finally realize that the blame and recrimination they have directed toward other people, situations or events has not helped to stop their pain or improve their life. It has kept them stuck in the meaninglessness of purgatory, and so they finally let go of the idea that someone else is to blame and look inside. As they do, they swallow the red pill they ignored 20 years earlier and finally unplug from the Matrix. This is what Joseph Campbell called 'crossing the threshold'[16] – the liberating realization that the move from ignorance to enlightenment is down to us and us alone.

At Level 5, individuals are said to 'talk the walk'. People at the early stage of this level have read a few books, attended a few courses, they may be saying things like, 'Well of course we all have to be more emotionally intelligent.' But often they are practising 'aboutism' – they know 'about' the subject they are discussing but there is no deeper intellectual understanding and they have certainly not converted the knowledge into wisdom or put the knowledge into practice in their lives.[17]

Level 6: the integrated self

Getting to the sixth level of consciousness development requires considerable effort and, for most, years of personal development. When an individual has taken ownership of their own development, they can often become deeply engaged by the need to do some serious personal vertical development. This may take many forms.

In the early days of the upper reaches of Level 5, an individual may start to read personal development books, explore religion or take classes in psychology, yoga and philosophy as they try to figure out what will make them happy and what they want to do with their life. For some it's not as ordered or structured as courses or books, but rather just a growing awareness of their own behaviour, a matter of having time to reflect on their life, the decisions they've made and why they made them. Many individuals become preoccupied by the concept of purpose. Being able to accurately uncover your personal purpose is a breakthrough. But it's a step on the journey, not the destination itself.

Some executives take a career break or a sabbatical. If this is just another distraction strategy, little may be gained, but if there is genuine insight there may be developmental progress. Critical to reaching the sixth level of awareness is the ability to own up to our own unhelpful patterns, or the dark side of our nature. It can be as simple as recognizing when we were wrong and owning those errors. But to really make it to Level 6 there has to be a deeper understanding of why those errors occurred and how to prevent them occurring in the future. This is often called 'shadow work'.[18] It involves working on those aspects of ourselves that are not easy to see, let alone address and ultimately heal.

But, like any difficult mountainous ascent, there are real dangers when you reach the upper fifth level of personal development. Not only does the terrain include many dead ends, false paths and redundant routes but there are also many false guides who tempt us with promises of the 'summit'. Unfortunately, they can't actually take us there as they have not done the journey themselves. Many coaches might argue that they don't need to have made the journey in order to be an effective guide, and whilst that may be true for time management or the cultivation of technical capabilities it's not true for personal vertical development.

Someone who has ascended to a later level can understand the issues facing someone at an earlier level. But an earlier level traveller has no way of conceptualizing the challenges or thought processes of someone at a later level – this is simply a fact when it comes to vertical development. If an executive is already at a later level than the person who is coaching them, the coach will have no way of conceptualizing the challenges and thought processes of the executive and so is totally unable to help that executive move up to an even more sophisticated level. As a result, few people make it out of the forest of the upper fifth level of consciousness because there are very few guides or executive coaches who can actually help.

I have witnessed many people who have been stuck in the forest of personal development for 20 or 30 years. They are still attending all manner of courses and, sadly, they are still unpleasant to their spouse or themselves.

In order to exit Level 5, the development effort must work. The individual must change, to transcend the patterns of the old and become a fully integrated human being. At Level 6 the individual is no longer constrained by the scars of the past; they are aware of all aspects of self, good and bad, and have taken ownership of those traits. They have healed themselves and are free to make different choices, instead of being locked into reactive behaviours driven by early life conditioning.

In the conditioning example in the last chapter, had William transcended to Level 6 consciousness or above and achieved physiological and emotional coherence, he would not have reacted to the interview candidate in the yellow shirt without knowing why. Instead, his frontal lobes would have remained fully 'on', allowing him to draw on all his skills, knowledge and experience to assess the candidate's suitability and find the right person for the role. At Level 6 consciousness the individual ceases to be a victim and realizes that there is no merit in allowing other people to control their emotions. This can be an incredibly joyful and liberating experience because we come to appreciate that we really do have free will and it is not just a trite soundbite from the personal development industry.

Demonstrating Level 6 awareness, Eleanor Roosevelt once said, 'No one can make you feel inferior without your consent'.[19] As explained in the previous chapter, we can't control what others do or what they say but we can always control what we make those things mean. Without this expanded awareness or emotional self-management, we are at the mercy of other people and their actions and reactions. When someone says something hurtful, they've behaved badly; it's therefore their issue, not ours. If we choose to feel upset about that, we punish ourselves for someone else's transgression. That doesn't make sense. If we have the power to create the upset, we also have the power to 'un-create' it, or even better just not create it in the first place.

When we don't appreciate our own free will at a deep level, we give people we don't even know, or people we don't like or respect, permission to ruin our entire day. And knowing what you now know about emotions and how toxic negative emotions can be for your health, are you really going to let someone else fur up your arteries? When we realize we don't have to give that permission and that if someone behaves badly that's their choice not ours, we have achieved ownership and emotional sovereignty.

Only when we take that ownership and master emotional sovereignty can our life really improve. At Level 6 there is complete ownership of all aspects of 'self'.

This moment of ownership is a game-changing shift – the clumsy caterpillar has transformed into the butterfly capable of flying above the crowd. When we cross the threshold, we leave the world as we knew it behind. Of course, it doesn't stop other people from behaving badly, but we can choose how we feel about it.

Austrian neurologist and psychiatrist Victor Frankl talks about this moment during his experience in a Nazi concentration camp.[20] The Nazis took everything from him, including his wife, brother, parents and his life's work – a manuscript that had been sewn into the lining of his jacket. He experienced unspeakable horror and a daily struggle to survive, but he also realized that they could not take his self-esteem or his ability to choose how to feel about what was happening. When Frankl was eventually liberated by the Americans in 1945 he wrote *Man's Search for Meaning* and developed a type of existential therapy that helped millions of people to find meaning in their own lives – regardless of the challenges they faced.

As I said in the last chapter, if we want to be a responsible human being, we have to learn to be response-*able*; in other words, to be able to respond rather than to react. We choose the response – as opposed to victimhood. Or, as Frankl said, 'Between stimulus and response, there is a space. In that space is our power to choose our response. In our response lies our growth and our freedom.'

At Level 6 individuals are said to 'walk the talk'. These people convert 'aboutism' into action by putting the things they read about or know about into practice. In other words, they are not just talking about being compassionate, they are compassionate. They may still have good days and bad days, but they can self-correct much more rapidly.

Level 7: pure being

Individuals at this level have dealt with all their baggage so that they are a living example of what they've learnt. There is a warm radiance to human beings operating at this level. They have a nourishing personal presence, phenomenal energy and powers of concentration as well as incredible selflessness.

This is how people describe meeting the Dalai Lama, for example. I remember talking to Matthieu Ricard, the Dalai Lama's right-hand man in

Europe, and he was talking about witnessing the difference between the queue going in and the queue coming out from seeing the Dalai Lama. Going in, people were full of their own importance and preening themselves, adjusting their ties or brushing their hair – all fluffed up in their finery. And they'd all come out in tears. His Holiness just melted them with his loving compassion.

I experienced this myself when I and a colleague of mine spent an evening with Matthieu and his mum in their tiny little house in the Dordogne. We were conducting a research study with Tibetan monks and looking specifically at their physiology when they were in different types of meditative states.[21] Matthieu's mum had converted to Tibetan Buddhism too and is also a brilliant painter in her own right. We were sitting in their humble home chatting around the table. After about 30 minutes I realized I was talking to two of the most spiritually important people on the planet and we were getting on like a house on fire. Both Matthieu and his mum were so utterly unconcerned with their own importance, and it really emphasized one of the key personal qualities of this level – selflessness.

Nelson Mandela was another powerful example of Level 7 consciousness. He too had a nourishing personal presence and selflessness that was beguiling. When Mandela was having his 90th birthday celebrations a host of celebrities and international dignitaries flew in from all over the world for a photo. Mandela patiently and graciously did what everyone else wanted although it probably wasn't actually what he wanted. The story goes that when it was all over, he turned to the photographer who had been taking pictures all day and asked him if he would like a photo. To Mandela, the photographer was no more or no less important than the people who had been visiting all day. But Mandela wasn't always this selfless or gracious. When he went to prison, he was an angry man, yet he emerged after 27 years an extraordinary mediator, philosopher and president-in-waiting. He could have emerged from prison even angrier, but instead he did the personal development soul-searching work necessary to evolve as a highly developed human being.

Level 7 consciousness is non-judgemental, incredibly perceptive and loving. When we meet these people, it can feel as though they really 'get' us – they see the warts and all and it's OK; all that exists is a profound loving empathy without criticism. That's what happens to the people in the queue to see the Dalai Lama. They feel understood and appreciated just for who they are and the energetic boost this creates can sustain them for weeks if not years!

And finally, because these individuals have evolved and developed as human beings, not just physically from childhood to adulthood, but adult to mature adult, they have incredible energy levels. They don't tend to drain their energy tanks with frustrations, judgement and negative emotion. Their mind is no longer fogged up and they don't lobotomize themselves, so they demonstrate crystal clarity and impressive powers of concentration.

At Level 7, individuals are said to 'walk the walk'. These people have fully integrated the knowledge and personal growth they've accumulated and are living expressions of whom they seek to be. Although how sophisticated and mature they are can often only be fully appreciated by others that live at this exalted level of development.

Level 8: unity in duality

This level of development, unity in duality, used to be considered as the ultimate state of consciousness. In the East it was called 'classical nirvana' – the ultimate destination of the spiritual journey when the student has achieved a joyful union with the 'divine'.

Many people will have experienced a glimpse of unity at some point of their life. Where and how that glimpse is experienced can alter their life forever because it can profoundly influence what they become interested in. It might, for example, occur as the person looks at the magnificence of the Grand Canyon. In that moment of wonder their ego evaporates, and they merge with the Grand Canyon. Often these nature-induced experiences can feel semi-spiritual and can ignite a passion for the environment.

Others experience this moment of unity through sport. The reason some people become obsessed with golf, for example, is because they experienced the 'perfect shot', one moment where they struck the ball so perfectly that they merged with the ball and become 'one with the ball'. This blissful glimpse is so moving that they spend the rest of their golfing life trying to recreate that moment of unity. The same happens in many sports – the perfect backhand in tennis, the perfect strike in football or the killer wave in surfing.

For others, they experience moments of unity in church and people will describe it as 'seeing the face of God' so they become devout Christians, Muslims or Hindus – or whatever denomination they experienced unity in.

The vast majority of people on the planet have, however, never experienced unity in any other form than during sex. Individuals literally forget themselves at the peak of orgasm, which is one of the key reasons why sex becomes the primary and most powerful motivator for most human beings – because it's the only time they ever experience unity.

But all of these experiences are not a pure unity. They are a unity in duality. There is a realization that even if we have experienced unity it's not complete unity because there is an internal observer, observing the unity experience. As soon as we label an experience, we separate ourselves from that experience. The person looking at the Grand Canyon can feel unity for a moment but as soon as they mentally or verbally acknowledge the magnificence of that spectacle they immediately create duality in the unity by splitting the observer from the observed – subjective (I) is separate from objective (Grand Canyon).

Even at Level 8 consciousness it can be difficult to describe the experience, but we know if we have experienced it. And that is definitely the case at Level 9.

Level 9: pure awareness

Any attempt to describe Level 9 awareness immediately drops us into Level 8 because we become the observer observing again. To really understand these higher levels, we have to physically experience them because it's a bit difficult to capture them with the rational mind.

But let's have a go. Pure awareness: the Tibetans call it nothingness or emptiness, which frightens a lot of people. It is also referred to, by some, as the 'vast blue sky'. When truly experiencing this, there is no longer an observer observing, there is just the experience of 'formless union'. There is not someone noticing that they are looking at the Grand Canyon, just the individual and the Grand Canyon in a formless union that transcends the subject–object relationship. When someone experiences Level 9 they also transcend time and space: ie they start to realize that time is a construct and there is no time. Space, too, is infinite; there are no boundaries to space and the person is connected to the entire universe – a universe without end. There isn't an observer making this observation; there is just the experience of it. 'I' stops being in here and 'everything else' out there – it's all one. Pure awareness is a first-hand experience that we are all that is. It's a massively expanded state of consciousness.

When we are in Level 9 the good/bad, right/wrong, black/white, up/down duality of life is seen for what it really is – an artificial construction of lower levels of consciousness. There is no duality, no right, no wrong – it just is.

The ramifications of this viewpoint were driven home to me when I watched an episode of *Life on Earth*. The brilliant David Attenborough explained that if we shrink the evolution of the planet and all living things into one year, living organisms didn't emerge until August. At the beginning of November back-boned creatures emerged and left the water to colonize the land. By the beginning of December those back-boned creatures broke their dependence on water and by the middle of the same month they could generate heat in their body and the scales turned to feathers. On 25 December the dinosaurs disappeared and mammals and furry animals emerged. In the early morning of 31 December apes arrived, and human beings arrived two minutes before midnight.[22]

Surely, it's difficult to get terribly upset about anything when we realize that human beings have been around for about two minutes! But Level 9 isn't really about knowing that fact intellectually but experiencing it in our body. To say that we are in our infancy in terms of human development would be a vast understatement and yet we strut around thinking we've got everything figured out. We haven't.

When seen from this perspective, the slights, upsets, challenges, disasters and traumas – large and small – are just tides of stuff. At pure awareness we cease to have preferences and transcend dualistic concepts of good/bad, right/wrong, etc. They are all just lesser conscious states to help us interpret the world, but actually the world is much more expanded and is all those things. It's everything. This is a blissful state of being. It's not someone observing the bliss, it's just bliss – a vast space with a tinge of blissful delight. This doesn't mean we can't make a choice; we still can, but the way we perceive choices is completely different.

Level 10: non-dual

This is very similar to Level 9 consciousness, only Level 10 also has an evolutionary spin. When an individual transcends time and space, it's not as if they cease to exist. There is still a desk, an office and they can still see themselves in the mirror. But the relationship to the notion of desk, office and self is completely different – we are those things and see those things and experience those things, but we are also not those things.

In Level 10 it's still pure awareness but the universe is evolving so it's not just static being; it's being in motion. There is momentum and things are changing and evolving all the time, so the awareness too is in motion.

Where are you?

A preliminary indication of what level you are currently operating from can be gauged when you read the above descriptions. The minute you thought to yourself, 'What the hell is this guy talking about?' is a pretty good indication that you are operating at one or two levels before that level!

If you are resting in your garden and you notice a line of ants carrying a leaf back to base, you see the ants and understand what the ants are doing because you see the scene from a bigger, broader and more expanded perspective. The ants, on the other hand, are oblivious of you. They are busy with their task and they simply don't have the perspective to appreciate that they are being watched. Even if you could speak 'ant' and tell them that you were watching them, they would still not understand what you were talking about because they don't have the necessary frame of reference. Their experience of human beings is usually short-lived, as they are stood on or their tasks are interrupted in some way. We can't understand the levels beyond our own development any more than the ant can understand you watching him and his mates carrying a leaf. If you have reached one of the upper levels of maturity (which means you definitely didn't deliberately stand on the ants) you can understand all the levels of maturity that you evolved through on your way to your current level but someone on a lower level can't understand someone on a higher level.

Everyone on the planet can relate to all the levels up to Level 5 because all adults have made the physical development that coincides with that journey. Most adults therefore reach Level 5 without any thought or consideration on their part – it just happens by virtue of the passing years. Most drop back into Level 4 and others get stuck in the foothills of Level 5 forever, never finding enough motivation to engage in genuine vertical development.

These people may have a conceptual understanding of higher levels of consciousness but no real experience of them. They may get glimpses or realize there is something very special and different about the Dalai Lama or Nelson Mandela but they don't recognize those qualities in themselves. Very few people experientially understand beyond Level 8. What really matters in the context of adult development and maturity, however, is that we appreciate that adults develop differently from children and that a certain amount of effort and self-reflection is required to develop maturity, which can in turn transform thinking, behaviour and therefore results.

These maturity models are not a competition or an assessment of bad, better, best. The ant is no better or worse than a human being – just different, operating at different levels of awareness. A monkey is no better than a rock – just different, operating at different levels of awareness. A rock is still very useful in the right situation – if you want to break a coconut, for example, a rock is considerably more useful than a monkey.

The same is true of people. These levels of maturity and adult development are not bad, better, best – their merit is in giving us a framework for development rather than a tool for comparison. They simply relate to the various ways we gain wisdom and maturity and make meaning. Each level of maturity is more comprehensive, with increasing levels of differentiation that in turn allow us to deal more effectively with elevating levels of complexity from baby to adolescent to adult to mature adult. The self-centred life of an infant is, after all, considerably less complicated than the life of a global CEO.

At Complete we work with CEOs and business leaders to unlock the potential from vertical development, using a number of assessment processes and tailored coaching programmes. One of the most profound metrics for helping leaders assess their current location and where they could progress to is the Complete Maturity Report (CMR). The CMR uses Susanne Cook-Greuter's sentence-completion questionnaire to measure maturity – the most rigorously developed, tested, unbiased and reliable stage measure currently in existence. Unlike many questionnaires it's not possible to 'fix' or 'game' the right answers to the questions, because there are no right answers to the questions. Nonetheless, the CMR provides leaders with an accurate insight into their own leadership maturity and personal integration and that of their individual team members. When leaders know the characteristics and behaviours associated with each level of adult maturity and how they manifest in business, much of the dysfunction in modern business is immediately explained. The CMR allows the leader to locate their own and their team's collective centre of gravity for personal and group maturity. This indicates where individuals operate from normally, where they can fall back to under pressure and where their opportunity for greatest growth lies. As a result, the CMR often explains individual performance shortfalls, why a team isn't working as well as it might or why it seems to be stuck in a destructive or unhelpful holding pattern and, perhaps most importantly, what to do about it.

Whose rules are they anyway?

Transformations of consciousness or awareness that alter an individual's world view or perspective are infinitely more powerful than the accumulation of more skills, knowledge and experience. It is these transformations that elevate thinking to a whole new level. Marcel Proust clearly understood vertical development when he said, 'The real voyage of discovery consists not in seeking new landscapes, but in having new eyes.' When we see the world through new eyes, the world itself is changed, and this awakening changes our interpretations, experiences, thoughts, feelings, behaviour and results.

What we therefore must appreciate is that our experience of the world, and specifically business, may be nothing more than the result of following a very sophisticated set of rules about the nature of business, and we are, in fact, stuck in concrete consciousness. These rules may lead us to believe that 'it's a dog-eat-dog world', and 'every man for himself', you need to 'muscle your way to the top', 'it's about shareholder return'. The list of 'rules' on how to successfully run a company, team or division is endless and most executives subscribe to them even though no one really knows where they came from, who wrote them or when they were created. And these rules are very rarely questioned. As soon as leaders reach the C-suite they quickly learn all the rules of the C-suite and behave accordingly. It takes a huge amount of leadership to pull back and say, 'Hang on a minute, what rules are we following and are they the best rules for this company?'

The stereotypes are not working. Based on the evidence, executives the world over are reaching middle age burnt out and miserable; they don't know their partners anymore and rarely see their kids. They've followed a set of rules and live firmly rooted in the concrete awareness, only to discover that the promised rewards did not materialize. They've worked their hearts out (sometimes literally) only to learn the 'promise' never really materializes. The rewards didn't come, or if they did arrive, they also came at a huge personal cost either through the loss of important relationships with their family and friends or the loss of their health.

If we as a species have only been around for a couple of minutes in the context of all life on earth, surely, it's realistic to consider that as a species we've not finished evolving. We may have physically grown into adults, we have clearly mastered the accumulation of information, knowledge, skills and experience (horizontal development) but we have barely begun our vertical development journey. If we don't wake up to that reality there may be very little growing up and meaningful progress in our lifetime.

And the only way we can do that is to push through the transpersonal swamps so we can learn what happiness is really about and how to live a life of service. We need to grow up to the realization that the rules don't always deliver what they promised. Part of growing up is owning up to our 'shadow' or the unhelpful, destructive and unpleasant behaviours we have previously engaged in. When someone owns up to their shadow and really integrates that healing on the inside, that will always influence how that individual shows up, in the world.

Truly mature and developed leaders show up differently. They cultivate the ability to really think and pull back from the day-to-day short-termism of modern business. They question the corporate rules, culture and myths and ask the hard questions, and they are willing to go against the grain if that position serves the long-term good of the business, society and the planet.

How to be smarter

Good-quality thinking is critical in any business; new ideas, new products, creative problem solving, the ability to see the future before it arrives and adapt accordingly are all cognitive functions that offer a vast opportunity for strategic advantage and growth.[23]

I'm incredibly optimistic about human potential because I know that once we get control of our physiology, appreciate emotion and integrate it into our commercial experience whilst also managing to avoid the DIY lobotomy, expand our consciousness and develop our level of maturity, we will finally realize that we are significantly more complex, more sophisticated and more capable than we have been led to believe.

Building on the physical skills outlined in Chapter 1 and the personal skills of Chapter 2, the next step toward smarter thinking and consistently brilliant performance is cognitive coherence. Cognitive coherence is facilitated by changing the energy within your system to unlock greater perceptual awareness, and this can be done using the SHIFT skill. John Browett, who has been the CEO of many retailer during his stellar career, discusses the importance of combining the rational with the human side of business, stating:

> In business, you're dealing with people, and people aren't rational machines. You may not make what is technically the perfect decision because you know it will cause more problems than it would solve. Instead, perhaps there will be another solution that everyone is happy with and that gets you 80 per cent of the way there... If you're really cold and calculating, people won't like you, and being liked in business is helpful. That's not to say you shy away from difficult decisions, but you reserve them for a time when it really matters. Taking people with you is critical... In the end, it's like water flowing in a river; if you do the right thing, there's only one direction it's going to go.

The SHIFT skill facilitates productive interaction and cooperation, as John reiterates:

> Your ego, or the smaller version of you, can be nervous, worried and unhappy. So learning to operate from a position of inner peace and calmness is transformational. In a transcendent state you are going to be more capable of helping people. I can think of so many examples where I've been able to put myself into that state and it has been incredibly helpful and powerful.

Cognitive coherence – the SHIFT skill

How do we develop a new level of thinking? Imagine someone is in the middle of writing an important report or tricky email and they get stuck. How best to phrase a critical point or argument? What do you do to come up with a new idea? Some people stop and go for a coffee. Others may go out for a walk to clear their head. Some will delay making a decision so they can sleep on it. Some prefer to exercise, and in the gym the new idea may appear. Some listen to music, have a glass of wine or phone a friend. All of these techniques work sometimes, which is why they are still widely used and recommended. However, they don't work every time. They are hit and miss solutions. Plus, perhaps most importantly, they can't all be done at work and they can't all be done in the heat of the moment. If we are in the middle of a board meeting, we can't nip out for a five-mile run or dismiss everyone until we've slept on it or start pouring the whisky at 10 am. But if we look at why these techniques work, on the occasions when they do work, we discover something interesting – a common active ingredient. From this analysis the SHIFT skill was born.

THE SHIFT PROCESS

Work through the following instructions:

1 First describe an area in your life or work that is currently challenging you. Write down the associated thoughts, feelings and associated actions.

2 Once you have made a note of your thoughts, feelings and behaviour, work through the shift process. SHIFT is an acronym and the process takes you through each stage as follows:

Stop everything that you are doing and simply shift your attention to your…

Heart, breathe through this area of your chest and then…

Induce a positive emotion.

Feel it in your body, enjoy how it moves through your body for a good 40 seconds or so and allow it to…

Turn the brain back on. Notice your insights and write them down.

How did it go? Do you see a difference in what you wrote down? Do you see a difference in what you wrote? Did your perception of the issue change or shift? What did you learn?

Say for example you've got to write a letter to an employee and it's awkward and you don't know how to phrase the letter. It may be that you've already agonized over it for 30 minutes and you still can't get the words right.

Shifting your attention   The first thing to do in any problem is stop what you're doing and shift (S) your attention. If you are struggling with the email, for example, you may get up and move away from the keyboard and move your attention to something else. You might shift your attention by going for a coffee, a walk, a cigarette, calling a friend, counting to 10, exercising, doing something else – anything else. All these techniques result in the same thing – you shifting your attention from the issue to something else.

Inducing a positive emotion   This conscious shift in your attention may, if you're lucky, induce (I) a positive emotion. When going for a walk you may notice the beauty of a tree, a certain way the light hits the pavement, the gentle breeze on your skin, the far-off laughter of people enjoying themselves. When you phone a friend, they may lift your spirits by recounting an amusing story of their own woes. When you sip your macchiato, you may experience the simple pleasure of a delicious coffee. Again, all of these different experiences are helpful because they induce a positive emotion.

Feel it in your body   It's not enough that the emotion has changed; you have to really feel the change in energy and feel (F) the positive emotion in your body. The more you can feel the feeling, the joy, the connection, the more you can sustain that energetic state, the more your physiology changes and this physiological change will affect your brain function.

Turn the brain back on   As you feel the feeling, you shift into a state of biological coherence and your thinking shifts too; your brain turns (T) back on. And once you've turned your brain back on you will have far greater access to your cognitive capabilities and a new thought or perspective will emerge.

You will no doubt already have experienced this process in action. Perhaps you were confused about how to fix a problem. You had been stewing over it for days and then one evening an old friend calls and this exchange shifts your attention away from the problem. You end up laughing about a shared memory and as you put the phone down, a smile plastered across your face. You suddenly have an epiphany that solves your problem. This was no coincidence or accident; it was simply the predictable consequence of shifting your emotional state from a negative to a positive state.

As I explained, SHIFT is an acronym, so you may have noticed that the explanation above misses out the H. The missing ingredient is to engage the heart (H). If we breathe smoothly and rhythmically while focusing on our heart in the way I explained in Chapter 2, we rely only on ourselves. And we can do this any time, anywhere. Remember our heart is the location of most of our positive emotions, so paying attention to our heart will help to shift attention (S) and induce a positive emotion (I). Once we have 'hold' of that positive emotion we need to feel (F) the emotion in our body, which will in turn switch our brain back on (T) – giving us answers we could not access only a few minutes earlier.

This process allows us to shift from a negative emotion to any one of the positive emotions that we've mastered through the emotional MASTERY skill from the previous chapter. Just like the executive who learnt to shift to contentment to improve his business decisions, we can also shift into a helpful and constructive emotional state that will give us access to our full cognitive capacity and drive cognitive coherence. Once we have embodied the new positive state and held on to it for 30 seconds, we will then get access to new insights. After just 30 seconds we can go back to the challenge we were facing and write down any new ideas or insights that emerge.

This exercise is often very revealing for people, because they can immediately see the difference between the initial explanation of the challenge and the insights that follow once emotional coherence has been achieved – even for as little as 30 seconds. The solution they have access to now seems simple and obvious, but without coherence it was obscured by a negative emotional state. Human beings are brilliant and we already know the answers to almost all our problems. It's just that we can't access those answers until we SHIFT out of a negative state and into a positive one.

COLLECT POSITIVE EMOTIONS

Having developed emotional literacy, we may now be very familiar with 15 or so different positive emotions. The MASTERY skill helps us to be increasingly familiar with the biological landscape of those positive emotions. Think of these positive emotional states as different outfits that can be worn at different times for different occasions. No one in their right mind would go to an important function in their shorts and slippers, so why would we consider going to an important meeting frustrated or angry?

Or think of these different emotions as different CDs in your music collection. If someone was feeling upset about the state of their marriage it wouldn't be helpful to listen to power ballads, and they are not going to be in a constructive emotional state to fix the problems if they listen to thrash metal all day long! They need to change the record. Break the negative emotional state by listening to more inspiring, positive upbeat music so they can solve the challenges they face.

Emotional MASTERY adds to our collection of positive emotions so we can SHIFT into that emotion when we need it rather than just hoping it shows up. Of course, it's not enough to have the positive CD – we need to play it. This means that we need to practise shifting from the emotional state that we are in to a more positive, constructive emotional state.

We will always experience emotional triggers in our daily life. We will still feel irritated and frustrated and angry, but these emotional skills mean that we are finally in control of how we respond. If we are aware of our negative emotional state, we will have the emotional flexibility to step back for a moment and re-adjust our state so we can move forward confidently in the right direction.

The good news is that we already shift emotional states very easily. If you are frustrated, for example after a particularly pointless meeting, you may get in your car to drive to see a client. As you are listening to the radio your favourite song comes on and you turn up the volume, singing along at the top of your voice. By the time the song has finished you are feeling completely different and you have a smile on your face. The music just shifted your emotional state. Or perhaps you get a letter from your boss informing you of a large bonus – that shifts your emotional state into delight. Then you realize the letter isn't addressed to you and you shift again, only this time you feel offended. You are constantly shifting your emotional state – you're just not currently doing it consciously. At the moment you are at the mercy of external events, people and situations that will shift your emotional state whether you want those emotions or not.

What we need to do is take back control so that we decide what we feel, not our boss or our partner or our kids or our clients or our colleagues. Shifting your emotional state in itself is not difficult; doing it deliberately when we need to does, however, require practice.

Cognitive coherence facilitates behavioural coherence

Companies succeed or fail based on their collective awareness and on their ability to consistently access the very best thinking possible. Business needs to foster the ability, particularly within the C-suite, to come up with better answers to commercial challenges than their competitors; they need to be more creative and more innovative, and they need to expand their perceptual awareness because that is what ultimately differentiates the winners from the losers.

The cumulative benefit of access to more energy and better energy utilization, emotional intelligence and literacy combined with vertically developed cognitive ability and maturity can have a profound impact on the quality of thought and, ultimately, business success. Being smarter is only possible when we systematically improve all internal lines of development. Each line builds on and facilitates the next. The emotional MASTERY skill provides us with emotional resilience, a quality that can massively impact performance and bottom line results. When applied, emotional MASTERY can ensure that we have permanent access to our frontal lobes! When we also expand our awareness and understand our values, we facilitate cognitive coherence. Physiological coherence facilitates emotional coherence, which facilitates cognitive coherence, and cognitive coherence facilitates behavioural coherence, which we will explore next.

Summary of key points

If you don't remember everything in this chapter, remember this:

- Growing a business requires clarity of thought, or at least better thinking than the competition.

- Smart thinking requires us to be able to access higher-quality content (or what we think) and work it more effectively (how well we think it through).

- In an emergency or when under pressure our brain goes binary and we can experience a DIY lobotomy. This is an evolutionary mechanism that shuts down all the clever thinking parts of the brain to leave only two options: fight/flight (adrenaline driven) or play dead (acetylcholine driven).

- The only way to keep our brain 'on', under pressure or otherwise, is to develop physiological and emotional coherence, especially cardiac coherence.

- When we create cardiac coherence through smooth, rhythmic heart-focused breathing, the coherent signal from the heart travels up the vagus nerve and liberates our very best thinking.

- While physiological and emotional coherence will certainly facilitate a significant improvement in cognitive function, it's vertical development or adult maturity that can transform results.

- Our primary goal is to 'wake up' and 'grow up'.

- Without a 'burning platform' for personal growth, most people stop developing once they have physically matured. Physical development from child to adult is, however, only one type of development. The real game changer happens after we have become physically mature when we move from adult to mature adult – this is where all the real magic lies.

- Over half of all leaders are currently operating with insufficient awareness or maturity to survive and prosper in our complex world.

- The only way to vertically develop awareness and maturity is to do the personal work and practise. The rewards are significant and can unlock a vast reservoir of potential.

- The quality of our thoughts is very much dependent on our emotions and emotional self-regulation. The SHIFT skill allows us to move from a negative emotion to a positive one at will so we can access our very best thinking when we need it most.

Notes

1   Watkins, A and May, S (2021) *Innovation Sucks! Time to think differently*, Routledge, London
2   Rooke, D and Torbert, W R (2005) Seven transformations of leadership, *Harvard Business Review*, 1 April 2005
3   Piaget, J (1972) *The Psychology of the Child*, Basic Books, New York
4   Kohlberg, L (1981) *The Philosophy of Moral Development: Moral stages and the idea of justice*, Harper & Row, London
5   L-Xufn, Hy, Loevinger, J and Le Xuan, Hy (1996) *Measuring Ego Development: Personality and clinical psychology*, 2nd edn, Lawrence Erlbaum Associates, Inc, Hillsdale, NJ

6 Wilber, K (2000) *Integral Psychology: Consciousness, sprit, psychology therapy*, Shambhala Publications, Boston

7 Watkins, A (2016) *4D Leadership: Competitive advantage through vertical leadership development*, Kogan Page, London

8 Graves, C (1981) Summary statement: The emergent, cyclical, double-helix model of adult human biopsychosocial systems, presented in Boston, May 1981

9 Watkins, A and Dalton, N (2020) *The HR (R)Evolution: Change the workplace, change the world*, Routledge, London

10 Watkins, A (2016) *4D Leadership: competitive Advantage through vertical leadership development*, Kogan Page, London

11 Phipps, C (2012) *Evolutionaries: Unlocking the spiritual and cultural potential of science's greatest idea*, HarperCollins, New York

12 Prochaska, J O, Norcross, J C and Diclemente, C C (1994) *Changing for Good*, Avon Books, New York
Wilber K (2017) Trump and a Post-Truth World Shambhala Publications, Boston

13 Rooke, D and Torbert, W R (2005) Seven transformations of leadership, *Harvard Business Review*, April

14 Hameroff, S and Penrose, R (2003) Conscious events as orchestrated space-time selections, *Neuroquantology*, 1 (1), pp 10–35

15 Wilber, K (2001) *A Theory of Everything: An integral vision for business, politics, science and spirituality* Shambhala Publications, Boston

16 Campbell, J (2012) *The Hero with a Thousand Faces*, Novato, New World Library

17 Kaipa, P and Radjou, N (2013) *From Smart to Wise: Acting and leading with wisdom*, Jossey-Bassey, San Francisco

18 Bly, R (2001) *Iron John: A book about men*, Rider, London

19 Roosevelt, E (1960) This is my story, *Catholic Digest*, August

20 Frankl, F E (1959) *Man's Search for Meaning*, Beacon Press, Boston, MA

21 Watkins, A (2014) *Coherence: The secret science of brilliant leadership,* Kogan Page, London

22 Attenborough, D (1979) *Life on Earth*, episode 13, BBC, 10 April 1979

23 Watkins, A and May, S (2021) Innovation Sucks! Time to Think Differently, Routledge, London

05

Be successful

Do you ever wonder why you bother with annual performance appraisals because you seem to be saying the exact same thing year after year? Have you wondered why your team don't quite do what was agreed, even when you feel you made things absolutely clear? Are you frequently confused by the behaviour displayed by key personnel? Have you ever spent a small fortune recruiting the best and the brightest talent you can find, only to be disappointed with the results? Are you frustrated by the lack of execution in the business? Is there a constant discrepancy between what is supposed to get done and what actually gets done? Are you confused at the inconsistency of performance or output in your business? If so, you're not alone.

We have been taught that success is the ultimate prize – the final destination. All our life we've been encouraged to play by the rules, get a good education and climb the career ladder to the C-suite. We work hard, put in long hours, and if we are lucky, smart or both we 'arrive'. When we work with leadership teams and ask about their level of ambition for the team, the short-term team goal is that the team wants to deliver consistently high performance. That's because, for most teams, consistent high performance remains elusive, even when expensive new talent has been recruited to power up the team. There may be ambitious chatter about becoming 'best in class' or even somewhat delusional hyperbole about being 'world class'. But unless teams can unlock the secret of consistent high performance, anything more is a pipe dream.

But even when executive teams know that something isn't working, they are wary of changing course. They stick with the same dynamics, often because they don't know what else to try. If we look at the banking crisis, for example, there is now a mountain of robust evidence that proves that the bonus culture is toxic.[1] It doesn't work and it caused or at least massively contributed to the biggest financial collapse since the Great Depression, and yet as soon as the dust settles it's 'business as usual' for banking. To paraphrase Einstein, we are insane – blindly doing the same thing and expecting a different result. As a consequence, there are many well-informed individuals who believe that another financial crisis is inevitable.[2]

Performance anxiety!

Whatever you do in life, you should always aim to improve and generate better results: better results for yourself, your team, your family or your organization. If we want to generate better business performance, physical performance, relationship performance or academic performance, we need to make the right behavioural choices. Behaviour is the final common pathway to all types of success. This is why large sections of society, be they business, education, health or crime prevention, put so much emphasis on behaviour (and correcting behaviour), from leadership behaviour to antisocial behaviour.

Many organizations are very preoccupied with behaviour and have spent considerable time and money building behavioural competency frameworks. If performance and results are not as good as we hoped, behaviour is almost always considered the 'problem' that needs fixing. This seems like a logical argument; after all, what we do determines the results we get. But if results are still inconsistent and performance is still erratic, something is clearly missing. Going back over the same behaviours will not solve the performance problem. There is clearly something else going on, and organizations need to look deeper than just the surface behaviours they have been focused on.

It's certainly been my observation in working with global CEOs and leaders since 1996 that most can perform really well sometimes, but being exceptional every day is much more difficult. This is why most continue to experience variable results and don't know why.

To achieve consistent brilliance requires a much more sophisticated approach. It requires us to look deeper at what determines whether behaviours do or don't appear. That means we need to look at what we think, what we feel and the amount of energy we have at any given time. That's exactly what we did in the previous three chapters. In unpacking all the levels of the human system from physiology ('Be younger'), emotions and feelings ('Be healthier and happier') and thinking ('Be smarter') and exploring how they interact, we can begin to appreciate why performance and results are so difficult to predict and why they seem so arbitrary and mysterious.

Obsession with results

In modern business and life in general, results, particularly financial results, are the primary measure of worth. This obsession has created several unintended consequences, not least that no matter how much money you have, most people always want more.

The World is Not Enough may be the title of a James Bond movie, but this notion is deeply embedded into most people's personal and professional lives and it goes a long way in explaining our obsession with performance and results. As Mike Iddon, Chief Financial Officer of Pets at Home and one of the most perceptive CFOs in the FTSE, explains, this 'not enough' mindset can have serious negative consequences on teams and the business:

> [Delivering] bad news creates a drop in energy levels. I felt it too. I was almost taking the blame for any missed figures myself. With new framing, we delivered a more positive contribution and could start to figure out why the numbers were as they were. This has an effect on the energy levels in the team, but it also changed the belief structure. People had previously lived with a 'not enough' mindset; their emotional state was very much aligned with the day-to-day performance of the business. A change in this perspective helped us towards a goal of more self-belief.

There is a relentless, restless drive for more, bigger, better, higher, faster, stronger, that pervades many lives and many businesses. Growth is the goal, and volume, size and scale are the main markers of greatness. Quality, value and meaning are subordinate. Bigger is better and the bar is set higher and higher. Cheaper is rarely challenged as a commercial target. If we are not delivering cheaper, bigger, more for less, we are not performing well enough, are somehow deficient or 'not enough'.

The first thought on waking up for many busy executives is: 'I didn't get enough sleep.' This is replaced by other thoughts and feelings of insufficiency: 'There aren't enough hours in the day'; 'I am not earning enough money or being paid enough'; or 'My career is not progressing fast enough.' A common fear of many is that they will be 'found out' and they are 'not good enough, smart enough or able enough' to do the job they are doing.[3]

The mindset of 'lack' may relate to a leader's team or organization: 'I can't find good enough people'; 'My team isn't skilled enough'; or 'This organization isn't ambitious enough.' The thinking may relate to customers: 'There aren't enough customers'; or 'The customers aren't loyal enough.' Even people we might think of as very successful often aren't satisfied. A very successful businessperson might frequently think their business should be more profitable or growing more quickly and generating more money.

Business can, particularly in tough economic times, become a grown-up version of musical chairs. Executives can become very focused on securing their slice of limited resources. Everyone keeps busy, wondering when the music might stop and if they will need to shove others out of the way to ensure they keep their seat. The rules of the game have changed, which now means that leaders often fight to get to the top, cling on there for a few years while they 'build their stash', only to be fired when they can't deliver the excessive promises they themselves had almost been encouraged to make in order to secure the position in the first place.

Because the pecuniary prize of reaching the C-suite is now so great it can, even in the saintliest organizations, foster a culture of greed and aggression as well as an erosion in humanity. For example, I spoke to a very senior executive who had given 20 years' loyal service to one company and had created a world-leading business unit in her area. Unfortunately, she refused to play the politics that were rife at the top of this particular organization. When a new boss was appointed over her, she shared her thoughts about him with him, after being encouraged to do so in a poorly facilitated 'team away-day'. A couple of weeks later she was summoned to the boss's office, informed she was surplus to requirements and told she would be escorted from the building. When she asked if she could go back to her office to 'get her things', she was told she could not. When she asked what she should say when her PA called her to ask where she was, her boss said, 'We want your phone too.' And, the group HR director sat throughout this entire exchange and said nothing.

When we hear of such stories, we wonder what has happened to the humanity of the people dishing out such news. Some organizations have inadvertently created a system that is set up to promote aggression and hubris instead of teamwork and elevated collective performance. There is little doubt that our overt obsession with results has fuelled this 'never enough' mentality, which in turn has contributed to the erosion of humanity and the creation of a culture of greed and entitlement so often experienced in business and society as a whole.[4]

And the really disheartening part to all this is that the 'not enough' mind-set actually renders the results irrelevant, because no matter how great the growth or how amazing the like-for-like results, they will never be enough. More recently, the head of supply chain for one multinational was able to restructure his operation during the pandemic, get his factories working in shifts 24-7 and deliver 15 per cent growth to meet a massively increased demand. His workforce was shouldering significant levels of exhaustion as they worked incredibly hard, only to be berated for not maintaining normal 90 per cent availability targets, which were completely impossible in the face of 15 per cent growth.

To make matters worse, our obsession with results doesn't actually work! Our singular focus on behaviour and results isn't actually improving behaviour or results. It's often making them worse. The only way to deliver a sustainable improvement in results is to have a much deeper understanding of the real drivers of performance and what impairs it.

Optimizing performance

In 1908 two scientists, Yerkes and Dobson, conducted a series of experiments with 'dancing mice'.[5] They put mice under pressure by heating the floor of their cage (hence 'dancing mice') to see how this affected their ability to perform. Yerkes and Dodson were able to demonstrate a clear and definitive relationship between pressure and performance that has stood the test of time. This relationship has since been verified for people, computers, complex systems and corporations.

This is not really surprising, and when asked to describe the relationship between pressure and performance most people can accurately describe how one affects the other. Most people know that pressure improves performance up to a point and then impairs it (Figure 5.1), and yet few managers, leaders or organizations apply these lessons to their own lives, teams or companies.

We all need some pressure or 'stress' in our lives in order to perform well. This is why many of us work well to deadlines. This is the healthy 'upslope' of the performance curve and it is often referred to as 'good stress'. However, if we become overloaded with an increasing number of tasks, conflicting deadlines and escalating pressure, eventually we will 'peak' and find our limit. The top of the performance curve or 'peak' forms an apex because most of us can pinpoint when we are working at our peak. This is our 'peak

FIGURE 5.1   The pressure–performance curve

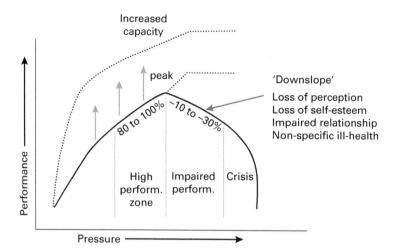

performance' and represents the physical, mental or emotional limits to how much we can take in one day.

If we're working flat out at or near our peak and somebody asks us to do an additional task, our performance cannot improve any further. All that happens is the pressure increases and performance declines.

When we are overloaded (or we overload others), performance doesn't plateau, it actually drops. We might think our performance is tracking upward along the first dotted line in Figure 5.1 but it's not. We have crossed a threshold and entered the 'downslope'. In the early days of impaired performance, we may not even notice that we are starting to underperform, partly because the gap between what we intend to do and what we are actually doing is small. Most people don't know that their performance has become impaired until they are a significant way down the downslope. Of course, once we realize there's a gap between our actual performance and our expected performance, that often makes us feel even worse and pushes us further down the downslope.

Getting the balance right

Underperformance in any organization is due either to insufficient pressure or, much more commonly, too much pressure. Unfortunately, the commonest organizational response to poor performance is to 'push harder', ie increase the pressure and demand even more by putting more pressure into the system or onto the person. This approach simply exacerbates the problem and drives the individual or team towards failure, faster.

We need to understand where we are on the performance curve and how to get the balance right, for both ourselves and our people. Too much pressure results in impaired performance and too little pressure results in sub-optimal performance. Most people in organizations live their life on the downslope because there is too much pressure in the system.

Part of the problem is that in business we demand '110 per cent' or '120 per cent effort'. People who make such demands are simply revealing how little they know about performance (and maths!) It's not possible to deliver a 120 per cent effort and such demands do nothing but perpetuate the 'not enough' mentality.

Any athlete will tell us that it is impossible to perform continuously at 100 per cent. Most elite athletes work on the healthy side of the performance curve at 80–85 per cent of maximum capacity. This is what enables them to raise their game for competition. Leaders, senior executives and teams need to be doing the same – leaving some spare capacity for a crisis or a busy time of year.

If we put too much pressure on ourselves or our team, performance will tail off until eventually performance falls off a cliff. Often this can happen when there is just too much on someone's plate and they have too many competing priorities. As a result, one of the most productive leadership interventions is to narrow the focus by clarifying and simplifying everything. Warwick Brady is President and CEO of Swissport International, formerly CEO of Esken (Stobbart Group) and the ex-deputy CEO easyJet. While at easyJet, Warwick used this approach to transform its performance and improve employee morale. easyJet is one of Europe's leading airlines, operating over 1,000 routes across 34 countries and serving around 96 million passengers annually. The company employs over 10,000 people, including 2,865 pilots and 6,516 cabin crew and as Warwick explains:

> Day-to-day delivery was poor, customer service was low, and the business was
> struggling to control costs. This all culminated in a collapse of performance
> in summer 2010. The number of easyJet planes arriving on time dropped to
> around 40 per cent. Gatwick Airport published the league table of airline on
> time performance (OTP) and easyJet came out below Air Zimbabwe – a fact
> shared with the wider world when Ryanair, a main competitor, used it as a
> headline in a national newspaper advertisement... The company was not in

good shape. I stepped into the COO role in October 2010. What I found was a team of people who had worked really hard for three to four years with little to show for it. For many it had become embarrassing to work for easyJet – performance was poor and everyone knew it… I had a lot to sort out.

Despite the apparent scale of the turnaround required, I decided we needed to really focus and fix just one thing: OTP. We needed to keep safety where it was, but essentially, we had to fix OTP, that's it, nothing else. The only way to achieve that goal was to work together as a team on that single focus… It worked. Within six months, we had stabilized the operation… Within 12 months we had not only fixed the problem, we had become number one in the industry for OTP. We had fixed the core. Our customers could trust that we would get them to their destination on time. Our crews could trust that they would be able to get home on time after their shifts.

My top team was predominantly made up of the same people as it was when we were failing back in the dark days. We went from being the worst-performing airline to being the best. The team became highly respected and operated like a well-oiled machine. All of this was down to the singular focus on OTP and teamwork.

Having achieved such a dramatic turnaround in performance, his team went further implementing a step-change to their meeting process, focus and discipline. This included reviewing all non-critical projects and literally stopping work to enable other projects to really succeed. Getting executives to stop doing things was quite a performance breakthrough.

When it comes to performance, there really is no need to overcomplicate the agenda. When a leader reduces the pressure, the performance will often improve immediately without any other intervention being required. Therefore, one of the most important responsibilities of a leader is to keep it simple and keep it clear. Getting the balance of pressure right is absolutely crucial for any leaders who are interested in increasing their own, their team's and their organization's results.

Living on the downslope

Often, leaders slip onto the downslope and don't even realize they are on the wrong side of the performance curve. Many don't notice anything is wrong until things reach a crisis point. If we want to get things working properly, early detection of underperformance is crucial. If action is only taken once the system has failed, it will be extremely costly, and recovery may even be impossible.

The more perceptive we are, the sooner impaired performance will become apparent and the sooner we are able to step in and reverse the trend. Without that expanded perception and awareness of the performance curve, we will simply drive harder and shout louder, which often brings about the very thing we are trying to avoid. If left unchecked, the highly pressurized individual will slide all the way down the downslope toward serious health issues and breakdown. If we don't want to keel over at our desks and we don't want any of our team to suffer the same fate, we must appreciate the signs of the performance curve and adapt accordingly.

There are several key signs that can tell us if we, or our people, have been tipped from peak performance into the downslope. The first is loss of perception. Most people don't even realize they're on the downslope. When challenged, they normally deny there is anything wrong. They just don't see their predicament.

There are also valid and relevant neuroscientific reasons why there is a loss of perception, as discussed in the previous chapter. When we are under pressure, the physiological signals generated in our body – particularly from our heart – create a chaotic, incoherent signal that causes a DIY lobotomy. Unfortunately, without access to our frontal lobes and the full depth and breadth of our own intelligence and cognitive ability, our perceptual awareness is seriously impaired. In addition to a loss of perception, there is often a loss of self-esteem and irritability, and all this can lead to impaired relationships.

Another tell-tale sign of the downslope is non-specific ill health. People on the downslope may wonder if they should go to a doctor. Unfortunately, doctors are trained to spot pathology and the early detection of dysfunction or instability before pathology occurs is not part of their training. As a result, the doctor will often dismiss the symptoms because there is nothing 'specifically' wrong or serious going on. It is these non-specific things that doctors should be paying much more attention to. These are the early warning signs of a destabilized system and the precursors of major disease and ill health. When things are just mildly dysfunctional and we're not quite sure what is wrong, that's exactly when we should be paying the most attention, because these are the early and highly reversible signs of poor performance and ill-health.

Left unchecked, more obvious psychological issues such as depression, dissatisfaction, frustration, pessimism, agitation and demotivation start to occur. These create behavioural problems in the workforce, poor relationships at work, excessive union issues, reduced productivity, impaired or

FIGURE 5.2   The individual and organizational impact of excess pressure

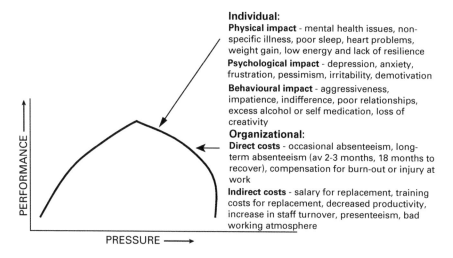

absent creativity, increased aggressiveness, impatience or indifference. Ultimately, the non-specific health issues such as low energy, poor sleep and weight gain will give way to more obvious conditions such as heart problems, high blood pressure and infections. The increased consumption of pills and alcohol is also a clue that we are on the downslope.

In addition to the impairment of individual performance and health, there are organizational costs to being on the downslope (Figure 5.2). At the team level, poor system health would be indicated by poor interpersonal dynamics, excessive silos and frequent ego battles. At the business unit level, poor health could be indicated by an unhelpful culture. At an organizational level, it would manifest itself as tribal behaviour and turf wars. Absenteeism is likely to rise, because people are demotivated. This can drift into long-term absenteeism and ultimately increased compensation claims against the business for ill health or injuries at work. Such activity also has indirect costs in terms of salary replacement and increased head count required to cover the absence. Staff engagement can be stubbornly resistant to change, leading to perpetually sub-optimal performance.

If we want to increase our own or our organization's performance, we will need to increase our own and other people's capacity. This can only be done effectively from the healthy side of the performance curve.

Exceptional Leadership unpacked

Having introduced the Exceptional Leadership model in Chapter 1, it's now time to unpack it in much more detail, because it is this model that explains why we are not getting the results we want, despite our very best efforts.

Adapted from Wilber's 'all quadrants all levels' (AQAL) model,[6] which seeks to map how the world and the individuals in it really work, the Exceptional Leadership model (Figure 1.6) focuses exclusively on how business and the people within business work. In order to make the model more business and commercially relevant we simply rotated Wilber's AQAL model anti-clockwise and simplified the perspectives into 'being' ('I'), 'relating' ('WE') and 'doing' ('IT'). We placed the individual at the centre, looking forward into their rational objective world ('IT'). By doing so, leaders can immediately see their business landscape depicted in a practical and powerful intellectual framework that can help them better understand the breadth of the challenges they face.

We stand in the centre of our own life looking forward, and the reason we are not getting the results we want despite our best efforts is because we rarely see what's behind us ('I' and 'WE'). Instead, we are predominantly focused on the 'IT' – especially the short-term 'IT', which takes up anywhere between 80 and 95 per cent of our time. And unless we realize that our efforts in the rational, objective world are built on 'I' (physiology, emotions, feelings and thoughts) and that the success of what we want to build requires our connectivity at the interpersonal 'WE', there is no solid foundation on which to build outstanding effectiveness in the rational, objective world.

The game of business causes leaders to become 'IT addicted' with an almost exclusive obsession on the short-term 'IT' targets, goals and metrics in the drive for quarterly results and shareholder value. A few leaders may, if time permits, also focus intermittently on strategic issues. And while many may appreciate the importance of 'WE', understanding the relevance of culture, values and relationships, they often struggle to move the dial on any of them.

And as for 'I', very few leaders spend any time thinking about their own awareness or their own individual development, the quality of their own thinking or their energy levels. And virtually no one ever thinks about their physiology, other than to notice they are exhausted. The four dimensions of leadership are rarely discussed in business; they are almost never taught in business schools and hardly ever appear in management and leadership journals.[7] And yet, at Complete we believe that it is the long-term 'IT', the interpersonal 'WE' and the 'I' that hold the key to business transformation and rewriting the rules of business.

To be an exceptional leader we have to be aware of and develop in all four quadrants simultaneously. We must cultivate our self-awareness; we have to develop much better interpersonal skills and we need to build innovative and resilient businesses. There are very few leaders who are outstanding in all four quadrants. The handful of truly world-class leaders are characterized by their ability to coherently move between all four quadrants.

Personal performance: the subjective, inner world of 'I'

If I was to summarize virtually all leadership books into one phrase it would be: 'Be yourself.' Whilst it is true that the leadership journey starts with 'I', it is also true that most leaders have not studied and do not have a detailed understanding of what 'I' or the 'self' really is. Leaders might understand intellectually the notion of authenticity, but very few, through lack of time or inclination, spend any time reflecting on the 'I' quadrant or thinking about who the person is that is turning up each day to do the doing. If you don't really know who you are then what are you being authentic to?

As I said earlier, this isn't that surprising considering that leaders are almost entirely focused on looking forward and they rarely look back over their left shoulder to the inner personal world of 'I'. Leaders are therefore encouraged to be themselves but given no time or intellectual framework to even consider who they are and what really makes them tick.

Much of what we have covered so far – physiology, emotion, feeling and thinking – seeks to provide that necessary intellectual framework so as to foster a much more sophisticated appreciation of what's really driving leadership behaviour and personal performance in the 'I' quadrant.

People leadership: the interpersonal world of 'WE'

Behind the leader's right shoulder is the interpersonal world of 'WE' – which will be discussed in greater detail in the next chapter. Obviously, successful leadership requires followership, so how a leader interacts with others is critical.

People interactions occur at three levels of scale for every leader – one-to-all, one-to-many and one-to-one. At the highest level the leader is the single biggest determinant of organizational values and culture (one-to-all.) The leader's impact (or otherwise) is determined by their ability to work effectively through the executive teams around them (one-to-many). The ability to build and bind teams together is therefore critical to organizational success, yet working their way up through the commercial, financial, operational, marketing or legal 'ranks' doesn't necessarily train a leader in the ability to build and bind teams successfully. It is often simply assumed that a leader can do this or they will work it out. Finally, a leader's ability to develop and nurture productive relationships with staff and stakeholders is also vital (one-to-one). How a leader shows up with every person they encounter determines their personal leadership brand and influence. Most leaders have not spent much time thinking about their own personal leadership qualities, their personal brand or how genuinely influential they are.

Both 'I' and 'WE' are aspects of reality that are not usually that visible. Instead, leaders are fully focused on the visible, external and objective world of 'IT' – the business. Despite many leaders claiming that 'people are our most important asset', they spend most of their time and attention on operations and finance. I remember asking a CEO, 'If people are your most important asset, why don't you spend most of your time with your human resource director (HRD)?' 'Because the guy's an idiot,' came the replay. This is a classic example of actions speaking louder than words. If that same CEO thought his finance director or his COO was an idiot, they wouldn't survive for five minutes because finance and operations are seen as absolutely vital to success. The fact that he thought his HRD was an idiot and the guy still had a job demonstrated how unimportant he really considered the people agenda to be.

When we interviewed Nick Warren, one of the boldest and most innovative HR specialists in mining and Head of Development for First Quantum Minerals Ltd, he explained what's possible when people leadership is considered important. Quantum Minerals is an established and rapidly growing mining and metals company producing copper, nickel, gold, zinc and platinum group metals across several mines worldwide, and as Nick explains:

> We've really committed to people development in a practical way. We wanted it to become a normal part of our culture. A few years ago, we started a graduate programme, which is not unusual in itself, but the real reason we did it was to give people-management responsibility to every manager in the organization. Each manager now has at least one graduate that they need to develop. While the graduates come with academic qualifications, they need to be developed and the managers take up that responsibility. Initially there was some resistance, but the managers soon saw the benefits of developing talent within their team and it has resulted in managers not just developing their graduates but other employees as well. In this way, we're building a culture of people development.

Market leadership: the future world of 'IT'

Driving an international business is very complex and intensely pressurized, so most leaders spend their time looking forward and only forward. Our top right quadrant, market leadership, is the long-term 'IT' (see Figure 1.6). Here the leader is focused on 'what' 'IT' is that needs to be done, and the emphasis is on the future and how to create the future. Even though business leaders the world over know that the long-term picture is important, few get out of the 'weeds' of the day-to-day so they can focus on the other three quadrants. However, the greatest businesses leaders spend just as much time building the future as they do managing the present.

As mentioned in Chapter 1, most businesses struggle to build their own future because they have not clearly differentiated the key concepts in the top-right quadrant of market leadership. In the absence of detailed training in strategic thinking, many companies outsource this to a strategy house that may deliver some detailed market analysis and some commercial options. As a result, the internal strategic thinking capability in many organizations is absent or underdeveloped. Often when I ask leaders to describe their strategic intentions to me I am presented with a series of thoughts about the 'in-year plan', which is not the same thing at all. The lack of high-quality strategic thinking or a strategic development process has a knock-on effect, impairing growth and innovation.[8] Insufficient detail on the scale of the ambition can make it very difficult for the CEO to make effective calls at pace, especially when those speedy decisions require a sense of urgency to be injected into the organization. The absence of an effectively articulated purpose can set in stone intractably low levels of employee engagement. A poorly defined vision confuses the customer and adds to the low engagement levels internally. Finally, massively inefficient governance dramatically slows down decision making and burns a huge amount of executive time in laborious meetings that don't take the organizational performance forward.

Quality focus on all these areas of market leadership can create 'clear blue water' between your business and your competitors.[9] Despite there probably being more competitive advantage to be had in the upper right quadrant than the upper left (commercial performance), many leaders find it immensely difficult to stay focused on anything other than the immediate short term. This problem is exacerbated by the volatile market conditions that create uncertainty and more insecurity.

Commercial performance: the here and now world of 'IT'

This quadrant is concerned only with the short-term 'IT' of money, profit, costs, product, service, marketing, target operating model, performance management systems, like-for-like sales comparisons and success metrics. The short-term 'IT' is purely focused on today and the quarter-by-quarter battle. We've talked to over 500 global CEOs and it's clear they spend most of their waking hours consumed by thoughts of 'what' 'IT' is that needs to be done now.

Short-term results are absolutely critical for an individual career. What's more, if leaders don't deliver today, they won't get permission to even explore the potential that lies dormant in the other three quadrants. The irony of this scenario is that the big commercial wins are virtually all to be found in those other three quadrants. It is, after all, difficult to outperform the competition just by having a tighter grip on the day-to-day metrics. But getting really tight cost control, driving down suppliers and squeezing the operation for maximum efficiency, measured via a myriad operational metrics, KPIs and 'steering wheels', is the standard combination a CEO employs to try and deliver shareholder returns.

While such a grip will always be necessary in the absence of activity in the other quadrants, it often creates a dry business seeking to grind out a result. Such organizations are often not that exciting to be part of, and over the long-term morale suffers, talent becomes increasingly difficult to attract and keep, leading positions are eroded and eminence is lost.

Leaders need to focus on building a business system that works independently of their own efforts. If they do not free themselves from the day-to-day operational focus, they are probably just managing the business, not leading it. The challenge for most leaders is getting out of the tyranny of 'today'. Until leaders start to make themselves redundant in that top left-hand quadrant it is very difficult to effectively lead the business. Exceptional Leadership only really emerges when leaders operate coherently in all four quadrants.

Leading in a complex world

Making the transition from managing the business to genuinely leading the business by not managing it is a very difficult step for most leaders. Often, the comfort zone is to continue to focus on tasks and driving short-term results. Management is mainly about the top left-hand quadrant whereas leadership is really about the other three quadrants. Management is about doing, whereas leadership is more about being. And who you are being often comes down to maturity. It will therefore come as little surprise that one of the key lines of development for an exceptional leader is maturity. Research has shown that leadership maturity can predict the ability to drive organizational transformation.[10] A number of academics have written and researched adult maturity and they have identified several stages of adult development. However, like so many of the insights shared in this book, adult development theory has until recently largely remained in the ivory towers of academia and has not made the transition into the places where those insights could really make a difference.

We explored one way to view maturity in the last chapter – Ken Wilber's 10-stage evolution of self. Other academics such as Susanne Cook-Greuter, Robert Kegan, Bill Torbert and Elliot Jacques have also all described different aspects of adult development. The research of each of these academics has something very useful to offer leadership development and yet it is surprising how few HR directors or leadership experts have even heard of, let alone studied, their work. Kegan, for example, provides some very valuable insights on the relationship between subject (the world of 'I') and object (the world of 'IT') and how this impacts the way we create our own destiny.

Of all the academics involved in this area, Cook-Greuter, who has spent 45 years researching ego maturity and how this plays out in organizations, is particularly useful. Her work provides a practical explanation for boardroom battles, the 'political manoeuvring' that so often occurs at the top of organizations and can distract leaders from building a great company and delivering results. It explains why leaders keep coming up with the same set of answers to the same set of problems. Specifically, her work adds real value and deepens our understanding of Wilber's description by providing greater differentiation of the transpersonal level and defines additional transpersonal levels of development. These additional distinctions go right to the heart of the leadership debate and why so many leaders struggle.

Bill Torbert explores adult maturity from the perspective of what drives action (called Action Logic) in a business setting. His descriptions of how the various stages play out in business are perhaps the most immediately recognizable to leaders. The labels Torbert uses to describe the levels of maturity, especially the three critical ones identified as being the 'centre of gravity' for most businesses, are a little more accessible than Cook-Greuter's descriptors.

We have built on Torbert and Cook-Greuter's work to try to make the key levels more comprehensible.[11] The two commonest levels seen in business are both conventional and called Expert and Achiever.

Maturity theory is a slowly emerging but profoundly insightful and practical framework for understanding much of the dysfunction witnessed in business (Table 5.1). As I said in the previous chapter, when leaders understand the characteristics and behaviours associated with each level of adult maturity and how they manifest in business, they are often immediately able to identify the maturity level of the other people in their team. As a result, understanding the different levels of maturity can shine a light on why their team isn't working well or why it may be stuck and, perhaps most importantly, what to do about it.

The majority of academics writing about adult maturity largely agree that the most important step-change waiting to occur in the development of leaders globally is the leap from the 'conventional perspective' to a 'post-conventional perspective'. Leaders who approach the world from a conventional perspective, which according to Torbert is at least 68 per cent of all leaders,[12] are focused on knowledge. In contrast, post-conventional leaders are starting to differentiate and understand the critical difference between knowledge and wisdom.[13] Not just as an intellectual distinction, but in terms of the implications of this distinction for organizational success and an organization's role in the world.

Torbert described how the conventional-level leaders have been promoted up through the ranks by being very proficient in a particular set of skills, but this proficiency did not automatically equip them to lead a business. And considering that the vast majority of learning and development (L&D) in any business is predominantly focused on the L with no real D, conventional leaders often find themselves in 'over their heads'.[14] And that's not good for either the individual or the business.

Conventional leaders like to know more and do more. As leaders mature, they develop an increasing ability to differentiate phenomena, which itself is a sign of their development. Experts and Achievers like to predict, measure and explain the world. This enables them to see ahead and they also like to look back in time to discover patterns, rules and laws at play. They notice more and appreciate more pieces of the puzzle, and this is what enables them to succeed.

In contrast, post-conventional leaders like to strip away illusions and see a deeper reality. As they move up the three levels of post-conventional

TABLE 5.1   The levels of leadership maturity

Descriptor	Level
12. Illuminated	Post-Post-Conventional
11. Embodied	Post-Post-Conventional
10. Unitive	Post-Post-Conventional
9. Alchemist	Post-Conventional
8. Integrator	Post-Conventional
7. Pluralist	Post-Conventional
6. Achiever	Conventional
5. Expert	Conventional
4. Conformist	Conventional
3. Self-protective	Pre-Conventional
2. Ego-centric	Pre-Conventional
1. Impulsive	Pre-Conventional

thinking, they develop an increasing ability to integrate the knowledge and wisdom they have accumulated, which is also a sign of their development. They prefer to approach issues without a preconceived idea of the answer. They take a much more holistic dynamic-system approach and like to see deep within, around and beneath the issue rather than just examining the context and the future possibilities. They are particularly keen to flush out hidden assumptions in thinking and explore the interplay between breadth and depth.

Many leaders have had no reason to focus on their own vertical development, partly because most have achieved a certain degree of success without ever doing so. However, as the world accelerates and becomes more complicated, leaders are increasingly recognizing they can't continue to succeed by just doing what they have always done. Leaders are starting to 'wake up' to the possibility that they need to consider their own development as central not only to their personal success but to their business success too. The more enlightened businesses have recognized this and have started to become deliberately developmental organizations (DDOs).[15]

Whilst the various developmental academics may look at their subject from different perspectives with different names and nuances, what they all agree on is that most leaders in business operate from 'Achiever' or below.

There are clearly leaders who have a more expansive perspective and greater maturity, but the current collective 'central tendency'[16] is that 85 per cent of leaders are hovering between Level 5 and Level 6 (Table 5.1).[17] And the effects of that are being painfully felt in the world today. For example, one of the main reasons that the world is still in turmoil is because of the predominance of unsophisticated thinking at Level 6 or below.[18] A new financial crisis seems inevitable[19] and our collective ability to navigate Covid-19 and come up with high-quality joint solutions has been woefully ineffective. This may also be one of the main reasons why leaders are struggling to grow their business in any other way than by mergers and acquisitions.[20] And it's probably at least partially to blame for the worrying number of exhausted, miserable executives that occupy the upper echelons of global business.

We need to evolve. We need vertical development. And we need new ways to lead business that will work for the human beings involved, the shareholders and the planet. We need more mature, more exceptional leaders.

Performance-driving behaviours

Over the last three decades, the popularity of leadership competency models or behavioural frameworks has grown to the point where virtually every organization has its own framework. Given the impact that leaders have on the organization, and what they do, this makes sense. However, despite investing huge amounts of time and money on such competency frameworks many organizations have been disappointed by how little this has delivered. Some experts have suggested that the assumptions behind the whole competency models are problematic.[21] Indeed, research suggests that many academics believe behavioural competencies are deeply flawed, which certainly raises questions about their practical and commercial relevance.[22]

So where does this leave organizations that are understandably keen to change leadership behaviours? Behaviours remain important because they are the final common pathway to improved performance. Thankfully, thinking about behavioural competency frameworks has moved forward significantly in the last couple of years. This thinking is rooted in some high-quality research that identified that the thousands of behaviours that companies have been building their frameworks around are all built from just 11 'letters' in the behavioural 'alphabet'.[23]

The behaviours that really matter

Harry Schroder from the University of Florida and Tony Cockerill from the London School of Economics identified an approach that avoids all the problems with competency frameworks.[24] They started with the right question: namely, what behaviours will leaders need to use to deliver high performance in a complex and dynamic environment? Next, they studied businesses that were experiencing a significant number of unpredictable changes (large and small), so as to pinpoint the behaviours that really matter and their practical applications.

Schroder and Cockerill's research found that when they studied people from initial idea through to successful implementation there were just 11 behaviours that determine organizational success.[25] All leaders must convert ideas into profitable action. The only difference between success and failure is how proficient each leader is in using these 11 foundational behaviours (see Figure 5.4).

We now understand that these behaviours are not just present or absent in a leader. The key question is to what degree they are present. There are six levels of competency within each behaviour, ranging from a 'limitation' to a 'strategic strength'. The more successful, senior and influential a leader is, the more behaviours they exhibit as a 'strength' or 'strategic strength'.

Most organizational frameworks are not rooted in this research. They often have detailed descriptions of behaviours, which can be a jumble of up to five 'letters' in the behavioural alphabet. This makes it impossible for organizations to accurately measure these behaviours and certainly makes it impossible for them to be developed within the talent pool. Furthermore, because most organizations don't realize that there are six levels of sophistication to each of these 11 behaviours, their competency framework often mixes several behaviours at different levels of sophistication. Finally, many companies don't have adequate coverage across the range of 11 critical behaviours. All of this means most organizations competency frameworks don't deliver what they are designed to deliver – and that is progress.

At Complete we therefore profile leaders using our Leadership Behaviour Profile, which provides leaders with an accurate insight into individual and team behavioural capabilities. This provides us with a map for further development so that individuals and teams can become much more efficient and

FIGURE 5.3   The six levels of behavioural competency

Rating	Definition
Strategic strength (level 5)	You consistently use the behaviour with high impact AND you promote its use by others and bake it into the organization.
Strength (level 4)	You consistently use the behaviour with high impact on a team, business unit or division to create a longer term outcome.
Developing strength (level 3 with occasional level 4)	You use the behaviour consistently to add value on the individual task and sometimes more widely.
Adding value (level 3)	You use the behaviour at a basic level to add value in the short term, on an individual task, but not consistently.
Undeveloped (level 2)	You understand the behaviour but don't use it or there is no evidence of use.
with Limitation (level 1)	You use the behaviour but in a way that erodes performance.

SOURCE © Complete Ltd

productive. This profile will assess an individual across the 11 performance-driving behaviours and illuminate what level of competency that individual currently demonstrates for each behaviour (Figure 5.3). If a behaviour is identified as a 'limitation', the leader inhibits the behaviour in a way that is eroding business performance. If a behaviour is identified as 'undeveloped', the leader either doesn't currently use the behaviour or uses it very rarely. Most leaders will have one or two 'undeveloped' behaviours. If a behaviour is identified as 'adding value', the leader is already using that behaviour at a basic level to add value to the business, but not consistently. Most leaders have three or four behaviours that are 'adding value'.

If a behaviour is identified as a 'strength', the leader is consistently using that behaviour in the business to great effect. The leader is making a considerable impact on the long-term outcome of the business through that behaviour. A sub-category of 'strength' is 'developing strength', which indicates that the leader is using the behaviour consistently to add value but is not yet using it consistently to create a significant impact in the business. Most leaders have four or five 'strengths' or 'developing strengths'.

Finally, a behaviour is identified as a 'strategic strength' if the leader is consistently using the behaviour with high impact *and* is baking that behavioural strength into the business through the coaching of others, implementation of systems or cultural change. It's possible, by comparing a leader's behaviours to our global benchmark, to separate directors from CEOs and global CEOs by the number of 'strategic strengths' that a leader exhibits in their business.

FIGURE 5.4   The eleven letters in the 'behavioural alphabet'

IMPLEMENT	IMAGINE
Maximize operational efficiency and enable organizational change to deliver commercial performance and customer value	Take a broad and deep view of the commercial context that ensures vision and strategy create competitive advantage
Being **P**roactive	**S**eeking Information
Continuously **I**mproving	Forming Co**N**cepts
—	Conceptual Fle**X**ing

IGNITE	INVOLVE
Connect with people to release their commitment, enthusiasm and support for ideas, plans and strategies that take the business forward	Fully engage and develop individuals and teams to build trust, nurture potential and get the best out of people
Transmitting Impactfully	**E**mpathic Connecting
Building **C**onfidence	**F**acilitating Interaction
Influencing **O**thers	**D**eveloping People

By identifying the current proficiency within these key behaviours, a leader and his or her executive team are able to focus, individually and collectively, on specific areas for behavioural development. Instead of wasting valuable time and money on generic 'leadership behavioural training' programmes, these insights effectively provide a very tight brief for leadership coaching with the sole aim of elevating behaviours that are currently 'adding value' to 'strengths', and, where appropriate, from 'strengths' to 'strategic strengths'. Massive improvements in individual and team performance are therefore possible with less effort than most organizations are currently spending.

The 11 performance-driving behaviours

The 11 behaviours that Schroder and Cockerill's research identified can be organized into four distinct sequential clusters with three behaviours in each, except 'Implement', which has two behaviours (Figure 5.4).

FIRST BEHAVIOURAL CLUSTER: IMAGINE

The Imagine cluster describes all the behaviours that leaders need to do to take a broad and deep view of the commercial context that ensures vision and strategy create competitive advantage. There are three behaviours that are critical in the imagine step:

- *Seeking information (S)*: How well does the individual seek out the information they need from a wide variety of sources, both directly relevant to the task at hand, and from the broader business environment?

- *Forming concepts (N)*: How well is the individual able to make connections to form ideas and solutions, linking data and ideas across the broader business environment to form high-level concepts?
- *Conceptual flexing (X)*: How well is the individual able to generate multiple viable options and hold them at the same time, analysing the pros and cons of alternatives to identify the optimum solution?

SECOND BEHAVIOURAL CLUSTER: INVOLVE

Once someone has completed the Imagine step and developed some workable concepts, the individual must fully engage and develop individuals and teams to build trust, nurture potential and get the best out of others. There are three behaviours that are critical in the Involve step:

- *Empathic connecting (E)*: How well does the individual seek to understand another person's point of view though listening, open questions and reflecting back to check their meaning?
- *Facilitating interaction (F)*: How well does the individual ensure contributions from all team members, facilitating team interaction towards a joint output built on everyone's shared inputs?
- *Developing people (D)*: In supporting others' efforts, how able is the individual to develop others and take personal responsibility to train, mentor, coach or stretch their development?

THIRD BEHAVIOURAL CLUSTER: IGNITE

Once the concept has been developed and others are engaged and able to deliver it, a leader needs to connect with others to release their commitment, enthusiasm and support for ideas, plans and strategies that take the business forward. There are three behaviours that are critical in the Ignite step:

- *Transmitting impactfully (T)*: How clearly does the individual get a point across with clarity and structure, broadcast in an engaging and compelling way so key messages are remembered?
- *Building confidence (C)*: How well does the individual state their position with confidence, and create optimism and enthusiasm in others by celebrating success and being positive?
- *Influencing others (O)*: How well does the individual persuade others with benefits and advantages and build sustainable, mutually beneficial alliances based on win–win relationships?

FOURTH BEHAVIOURAL CLUSTER: IMPLEMENT

Once everyone is on board with the idea or task, the final stage requires a leader to maximize operational efficiency and enable organizational change to deliver commercial performance and customer value. There are two behaviours that are critical in the Implement stage:

- *Being proactive (P)*: How proactive is the individual in taking action to assign roles and responsibilities and deliver plans, ensuring change happens by overcoming barriers, bureaucracy or inertia?

- *Continuously improving (I)*: How focused is the individual on setting and measuring appropriate goals to improve performance and manage quality by routinely tracking key performance indicators?

More detail regarding the variance of output within the 11 behaviours can be seen in Figure 5.5.

This behavioural research, often known as the High-Performance Managerial Competencies (HPMC) framework, is the most widely used basis for leadership behavioural assessment globally. This research has been independently validated in several separate studies, including Ohio State leadership studies,[26] Harvard, Michigan[27], Princeton strategy research, the Transformational Leadership Study[28] and the Florida Council on Education Management (FCEM) competency research[29] as well as Professor Richard Boyatzis' study for the American Management Association.[30]

The benefit of this work is that it enables us to focus only on these 11 behaviours, because these are the ones that really make a commercial difference and have the capacity to transform results. Like the four base pairs that make up DNA these 11 'letters' in the behavioural 'alphabet' can be used to understand thousands of other more complex behaviours.

When fully present at the 'strength' or 'strategic strength' level, these 11 behaviours will provide a competitive advantage because they enable leaders, teams and organizations to perform at outstanding levels in a complex world.

This framework also allows us to assess individuals and teams and identify strengths and weakness within both. Using the global benchmark in Figure 5.6, which is based on data from 55,000 executives, we can identify areas for improvement across a team so that individually and collectively the capacity of the team can develop. For example, we can look at the global benchmarks and identify that effective managers exhibit three of these performance-driving behaviours at the 'strength' level. However, if a

FIGURE 5.5 Details of the 11 behaviours

IGNITE

Transmitting Impactfully (T)

Score	Description
5	Creates communication strategies to promote the business unit's values, messages and profile to external and internal audiences; creates value for excellence in communication across the organization.
4	Makes communication more memorable using tools such as analogies, humour, compelling momentum, gestures, surprises and visual aids.
3	Verbal communication is clear, well-structured and easily understood.
2	Communication is impaired by poor diction, eye contact or ineffective visual aids.
1	*Communication is very difficult to understand due to high speed, impenetrable structure or rambling.*

Building Confidence (C)

Score	Description
5	Creates processes, tools and a climate that celebrates success and to boost morale and confidence across the organization.
4	Builds confidence of others in themselves, the company or the success of a project by making statements that build hope and optimism; celebrates success.
3	Speaks in a self-assured, confident way so that own position is clear to others; makes timely decisions and does not shy away from making difficult or unpopular decisions when required; holds own ground when challenged.
2	Changes own mind without good reason; avoids making a decision when needed; hesitates and shows doubts; creates uncertainty.
1	*Express lack of confidence in project or company; refuses to deal with contentious or difficult issues; creates climate of pessimism and despondency.*

Influencing Others (O)

Score	Description
5	Forms strategic alliances with other organizations to achieve joint goals; fosters a climate which values shared interests, mutual cooperation and win-win rather than internal competition or win-lose.
4	Forms win-win alliances with others by citing how a proposal can achieve mutually beneficial aims.
3	Aims to persuade others by citing advantages and benefits of an idea, proposal, product.
2	Presents own proposal to stand on its own merits with no effort to persuade others to buy in.
1	*Shoots down others' proposals to give own idea credibility; may use coercion or threats to get people's backing.*

INVOLVE

Empathic Connecting (E)

Score	Description
5	Creates an environment of trust where people feel valued for speaking honestly and openly and are encouraged to air their true ideas and beliefs.
4	Tests own understanding of another's ideas by reflecting back what has been heard; shares own feelings to encourage others to do so.
3	Seeks to understand another's viewpoint, beliefs or opinion by asking open-ended, non-judgemental questions.
2	Listens and acknowledges others' contributions.
1	*Closes down others' contributions by interrupting, over-talking, finishing others' sentences; shows lack of value for others' opinions or beliefs; interrogates others to verbally 'corner' them.*

Facilitating Interaction (F)

Score	Description
5	Creates process or strategy to encourage cross-boundary thinking and working; creates a value for open team interaction and development.
4	Facilitates dialogue until contributions of two or more team members' ideas have been cohered into a true 'team idea', not one owned by one individual.
3	Invites others to contribute; identifies links or themes between team members' contributions; facilitates dialogue to make sure everyone understands links.
2	Contributes to team discussions but does not facilitate.
1	*Shuts down contribution of others by imposing premature consensus, hogging the stage or not giving others air time; discourages others from interacting by channelling interaction through themselves.*

Developing People (D)

Score	Description
5	Implements a strategy or process to cultivate learning and development throughout the organization by setting up development, coaching or mentoring programmes; creates an open feedback culture; ensures people development receives as much priority as any other part of the business.
4	Takes personal responsibility for individuals' development, e.g. coaching or mentoring them; gives others challenging, stretching projects to develop them; gives regular, constructive feedback.
3	Sends people on training courses to develop their skill; supports others' efforts to develop themselves.
2	Recognises the need for development, but does nothing about it.
1	*Gets fixed on one plan, solution or point of view; will not consider or acknowledge alternatives or other perspectives.*

IMAGINE

Seeking Information (S)

5	Implements a system or strategy for collecting and disseminating information on an on-going basis; creates a value for research and knowledge gathering.
4	Looks for information from outside the situation being considered to get a better, wider, richer diagnosis of what's going on.
3	Actively searches for information about the task in hand; may search deeply rather than broadly; collects enough information to gain an understanding of the situation being considered.
2	Limited information search that fails to cover key categories; clarifies what is already known or stated, but does no original research.
1	*Makes assumptions based on existing information; prevents others from collecting information; distorts, rejects, ignores or denies information presented to them.*

Forming Concepts (N)

5	Implements processes or strategies to encourage the evolution of ideas and to support others' efforts to generate ideas.
4	Links information about apparently different topics to form powerful diagnostic concepts, visions or solutions; links information from the wider environment to form a deeper understanding of the situation.
3	Forms ideas, judgement or conclusions from the information available; concepts focus on or are associated with the task in hand.
2	Repeats others' concepts, but does not generate own; can organize and categorize information but does not use it to explain a situation.
1	*Squashes others' ideas before they've had a chance to flourish; recycles old concepts which may no longer be relevant; may struggle to understand complex ideas.*

Conceptual Flexing (X)

5	Implements processes or strategies to encourage flexible thinking in others; sets up strategic scenario planning at all levels in the organization.
4	Explores in depth two or more explanatory concepts, perspectives or alternative solutions simultaneously; models out the short and long term pros and cons of at least two viable options simultaneously before judgement.
3	Suggests or uses at least two viable options or solutions; suggests at least two possible diagnoses for a situation, sees the perspectives of at least two other parties; options held 'in parallel' not 'in series' and without judgement.
2	Able to explore one option or perspective.
1	*Gets fixed on one plan, solution or point of view; will not consider or acknowledge alternatives or other perspectives.*

IMPLEMENT

Being Proactive (P)

5	Implements strategies to train, empower and encourage others to take the initiative and drive change
4	Removes bureaucracy and red tape to allow freedom of action (within accepted parameters) and scope to take initiative, eg redesigns a job role to allow greater freedom to act.
3	Puts together effective action plans with phases, assigned roles and responsibilities; identifies sequences and phases of a project.
2	Responds to others' suggestions and plans without taking the initiative personally.
1	*Resists or stops other taking action if it breaks rules or is not 'what is normally done round here' or is outside formal boundaries; creates unnecessary rules or policies that restrict the performance of others.*

Continuously Improving (I)

5	Builds a culture that values performance measurement and makes measurement part of everyday language; measures are aligned to corporate goals and cascaded throughout the company.
4	Sets interconnected goals, target or measures to improve performance, regularly reviews against indicators at milestones.
3	Sets a goal, target or measure to monitor or raise performance. Takes action to improve performance.
2	Talks about improving, monitoring or measuring performance - but takes no action.
1	*Sets goals or targets that are irrelevant to the improvement of performance or measure the wrong things; prevent others taking action to improve performance.*

FIGURE 5.6   Benchmarking leadership behaviours

YOUR PROFILE	INDIVIDUAL CONTRIBUTOR	TEAM LEADER	HEAD OF FUNCTION	DIRECTOR	CEO	GLOBAL CEO
S	DS	S	S	SS	SS	SS
S	DS	S	S	S	SS	SS
S	DS	S	S	S	SS	SS
DS	AV	DS	DS	S	S	SS
DS	AV	AV	DS	DS	DS	S
DS	AV	AV	AV	DS	DS	DS
DS	AV	AV	AV	AV	DS	DS
DS	UD	AV	AV	AV	AV	AV
AV	UD	UD	AV	AV	AV	AV
AV	UD + L	UD + L	UD + L	AV	AV	AV
UD	UD + L	UD + L	UD + L	UD + L	UD + L	UD + L

manager wishes to develop into an effective director (vice president or VP in US terms) or chief executive (SVP), he or she must develop the 'strengths' and 'developing strengths' further and convert them into 'strategic strengths'. Based on the global benchmark, if that leader wishes to perform at a global or group CEO level, 4 of the 11 behaviours must be demonstrated at the 'strategic strength' level or higher.

These insights are invaluable and allow us to identify gaps in individual development and the development of a team that can direct learning and development initiatives. Instead of throwing everything at the learning and development wall and hoping that something sticks, we can address very specific issues highlighted through the Leadership Behaviour Profile and provide very tailored coaching for each member of the executive team.

Every individual has their own unique strengths, which means that leaders usually excel in four or five of these behaviours. Exceptional leaders, however, are also defined by the fact that they do not demonstrate any 'limitation' or 'underdeveloped' behaviours. In other words, they do not demonstrate negative use of a particular behaviour, which means that their impact on the organization is consistently positive.

This is not about turning weaknesses into strengths; it's about highlighting the behaviours where we are already 'adding value' or operating at the 'strength' level and taking active steps to develop those behaviours further so more of them become 'strategic strengths'. Operating at the 'strategic strength' level means that we bake the very best of our leadership into the business, thereby creating a leadership legacy.

We were asked to review a bank's behavioural competency framework. They had decided they wanted their leaders to 'make it happen' and had written some detailed descriptions of what this behaviour really meant. We reviewed their description and it was clear that this behaviour was actually a mix of four different behaviours or letters of the behavioural alphabet including 'being proactive' and 'facilitating interaction'. One of these four 'letters' was described at 'strategic strength' level, one at 'strength', one at 'developing strength' and one at 'adding value' level. Given this confusion, it was not surprising that they had found it impossible to develop this behaviour in their talent pool, let alone accurately assess whether this behaviour was present in the workforce at all.

Understanding the 11 behaviours also enables us to identify weaker behaviours or any behaviour that is being exhibited in an unhelpful way. A behaviour identified as a 'limitation' is almost certainly limiting career progression. The reality of human nature is that we will never turn all our limitations into strengths. It's not possible. Instead, focus on elevating the 'limitations' just enough so that they stop being a hindrance to personal and collective performance. Once we've done that, we are better served by switching focus to the behaviours that are currently 'adding value' or 'strengths' and elevate those still higher.

We must practise these behaviours daily because, as Geoff Colvin pointed out, 150 years of research now proves that there is no such thing as natural talent.[31] Instead, it is the predictable emergence of a skill following a considerable amount of deliberate practice. Elevating performance in behaviours where we are already 'adding value' or 'strengths' is therefore much easier and much faster because we've probably already clocked up a considerable amount of time in these areas.

Knowing where you and your people are in terms of these 11 performance-driving behaviours can transform results and direct learning and development within the entire business.

How to be *more* successful

Even when we know the behaviours that actually drive an increase in organizational performance, it's not enough to actually deliver better performance.

We still need the motivation to change and the optimistic belief that change is actually possible. In order to drive consistently brilliant performance and behavioural coherence, we need to master the last two personal skills of Exceptional Leadership.

Building on the emotional resilience of the previous chapter, we need to step-change our motivation for behavioural change, through the identification of personal purpose. In addition, sustaining that behavioural change requires us to develop an optimistic outlook. This can be achieved by cultivating the art of appreciation.

Behavioural coherence – self-motivation: identify your personal purpose

The pressure experienced by leaders and the punishing hours they work has often led me to wonder why they do it. When things become really difficult, many even wonder themselves. When I ask leaders why they do what they do, nearly all have no accurate sense of their own personal purpose.

Understanding personal purpose is critical in helping leaders to keep going when times are tough. Identifying purpose is also at the heart of being fulfilled and learning to live in the here-and-now. When we are clear about what really drives us and why we do what we do, we don't need to tie ourselves in knots about the past or the future. We don't need to second-guess every decision or ruminate endlessly over various options or choices. Once we know our purpose, everything becomes simpler because every course of action is either taking us closer to that purpose or further away from it. When we know why we are going where we are going, it's much easier to stay on track and make the right decisions quickly.

Working with a trained developmental coach can help to uncover a leader's personal purpose in a few hours of skilled exploration and discovery. When we work with executives, the question of purpose frequently comes up. Do they know why they do what they do, or are they simply going through the motions, following a set of corporate rules, playing different roles and just doing a job?

The late Clay Christensen suggested that often:

> we pick our jobs for the wrong reasons and then we settle for them. We begin to accept that it's not realistic to do something we truly love for a living. Too many of us who start down the path to compromise will never make it back. Considering the fact that you'll likely spend more of your waking hours at your job than in any other part of your life, it's a compromise that will always eat away at you.[32]

Yale psychologist Amy Wrzesniewski has spent many years studying how what we believe about our work affects our performance at work.[33] She found that everyone operates from one of three 'work orientations' or mind-sets about work. Everyone therefore sees their work as either a job, a career or a calling. Unsurprisingly, those with a job tend to be motivated by the money alone. Those with a career may enjoy the money but they work for personal fulfilment and self-actualization. And, finally, those who consider their work a calling would do it whether they were paid or not!

When someone is passionate about something, the 'work' becomes a source of energy and the more they work the more energy they have. This is why identifying purpose and motivation is so important because it can help to transform a 'job' into a 'career' or 'calling'. Interestingly, Wrzesniewski found the three orientations within every profession she studied – from surgeons with a job to janitors with a calling! In every case, however, those who considered their work a career or calling worked harder and longer, and were more productive, healthier and happier than those with a job. Meaningful work – whatever that means to you – is good for the soul. Unfortunately, very few people fall into blissful fulfilment in a profession that suits them perfectly. Most of us need to take conscious steps to uncover our purpose. When we are living 'on purpose' and tapping into our innate motivation, energy and fulfilment are never a problem.

In order to help uncover life purpose, take a moment to consider these questions:

- What was the first decision you made as an adult and why?
- Think about critical moments of choice in your life – why did you follow a certain path? What was it about that choice that attracted you?
- Look for threads that unite your moments of choice. These moments of choice are clues that can help you uncover your purpose.
- What was the greatest day of your life (excluding your wedding day, or the birth of a child) – when you were most fulfilled, when you were absolutely loving what you were doing and where were you at that time?
- What is the greatest compliment or greatest insult someone could give you? (Both can also provide clues to help you discover your purpose.)
- Think about both the tragic and the magic – the high points of your life are magic, low points of your life are tragic. These experiences also give you clues to your purpose. Try to identify a consistent pattern, and that will help you understand your core purpose.

Our purpose will almost always have something to do with strengths we already possess, so take the time to consider what those are or might be. Certainly, the Leadership Behaviour Profile highlights existing strengths that may help shed light on your purpose.

Most highly successful individuals are not well rounded – they are 'spikey'. In other words, they have developed a small number of unique talents that they leverage to maximum effect. These talents are almost always something that they yearn to do, learn to do easily and love to do, or that bring fulfilment and that they do with ease. Often it is this last characteristic that can throw us off the scent of purpose. Because most people use their talents effortlessly, they are often not aware of them, so they wrongly assume that it's nothing special, not difficult or that everyone can do it. It is often perceived as special and difficult by everyone other than the person who has that talent!

I believe it is possible to boil what we are really about at our core down to two, three or four words. The first word is 'I'. Once purpose has been discovered our life can start to make sense. Purpose has been guiding you whether you realize it or not. A skilled developmental coach can bring that drive into conscious awareness, and help you uncover your core purpose.

As Steve Jobs so rightly pointed out, 'The only way to be truly satisfied is to do what you believe is great work. And the only way to do great work is to love what you do. If you haven't found it yet, keep looking. Don't settle'.[34] Joseph Campbell, the great scholar of myth and mythology also suggests that the route to fulfilment and happiness is to 'follow your bliss', adding:

> If you follow your bliss, you put yourself on a kind of track that has been there all the while, waiting for you, and the life that you ought to be living is the one you are living. Wherever you are – if you are following your bliss, you are enjoying that refreshment, that life within you, all the time.[35]

Meaning, do what you are here to do, live according to your purpose. As with all matters of the heart, when you actually uncover your real core purpose, you'll know it. It often feels like 'coming home'.

Behavioural coherence – optimistic outlook: the appreciation skill

The second critical element to driving behavioural change is cultivating a belief that change is indeed possible. Children have no problem believing they can change their behaviour but unfortunately such optimism is usually knocked out by the time they reach adulthood.

If we strip back this optimistic childhood belief, we uncover something absolutely critical to behavioural change, and that's the ability to learn. In the absence of an ability to learn, behavioural change is very difficult. What is more, when we delve deeper to discover what really drives a child's innate ability to learn we discover something even more fundamental, and that is that learning requires us to appreciate the new. It's this appreciation that children are remarkably good at. They have open, curious minds and can appreciate the simplest of things.

Most children are natural learners; their curiosity makes them soak up information like a bone-dry sponge soaks up water. And it's almost effortless. For example, by the time a child is five he or she will have mastered 6,000 words and can operate 1,000 rules of grammar.[36]

But then we go to school and it is often slowly squeezed out of us as we are told to 'sit down and keep quiet' as the teacher pours information into our heads. We are rewarded for outcome not effort and are taught very early on that failure is unacceptable. As a result, we get to adulthood thinking we've made it and don't need to learn anything else, or feel uncomfortable at the idea of learning something new in case we fail or look foolish.

Extensive studies into success and achievement have found that it's not abilities or talent that determine success but whether we approach our goals from a fixed or growth mindset.[37] As the name would suggest, a person with a fixed mindset believes that what they were born with is basically what they have. If their parents were intelligent, they will be intelligent, and if not, there isn't that much they can do to change that. Someone with a growth mindset, on the other hand, assumes that what they start with in terms of genetics and upbringing is the start line not the finish line, and that they have the power to improve anything. As children we have a growth mindset. We try, fail and try again. But over time it becomes more and more fixed until eventually we forget how to learn anything new.

This pinpoints one of the fundamental problems for behaviour change, namely that many adults are poor at learning. They have to hear something seven times before the learning 'lands'. We fail to appreciate what we are taught, so we need to be taught the same thing over and over again. Some people constantly repeat the same error without any reflection and improvement. When we close ourselves off from learning and life, we are not receptive to new information or perspectives, which merely amplifies the problem and keeps us stuck in outdated and unhelpful thinking – a point not lost on William James when he said, 'A great many people think they are thinking when they are merely rearranging their prejudices.'

I believe that the best way to foster a growth mindset and develop an optimistic outlook is to practise the art of appreciation. When we appreciate everything – the good days and the bad – and convert every experience into a learning experience, we open ourselves up to life and can become wiser much more quickly. This boils down to a simple phrase:

We must first learn to appreciate in order to appreciate what we learn.

Of all the 17,000-plus positive emotions, appreciation is one of the most power-ful because it allows us to wake up every morning and see the world afresh. People get attached to various viewpoints and beliefs about themselves and others that make it impossible to wake up with fresh eyes and see their world anew, so they merely 'rearrange their prejudices'. The appreciation skill is there-fore about learning how to cultivate the state of appreciation as a default emotion. When we do, we see each day as a fresh and exciting opportunity for growth, learning and changing our behaviour or expanding our options.

THE APPRECIATION SKILL: YOUR BRAND

Most people are their own worst critics and have spent years judging them-selves and creating a belief structure that they are, in some way, not enough. As an antidote to this tendency, which drains energy, limits growth and interferes with creativity and innovation, it can help to develop the ability to appreciate ourselves.

This may sound simple, it may even sound puerile, but it doesn't come naturally to most people. Ask someone what they dislike about themselves and they can often talk for several minutes. Ask them what they appreciate and you'll be met with confused silence or a list of bravado-based state-ments that don't really ring true.

To make this exercise easier, think about what you appreciate about yourself across six distinct areas:

- *Mentally*: What do you appreciate about your mental prowess?
- *Emotionally*: What do you appreciate about yourself emotionally?
- *Physically*: What physical attributes or abilities do you appreciate about yourself?
- *Socially*: What do you appreciate about your social skills and how you interact with others?
- *Professionally*: What do you appreciate about your professional skills and capacity?
- *Spiritually*: What do you appreciate about yourself spiritually or ethically?

After greater consideration, you may realize that you appreciate that you are mentally thoughtful and quick-witted. You might appreciate that you are professionally 'dedicated' or that you are physically fit because you exercise regularly.

It might also help for you to know that no one will ever see this list. It's simply a private stocktake of the things you sincerely appreciate about yourself. Once you've written the things that really mean something to you, convert the list to bullet points and make a note of them on a credit card-sized piece of paper. You could even laminate it if you were feeling particularly creative. If anyone finds it, it won't make any sense to them, but you can bring it out of your wallet or purse and look at it every day.

The idea is that even if you've had a really bad day, you can take a moment to look at your list and you can remind yourself that you're still 'dedicated'. What you appreciate about yourself doesn't change because of the ups and downs of life. You don't stop being thoughtful; you may demonstrate an alternate behaviour now and again but that doesn't mean you are not thoughtful most of the time. You might have behaved like an idiot shouting at your partner, but you can still appreciate that you are 'empathetic and loyal' more often than not. You may have used your 'quick wit' in an unhelpful and hurtful way but you didn't stop being quick witted. And, you can still appreciate that quality.

Remember, psychologist Sonja Lyubomirsky's research that found people who took the time to count their blessings, even just once a week, significantly increased their overall satisfaction with life.[38] Psychologist Robert Emmons also found that gratitude (which is a sibling from the same family of emotions as appreciation) improved physical health, increased energy levels, and for patients with neuromuscular disease relieved pain and fatigue. Emmons added, 'The ones who benefited most tended to elaborate more and have a wider span of things they're grateful for'.[39]

The reason this skill is so important and so powerful is that people spend vast amounts of time in self-judgement and self-criticism. These types of personally directed negative emotions do not facilitate clear and creative thinking. They are the hallmark of mismanaged emotions and, as explored in Chapter 3, are extremely toxic to our health and happiness. Many of us have a natural drive to succeed, but when that spills over into excessive concern about our own performance it can and does contribute to ill health. One 10-year study of over 10,000 managers and professionals suggested that those characterized as 'perfectionists' were 75 per cent more likely to have health issues, including cardiovascular problems.[40]

We must learn to appreciate who we are instead of berating ourselves over who we are not. Forgiveness is not something we give to others; it's a gift we give to ourselves. When we truly forgive someone (and ourselves) we release the unhelpful energy or emotional charge from our body. As a result, that negative energy no longer wreaks havoc with our health, thinking or performance. We don't forgive someone to let them off the hook – we forgive them to let ourselves off the hook.[41]

I was reminded of just how powerful this idea is when I was asked by a friend to help his wife. She had become so anxious that she was almost agoraphobic. She grew up with a toxic mother who constantly criticized her and made her feel awful. She left home at 16, finally breaking free of her mother's negative influence. Since the age of 19 she'd had little to do with her mother. When I worked with her, she was 40 years old. She had spent most of her adult life physically away from her mother and yet her mother's influence continued to affect her every single day. Her mother, on the other hand, was totally unaffected by this situation. The only life being ruined was the 40-year-old daughter's. But she has a choice. We all have a choice. Bad things happen to many people. The choice is whether we let them define us for the rest of our life or whether we choose to forgive and start to appreciate our good points.

All too often, we are our own worst critics. We're not kind to ourselves and we don't care for ourselves. Being kind to ourselves is not all about having a massage or playing a round of golf; that's just addressing the surface! The real point is dealing with how we feel and what we think about ourselves every moment of the day. The appreciation skill breaks that negative and dysfunctional pattern of self-criticism and self-judgement so we can use our energy more constructively and foster an optimistic outlook. Cultivating the art of appreciation creates a different emotional default. If we learn to appreciate, we are much more likely to be able to appreciate what we learn. If we can appreciate what we learn, we are much more likely to be able to change our behaviour. We see other options; we feel good about ourselves and this optimism enables us to make better choices.

Behavioural coherence facilitates relationship coherence

Business leaders and managers are obsessed with behaviour, because they know that behaviour drives performance. But there are internal lines of development that need to be understood and strengthened first, otherwise any effort to improve performance will falter. Behavioural coherence is also facilitated by a clear understanding of our strengths across the 11 performance-driving leadership behaviours. Most people will instinctively know where their strengths lie. For those interested in a more definitive insight, the Leadership Behaviour Profile can provide leaders with an accurate insight into individual and group strengths. It can isolate areas for further development so that individuals, teams and the business as a whole can become more efficient and productive.

For decades we have been told repeatedly that success is the final destination, achievement is the goal. And yet there is a growing realization that perhaps there is something bigger and better that includes success but facilitates a different, more rewarding type of success. I believe that new finishing line is influence and the ability to foster powerful influential relationships inside and outside the workplace. And that's what we'll explore in Chapter 6.

Summary of key points

If you don't remember everything in this chapter, remember this:

- Our obsession with performance isn't actually improving performance. It can really help to understand the performance curve. A certain amount of pressure (good stress) is beneficial and can improve output. Too much, however, and we become unproductive.

- Like elite athletes, high-functioning leaders need to operate at around 80–85 per cent of maximum capacity so they leave some space to think or deal with a sudden crisis.

- Leaders need to appreciate the importance of performance across all four quadrants of the Exceptional Leadership model. Specifically, in relation to behaviour, leaders must extricate themselves from the weeds of day-to-day, short-term management and direct more of their attention to the long-term leadership of the business.

- What we do in business and the decisions we make are also fundamentally influenced by leadership maturity. Maturity theory is a slowly emerging but profoundly insightful framework for understanding much of the dysfunction within modern business.

- This topic is especially critical when we consider that the majority of academics writing about adult maturity agree that some 85 per cent of current leaders do not have the maturity, awareness or perspective to successfully lead their businesses in a complex world.

- Based on rigorous research, we now understand the 11 performance-driving behaviours that really matter when it comes to improving performance and results.

- We can assess leaders and their teams against these behaviours, identifying whether an individual demonstrates that behaviour as 'undeveloped' all the way up a scale of competency to 'strategic strength'.

- By identifying the current proficiency within these key behaviours, a leader and executive team are able to home in, individually and collectively, on specific areas for development that can massively improve performance with minimal effort.

- We still need the motivation to change and the optimistic belief that change is actually possible.

- Consistently brilliant performance and behavioural coherence is therefore facilitated by mastering the last two personal skills of Exceptional Leadership – identifying purpose and fostering an optimistic outlook.

Notes

1   Ariely, D (2008) *Predictably Irrational: The hidden forces that shape our decisions*, HarperCollins, London; Ariely, D (2010) *The Upside of Irrationality*, HarperCollins, London

2   Taleb, N N (2007) *The Black Swan: The impact of the highly improbable*, Penguin, London; Martin, R L (2011) *Fixing the Game: How runaway expectations broke the economy, and how to get back to reality*, Harvard Business School Press, Boston, MA; Roubini, N (2020) Ten reasons why a 'Greater Depression' for the 2020s is inevitable, *Guardian*, 29 April

3   Brown, B (2013) *Daring Greatly: How the courage to be vulnerable transforms the way we live, love, parent, and lead*, Penguin, New York

4   Rowland, W (2012) *Greed Inc: Why corporations rule the world and how we let it happen*, Arcade Publishing, New York

5   Yerkes, R M and Dodson, J D (1908) The relation of strength of stimulus to rapidity of habit-formation, *Journal of Comparative Neurology and Psychology*, 18, pp 459–82

6   Wilber, K (2001) *A Theory of Everything: An integral vision for business, politics, science and spirituality*, Shambhala Publications, Boulder

7   Watkins, A (2016) *4D Leadership: Competitive advantage through vertical leadership development*, Kogan Page, London

8   Watkins, A and May, S (2021) *Innovation Sucks! Time to think differently*, Routledge, London

9 Kim, W C and Mauborgne, R (2005) *Blue Ocean Strategy: How to create uncontested market space and make the competition irrelevant*, Harvard Business School Press, Boston, MA

10 Rooke, D and Torbert, W R (2005) Seven transformations of leadership, *Harvard Business Review*, April

11 Watkins, A (2016) *4D Leadership: Competitive advantage through vertical leadership development*, Kogan Page, London

12 Rooke, D and Torbert, W R (2005) Seven transformations of leadership, *Harvard Business Review*, April

13 Kaipa, P and Radjou, N (2013) *From Smart to Wise: Acting and leading with wisdom*, Jossey-Bassey, San Francisco

14 Kegan, R and Lahey, L (2009) *Immunity to Change: How to overcome it and unlock the potential in yourself and your organisation*, Harvard Business School Press, Boston, MA

15 Watkins, A and Dalton, N (2020) *The HR (R)Evolution: Change the workplace, change the world*, Routledge, London

16 Cook-Greuter, S R (2004) Making the case for a developmental perspective, *Industrial and Commercial Training*, 36 (7), pp 275–81

17 Rooke, D and Torbert, W R (2005) Seven transformations of leadership, *Harvard Business Review*, April

18 Watkins, A and Wilber, K (2015) *Wicked & Wise: How to solve the world's toughest problems*, Urbane Publications, Kent

19 Reich, R B (2020) *The System: Who rigged it, how we fix it*, Picador, New York

20 Martin, R L (2011) *Fixing the Game: How runaway expectations broke the economy, and how to get back to reality*, Harvard Business School Press, Boston, MA; Watkins, A and May, S (2021) *Innovation Sucks! Time to think differently*, Routledge, London

21 Hollenbeck, G P, McCall Jr, M W and Silzer, R F (2006) Leadership competency models, *The Leadership Quarterly*, 17 (4), pp 398–413

22 Cockerill, A P, Schroder, H M and Hunt, J W (1993) *Validation Study into the High Performance Managerial Competencies*, London Business School, unpublished report sponsored by National Westminster Bank, Prudential Corporation, Leeds Permanent Building Society, the Automobile Association, the UK Employment Department and the UK Civil Aviation Authority

23 Schroder, H M (1989) *Managerial Competence: The key to excellence*, Kendall Hunt, Dubuque, IA; Cockerill, A P (1989) *Managerial Competence as a Determinant of Organisational Performance*, unpublished doctoral dissertation sponsored by the National Westminster Bank, University of London; Cockerill, A P (1989) The kind of competence for rapid change, *Personnel Management*, 21, pp 52–56

24 Cockerill, A P (1989) *Managerial Competence as a Determinant of Organisational Performance*, unpublished doctoral dissertation sponsored by the National Westminster Bank, University of London; Cockerill, A P, Schroder, H M and Hunt, J W (1993) *Validation Study into the High Performance Managerial Competencies*, London Business School, unpublished report sponsored by National Westminster Bank, Prudential Corporation, Leeds Permanent Building Society, the Automobile Association, the UK Employment Department and the UK Civil Aviation Authority

25   Schroder, H M (1989) *Managerial Competence: The key to excellence*, Kendall Hunt, Dubuque, IA; Cockerill, A P (1989) The kind of competence for rapid change, *Personnel Management*, 21, pp 52–56

26   Stogdill, R M and Coons, A E (1957) *Leader Behaviour: Its description and measurement*, Bureau of Business Research, Ohio State University, Columbus, OH

27   Katz, D, MacCoby, N and Morse, N C (1950) *Productivity, Supervision and Morale in an Office Situation*, Institute for Social Research, University of Michigan, Ann Arbor, MI

28   Bass, B M (1999) Two decades of research and development: Transformational leadership, *European Journal of Work and Organizational Psychology*, 8 (1), pp 9–32

29   Croghan, J H and Lake, D G (1984) Competencies of effective principles and strategies for implementation, *Educational Policy Analysis*, Southeastern Regional Council for Educational Improvement, #410 Research Triangle Park, NC

30   Boyatzis, R E (1982) *The Competent Manager: A model for effective performance*, London, Wiley

31   Colvin, G (2010) *Talent Is Overrated: What really separates world-class performers from everybody else*, Penguin, New York

32   Christensen, C M, Allworth, J and Dillon, K (2012) *How Will You Measure Your Life? Finding fulfilment using lessons from some of the world's greatest businesses*, HarperCollins, London

33   Achor, S (2010) *The Happiness Advantage: The seven principles that fuel success and performance at work*, Crown Business (Random House), New York

34   Christensen, C M, Allworth, J and Dillon, K (2012) *How Will You Measure Your Life? Finding fulfilment using lessons from some of the world's greatest businesses*, HarperCollins, London

35   Campbell, J and Moyers, B (1988) *The Power of Myth*, Doubleday, New York

36   Attenborough, D (1979) *Life on Earth*, episode 13, BBC, 10 April

37   Dweck, C S (2007) *Mindset: The new psychology of success, how to learn to fulfil our potential*, Ballantine Books, New York

38   Lyubomirsky, S (2007) *The How of Happiness*, Penguin, New York

39   Wallis, C (2005) The new science of happiness: what makes the human heart sing? *Time Magazine*, 17 January

40   Rosch, P (1995) Perfectionism and poor health, *Health and Stress Newsletter Issue 7 (Newsletter of the American Institute of Stress)*, pp 3–4

41   Dowrick, S (1997) *Forgiveness and Other Acts of Love*, Norton, New York

06

Be influential

Have you noticed how incredibly difficult it is to change corporate culture? Do you often feel that some of your people are coasting or hiding most of the time? Do your people really listen to you? Do they really understand what you want? Do you feel accepted by others at work, or do you feel judged and underappreciated? Have you ever been passed over for promotion and didn't know why? Have you ever embarked on a merger or acquisition only to be deeply disappointed with the results? Did the merger only double your worries rather than fix the ones it was designed to solve? Have you ever wondered why it seems so hard to unlock the discretionary effort or improve employee engagement? Do you find that you have brilliant individuals in your team, but they don't work together well? Are you on to your second or third marriage? Are the people you work with a mystery to you? Do you find people management challenging and tedious? If so, you're not alone.

Most of us have experienced power struggles at work at some point or another. Most of us have worked in an environment that lacked leadership – where people were too busy bickering with each other, engaged in 'turf wars', back-stabbing or arguing about the wrong things instead of providing the team or organization with real direction. Petty boardroom squabbles and point scoring are common even though they actively inhibit performance.

We can spend 20 years working with someone, attend their retirement party and realize we don't actually know anything meaningful about them. The people we spend most of our lives with are virtual strangers. Business executives tell themselves that their business is customer-centric, yet if you walk into many stores or listen to customer conversations, you'll realize we pay scant attention to the actual needs of the human beings our corporations are set up to serve. We can be rude or indifferent, lacking in warmth and genuine care.

We understand the importance of relationships and social connections, but we have little idea how they really work. In business there is a huge industry around employee engagement, looking for ways to build productive working relationships and develop trust and camaraderie. But the vast majority of it makes little difference. Employee satisfaction and engagement is not great in most businesses. As employees, executives and leaders, we often feel we can't really say what we want to say, be ourselves and bring all of ourselves to work. Our diversity is not always honoured or appreciated. Instead, many of us simply homogenize to fit in or simply survive; and here begins the disengagement process.

Most people's experience of professional relationships is patchy at best because we're never really taught how to build and sustain productive working relationships. The frustrating part of business – any business – is the people, because we don't all think, feel or act in the same way. We are by our nature beautifully complicated human beings. And yet people, and specifically the relationships we have with those people, hold the key to phenomenal success and elevated performance over the long term – a fact acknowledged by Nobel Prize-winning economists Gary Becker, George Stigler and Milton Friedman, who all believed that modern economics fails to adequately account for human interactions, motivation and behaviour in a business setting.[1] It's the people in a business that make the culture, for example, and it's cultural challenges that are at the top of the list when it comes to explaining why most mergers and acquisitions fail to add value. A merger may look good on paper, but when the two organizations have even slightly different cultures it is almost certainly doomed to fail. Companies spend more than $2 trillion on acquisitions every year. Yet study after study puts the failure rate of mergers and acquisitions at somewhere between 70 and 90 per cent.[2]

When we fail to understand or appreciate the impact of individual and collective differences, we can end up steamrollering the changes through, which rarely works. When no attention is paid to the people involved and the relationships they have and how they will change, people simply disengage. But if we take the time to understand what makes people tick, and we engage with them as individuals rather than just employees, we can unlock discretionary effort and amazing things are possible. If we don't, our mergers and acquisitions will continue to fail, our work teams will continue to function poorly, and we will not bake success into our businesses.

But relationships are not just a work issue. Relationships in all their forms are the single hardest thing that we do as human beings.

For many senior executives and business leaders, the only family member that seems genuinely happy to see them is their dog. Many senior executives and leaders have already experienced at least one divorce. They spend so much time at work or thinking about work that relationships with their partner, family and friends are almost non-existent or simply break down, often with far-reaching consequences. When it comes to love and intimacy – felt and shared – renowned physician Dean Ornish states: 'I am not aware of any other factor in medicine – not diet, not smoking, not exercise, not stress, not genetics, not drugs, not surgery – that has a greater impact on our quality of life, incidence of illness, and premature death from all causes.'[3] Relationships are critical to everything we do in life. They are the ultimate prize in life. Success without connections – colleagues, friends and family – to share it with can often feel hollow and unfulfilling. That's why this chapter has been positioned after the chapter on success. We need a new finish line when it comes to measuring achievement that includes but transcends material success. Success is no longer enough; we need to build strong, enduring and productive relationships inside and outside work in order to live full, happy, healthy and successful lives.

Relationships are difficult

If you consider the number of people who have limited or no contact with their family, broken or neglected friendships, are divorced or experience problems in working relationships, it's pretty obvious that relationships are not easy. Relationships of all types are the hardest thing we do as human beings.

Lack of time, and a singular focus on results, means that too many leaders fall back on fast, superficial methods of 'communication' such as email, company-wide bulletins, video presentations, PowerPoint, etc, instead of detailed discussions or face-to-face interaction. Or they opt for the 'hairdryer treatment', which is not communication either. The irony is that once a leader reaches a certain level of seniority, success becomes all about high-competency people skills and much less about technical ability. It comes as a shock to many that they are poorly equipped for the demands of people leadership.

Ultimately, relationship failure comes down to two things: poor communication and low levels of trust.

Poor communication

When two people talk to each other, a huge amount of information is exchanged: words, tone, body language, pheromones, heat, energetic signature and a host of biological signals, including electrical, sound and electromagnetic signals. Interestingly, most of that exchange is still happening even if we don't speak. And yet we rarely pay attention to it and certainly don't understand it.

Effective communication has two basic aspects: transmission and reception. We are only ever taught half the formula. We are taught transmission, first from our parents, then from our teachers: 'You can't say "more better", it's just "better".' They help us to understand the correct tense, pronunciation and grammar. We are taught about using the right word and the power of metaphors, etc, and over time we become pretty effective at transmission. But we don't get trained in reception or how to receive information. Our parents rarely gave us instructions and never asked us to repeat those instructions to make sure we understood. They just say, 'Are you listening?' Or, 'Can you please listen to me!'

Little people grow up into big people, believing that listening is simply 'waiting to speak'. To most people, listening is the moment before they say something. When someone is sitting quietly in a business meeting, we assume they're listening, but they are probably either deciding what they are going to say or considering what to have for dinner. There is little or no reception going on. This is why people constantly talk at cross-purposes.

We see poor listening in game shows like *Family Fortunes* where one member of a team will give an answer and it will be wrong and the next member of the same team will give exactly the same answer. They were not listening to what was being said because they were so busy thinking about what they would say. This happens all the time in business, but we just don't realize it. We ask someone to do something and they seem to agree with the request and look confident. Only what they produce bears almost no resemblance to what we actually asked for – at least not in our mind. Most people are very poor at listening to each other. It's not deliberate or malicious or unprofessional; it's just that most of us have never been taught how. Our parents and teachers may have told us to listen all the time, but they never actually told us how to listen. Consequently, our ability to connect is very superficial; we haven't really heard each other so there is little chance that we really understood each other.

The training that leaders or executives often receive on communication occurs at what I call Level 1 or Level 2. The real value of most communication is at the deeper Level 3 – the meaning level. Since most people get stuck at Level 1 or 2, the message never truly lands as it was intended.

The first level of communication is what is often discussed in mainstream communications workshops and includes a focus on the words, tone and body language of the message. These component parts of Level 1 communication are often referred to as the '3 Vs' for verbal, vocal and visual.

We are able to gauge far more from the tone that someone uses and their body language than we can from the words they use, and it's tonality and body language that help us to go behind the words to understand the content of the message. We often know this instinctively and have usually experienced it many times in business. If, for example, we ask a member of staff to stay late, they may say 'Yes, that's fine', but it's crystal clear from their tonality and body language that they don't really believe it's 'fine' at all. The influence of tonality and body language in effective transmission is the reason why face-to-face is always better than phone, and phone is always better than email. This is why people often use emojis to try to inject some tonality into the basic message and assist accurate interpretation.

But the real gold in communication occurs when we seek to establish what someone means (Level 3) rather than what they say (Level 1) or what they think or feel (Level 2). The meaning level is also the domain of genuine influence. When a leader can get behind the words, tonality and body language of an interaction and accurately understand what that individual really means – sometimes clarifying a point that the individual isn't fully cognizant of until that moment – the individual can finally feel validated and heard. And making another human being feel heard is such a rare occurrence in most workplaces that it can be extremely motivating.

Often, leaders mistakenly believe that their job is to give people answers. Managers and senior executives come into their office and tell them stuff, but those communications are usually only partially true. The leader's real job is to get underneath the words, tonality and body language to discover the truth and what that truth means. Too often, we take conversations at face value, jump to conclusions and offer up a ready-made, albeit wrong, solution.

Instead, we need to pull back, get to the truth, uncover the meaning and guide our people to their right solution. Sir Ian Cheshire, ex-CEO of Kingfisher and one of the most sophisticated leaders in Europe, is a strong believer in this approach. Kingfisher is Europe's largest home improvement business, employing 77,000 people across several retail banners including B&Q, Screwfix and Tradepoint. The company operates over 1,300 stores in nine countries and serves millions of customers every week. When we interviewed Ian about Exceptional Leadership he said, 'It is fascinating to me that people who reach a certain level of seniority feel they have to know all the answers.' He added:

> I pay attention and unlock things within what others are saying. I go deeper than the words. In terms of external stakeholders and managing relationships with the city, the first thing to say is that you must have the right numbers. No amount of clever arrangements will disguise the numbers. Moving beyond the numbers, there is an odd intersect in the world of public companies, between shareholders, analysts and the press. There are mutually reinforcing pressures at work there and I observed two things. First, you must get out and put yourself about. You need to spend time understanding the motivations of the shareholders, analysts and the press. Second, you need to understand their way of looking at the world, but you must show up as yourself. You can't do this with spin. You have to be authentic. If you don't know what their view of the world is, you can't frame a message for them.

True leadership requires us to get beneath the surface, beyond the gesture and even beyond what people think and feel to get to the meaning: why has this union rep come in and threatened to call a strike? Why is this customer so angry when we think we've done a good job? If we can't get to the truth, we end up solving the wrong problem. And we solve the wrong problem because we are too focused on the words, tonality and body language of any communication rather than the meaning.

The only way to get to the meaning is to learn the other half of the communication formula. We need to get much better at reception. Again, we already know this. It's why we send our people on 'active listening' courses or rapport-building courses. But they rarely make much of a difference. If anything, they just make people more effective at not listening! It's all a bit 'relationship by numbers' – nod three times, repeat the phrase, 'I hear what you are saying…'; or when the person you are talking to leans in, you lean in; or when they cross their leg, you cross your leg! It's insincere, it looks ridiculous at times, and the very best outcome is that it allows people to get better at faking communication.

We can create better relationships, but only if we dispense with the unsophisticated interventions, go beyond the words, tone and body language and access real meaning. Then we will create more authentic connections with each other that facilitate genuine listening and genuine reception. The good news is that it's not a difficult skill to learn. It literally takes five minutes to learn the MAP skill, which we'll cover later in the chapter, and yet it can have a very profound effect on communication and the quality of all of our relationships, home and work.

Insufficient trust

Trust is known to be central to team development. Like listening, it's a profoundly simple concept but few of us have ever been taught what the component parts of trust are. Few have ever stopped to consider how trust is created or lost. If we want stronger, more productive and more influential relationships, it stands to reason that we need to unpack trust.

There are two types of orientation to the very notion of trust (Figure 6.1). There are 'trust givers' who naturally trust people immediately. This type of upfront trust is either validated or gets eroded over time. When validated, people who take this stance claim that they were 'right to trust them'. If trust is eroded, they end up disappointed in the other person. Relationships or even companies that operate in this trust mode tend to be more empowering and give others more autonomy. They expect the best of people. On the downside, they may not make the commercial goals explicit enough. When a leader is involved in the recruitment of an executive there is often automatic 'trust giving' – this can leave the leader blind to the executive's failings for a longer period of time.

FIGURE 6.1   Trust orientation – 'trust givers' or 'trust earners'

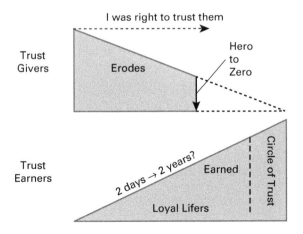

The second orientation is present in 'trust earners' where an individual doesn't naturally trust another and so trust must be earned and accumulated over time. People who take this stance tend to be wary and they don't trust others until the other person has proven themselves worthy. Once trust is earned, they may view others as 'loyal lifers'. Relationships or companies that operate in this mode tend to be more performance driven with more controls, checks and at times more fear. On the upside, what's required is usually much clearer.

In our work we often spend a significant amount of time exploring trust with leaders and senior leadership teams. We suggest that TRUST can be seen as an acronym for Taking Responsibility for Understanding Someone else's Traits. The central concept within trust is therefore understanding. If leaders want to increase the levels of trust in their organizations, they must take responsibility for building that understanding. And the thing they must understand is the other person's traits.

In working with leadership teams all over the world since 1996, we discovered that understanding someone else's traits requires us to spend some quality time with the other person to build a personal connection. It also requires us to understand their motives, their working style and why they may sometimes fail to deliver on their promises. Thus, we discovered there were four key elements to the 'trust recipe', and these are independent of culture or geography. Knowing this recipe can significantly fast-track results and performance. If leaders want to increase the level of trust in their relationships, their teams or their organizations, they need to focus on one or all of these elements:

- *Personal connection*: In order to trust someone, or have them trust you, and develop a strong relationship, we need to spend time with that person, building a quality connection with them.

- *Understand motives*: It is very difficult to trust someone if you are suspicious of where they are coming from and why they are behaving in a certain way.

- *Consistent delivery*: It is vital that people consistently deliver on their promise and do what they say they will do.

- *Working style*: Finally, if the way that a person works is very different from our own, this alone can impair the ability to build trust, because we find it difficult to resonate with them.

People leadership and the development of powerful teams

Exceptional Leadership is only possible when a leader and their executive team are coherent and increase their altitude across the separate but connected lines of adult development. Unfortunately, most leaders are so immersed in short-term commercial performance that they don't get time to address anything other than the top left-hand quadrant of the Exceptional Leadership model (Figure 1.6). Remember how this relates to Wilber's AQAL model (Figure 1.5). Modern business is almost exclusively focused on 'IT'.

There is no time to look over their left shoulder to personal performance ('I') or their right shoulder to people leadership ('WE'). They might know theoretically that these aspects of leadership are important, especially people leadership, but the noise created around shareholder value tends to drown out almost everything else.

If we really want to make a massive impact on our business, create a legacy and transform results in the long term, we need to make ourselves almost redundant in the top left-hand quadrant ('IT'). By doing so, we liberate ourselves to reap the massive rewards inherent in the other three quadrants. Real business transformation will only really emerge when we do the personal inner developmental work ('I'), step-change the top right-hand quadrant ('IT') and also truly embrace the bottom right-hand quadrant ('WE'). This requires us to develop leadership teams into high-performing units or even executive fellowships that we trust enough to take care of the majority of the commercial performance.

Iman Stratenus, reflecting on Exceptional Leadership and his time as Managing Director with TNT Express in China, explains:

> The most important moment of my development as a leader was when I realized that leadership was not about me. Of course, it matters greatly what I do and how I lead – my energy, my intentions and my actions – but the goal is not me, nor is it me who is judged. All that matters is the strength of the connections in the team and the impact we have through our collective efforts. For me, that shift was liberating. All my interactions – interviewing candidates, coaching conversations, leading team discussions, interacting with customers and suppliers – became a lot more worthwhile and satisfying when I could shift my interest from me to the other person.

Having a big ambition and a brilliant strategy will count for nothing if the executive teams are not pulling together and the culture is dysfunctional.

Senior executives need to focus on leading the people in their organizations as well as building companies that can lead their markets.

The stages of team development

Most leaders come up through the ranks, having managed teams of various sizes. They have learnt on the job how to work with others. Some have developed an ability to get the best out of others; some have simply learnt how to tell people what to do. Very few leaders have been formally trained in the stages of team development or know much beyond some generic clichés about 'norming, storming and performing'.

Despite this, many leaders still take their team 'off-site' for a 'team-building session' once in a while. Most leaders have become pretty cynical about such events. Experience has shown them that the best they can hope for is that such events will make no difference; otherwise, they may reinforce prejudices or cause the team to go backwards. After a questionable outward-bound programme or a strained supplier site visit, many leaders conclude that teams are not cost effective and they may as well continue in their command-and-control approach, meeting separately with the heads of the various business units and having individual meetings with each silo.

That's not to say that team development is a waste of time. Far from it, it's absolutely critical. But we must accept that great teams take time. Remember, the first critical component in building the trust necessary for high-functioning teams is 'personal connection'. We need to spend time together; it's simply not possible to foster the trust and develop exceptional teams without personal connection. As a consequence, when working with CEOs and senior executives we always advise that if they are not prepared to invest a minimum of eight days a year in developing their teams, they probably shouldn't even start because anything less is a waste of time and money. They would be better off giving the money they were about to spend on the team event to a deserving charity. Building a successful relationship between just two people is hard enough, so when we add a third person to the mix the challenge more than doubles. Add 10 more executives, each with his or her own agenda, and the level of complexity and dynamism goes off the charts. No wonder it's difficult to get an executive team to work well together. Needless to say, high-functioning coherent executive teams are pretty rare. And this task is significantly hampered by an absence of under-standing of the stages of team development.

The lack of knowledge about the inner workings of a team stems from two things. First, few organizations reward their leaders for working well cross-functionally or building coherent teams. Rewards are largely based on individual contribution. As a result, most leaders engage in 'symptom thinking' not 'systems thinking'.[4] Second, there is scant technical understanding of the stages of team development, how these stages can be measured and how to guide teams through the stages to much higher levels of performance. Research done at Princeton University and Southern Illinois University looking at hundreds of task-orientated teams over several months has helped to identify highly consistent ways in which teams evolve.[5]

As with all the developmental models shared in this book, it's not possible to skip a stage of development. Teams who put in the work can progress through the levels, and those that don't or are poorly guided will simply slip back to an early, less sophisticated stage of functioning. Experience has shown us that once a leader has a deeper appreciation of the stages of team development and has mastered the behaviours, practices, methodologies and disciplines required to achieve more advanced levels of team performance, they can facilitate more rapid development when they join a new team.

Making a strategic decision to properly invest in team development is one of the three most commercially important moves a leader can make in the 'people leadership' quadrant of the Exceptional Leadership model and such investment can create a strong competitive advantage.

The issue is how to build and bind teams together. Better team-working cannot be mandated. Leaders who demand team engagement will usually have the opposite effect and inhibit team development. There are certain conditions that, if present, increase the likelihood of genuine team coherence. They are:

- *Interdependency*: It can help to make one person's success dependent on another team member's input, thereby creating interdependency across functions.
- *Common purpose*: Teams are united by a common objective. This can be broken down into the team's vision or dream, their purpose, their ambition and their strategy. If a team has made the effort to build a shared version of any one of these, it can serve as a unifying force. If there is alignment across all of these differentiated concepts, team coherence is likely to be significantly higher, and such things can be defined at every level of an organization.

- *Authority*: Every team needs a degree of autonomy and the ability to determine its own destiny within the limits of authority given to it. A team that is clear around what delegated authority it has and what it can change is able to cohere around such authority.

- *Team size*: With increased size comes increased complexity. The optimal size of a team really depends on a number of factors, such as the team's purpose and the range of capabilities required in delivering its purpose. Many organizations think six is the magic number but we have seen dysfunctional teams of four people and highly effective teams of 18 people.

- *Commitment to development*: There is a justifiable scepticism about 'team away-days'. However, a shared commitment to improving the team's effectiveness and enhancing the team spirit, dynamics and inter-personal relationships can itself be a powerful cohering force. This has to be a sincere commitment, not lip service or 'box ticking'.

- *Leadership*: A leader's commitment to developing a team is the single biggest determinant of that team's success. This leadership can be supported or enhanced by other team members but if the leader is not behind the 'team journey', the team will never really develop.

- *One boat*: One of the most vital aspects of team success is the idea that we are 'all in this together', one team, one boat. The 'stroke' in the stern of the boat sets the rhythm and is the equivalent of the CEO or team leader who is responsible for direction and injecting pace. But everyone in the boat has their role, and that role is no more significant than any other. Everyone must play their part and if someone tries to be a hero, they will usually slow the team down. Organizational status or hierarchy is irrelevant; what matters is the team result, not anyone's individual expertise. Often, leaders who are keen to exercise their own power or authority are the primary reason why the team does not develop beyond the third stage of team development.

If the conditions for the team journey are largely in place, the stage is set, and it is possible to coach and facilitate the team through the nine stages of team development. Passively leaving teams to develop themselves or holding team events that are not integrated into a people leadership strategy may provide short-term improvements but are more likely to keep teams stuck below Stage 3. Such an unstructured approach to development is one of the main reasons why organizations that want to change fail to do so. Successful

FIGURE 6.2   The nine stages of team development

9	Unified Fellowships	INDUSTRY "this industry as part of society"
8	Broad Fellowships	
7	Integrated Pluralists	ORGANIZATION "this organization as part of the industry"
6	Diverse Pluralists	
5	Interdependent Achievers	TEAM "this team as part of the organization"
4	Independent Achievers	
3	Dependent Experts	INDIVIDUAL "me as part of this team"
2	Battling Experts	
1	Talented Individuals Pre Team	

transformation requires a much more sophisticated understanding of the stages of team development and how to navigate the stages to unlock the true potential teams offer organizations. High-functioning executive teams are often the difference between success and failure in many organizations, and this is becoming increasingly vital as organizations navigate a complex world.

Twenty-five years of research by Cockerill, Schroeder and others has provided deep insight into the stages of team development most commonly seen in organizations today.[6] It was their work that uncovered the 11 performance-driving behaviours we explored in the last chapter. Their efforts have also provided the foundations for the nine distinct stages of team development (Figure 6.2):

1 *Talented individuals*: This is where all teams start. It is a pre-team collection of individuals but with no common purpose or shared agenda.

2 *Battling experts*: When talented individuals realize that there is a legitimate reason that they need to work together then they naturally start to figure out a 'pecking order'. The dysfunction at this level is often concealed by a thin veneer of politeness or professionalism. Underneath,

power struggles and undercurrents remain. This is the *forming*, *norming*, *storming* stage of team development that most people recognize.

3 *Dependent experts*: Some of the struggles of stage 2 improve with leadership refereeing, adjudication and decision making. The team starts to deliver results. Most people have experienced this 'performing' stage of team development in their career. But the team is still massively sub-optimal, and hasn't unlocked its potential or got close to what's possible. Team members turn up, report in and seek guidance from the boss. There is more friendliness, members may even enjoy each other's company. But really the team is still just a collection of individuals doing their job, in their silo, all held together by the leader in charge (hence dependent).

4 *Independent achievers*: The big switch here is that team members stop 'reporting in' to the team and start 'leading out' from the team. Thus, they get in the boat together and become a proper team for the first time, rather than a bunch of silo experts working alongside each other. The team is not dependent on the leader for cohesion and to broker relationships. They proactively work to strengthen their relationship bonds themselves. Members openly share their thoughts and feelings. There is greater psychological safety. They take much greater responsibility for their own energy, their impact on others and their behaviour. They also start taking increased responsibility for the performance of the whole team, not just for their discrete areas. All this reduces the dependency on the team leader to propel the team forward. The team starts to achieve things without needing the leader to drive them forward all the time.

5 *Interdependent achievers*: As the team starts to really function properly the success of stage 4, the increased energy and the stronger relationship bonds encourage team members to work even more closely together. The team sees joint working as the route to greater success and starts to build joint outcomes. Tensions are seen as a positive thing in that when they are resolved they can speed the team up. There is a much greater interest and ability to accept each other's unique perspective and successfully integrate those perspectives into a solution. The desire for such integration comes from an understanding of the mutual advantages to be had if the team learns to effectively share and cooperate.

6 *Diverse pluralists*: Very few executive teams make it to stage 6. At stages 4 and 5 the team is largely focused on leading the business. At stage 6 the team conversations switch to how the business leads the industry. Having

learnt, at stages 4 and 5, that greater performance is achieved through working better together, stage 6 teams become fast and skilful at mining their differences, aligning and integrating multiple perspectives and leveraging their diversity. Silos dissolve.

7 *Integrated pluralists*. All of the capabilities that came online at stage 6 are accelerated. The leader becomes much more externally focused, not to manage the market or shareholder perceptions but to specifically bring the team even more diverse and complex external perspectives for them to integrate so they can lead their industry. Knowing how to leverage diversity, the team start to create organization-wide systems and processes that integrate a much greater set of internal stakeholders.

8 *Broad fellowships*: At this stage, teams are becoming world class. There is a significant shift again in the team conversations and ambition, from how to lead the industry to how to change society itself, for the benefit of all, including their own organization. Fellowships have moved way beyond the parochial interest of silos, teams and even single organizations. They understand that all organizations have a 'social licence to operate'. The interpersonal relationships within the team are now so strong that the relationship that the team is now collectively focused on is that between the organization and the society or country in which it operates. The external focus on the leader is picked up by several team members, who themselves start to operate more externally for the benefit of the team, the organization and society at large.

9 *United fellowships*. At this level, a team is beyond world class and has become world leading, able to teach world-class teams how to improve. Leadership is fluid, flexible, disseminated and inspires social change and individual action. There are unspoken bonds between team members and 'mudita' is the norm. Mudita is a Sanskrit word meaning joy, especially sympathetic or vicarious joy, or the pleasure that comes from delighting in other people's well-being. Such teams are extremely rare and may be seen once in a generation.

Network analysis

In order to facilitate rapid evolution through the stages of team development and to arrive at highly functioning teams and executive fellowships, it can be really helpful to understand the existing networks within an organization. In our work, we help senior leaders to define the current connectivity within an organization using our Complete Network Analysis diagnostic.[7] This assessment enables us to precisely define who is connected to whom and why. And we can identify how strong those connections are.

One of the interesting paradoxes in modern business is that we have more ways to 'communicate' with each other than ever before, but that communication is increasingly shallow, superficial or transactional, and as such we often feel *less* connected. We have the tools for greater connectivity but meaningful connection is still rare in most corporations.

It's now clear that top-down traditional 'roll-outs' of initiatives from the 'corporate centre' to the far reaches of the corporate empire are not effective. We encourage organizations to communicate and engage with their people through 'viral' mechanisms, rippling ideas through the existing organizational networks and forums. A nudge, a wave of excitement and an engaging dialogue with staff are much more effective than most traditional 'internal comms' processes. As Nick Warren, Head of Development at First Quantum Minerals Ltd, pointed out when we interviewed him about his experiences with Exceptional Leadership:

> For us, our culture creates the rules that help us manage the business. You feel it around you. You pick up the signs almost subconsciously and then start to behave in a certain way. We continue to foster that culture by paying attention to the symbols, rituals and stories that make up a culture. Limiting bureaucracy enables the culture to determine the rules of engagement in the business... Culturally driven interventions like storytelling are far greater drivers of behaviour than systems or forms... We want to get away from this Western, McKinsey rationale that it's always about solutions; for us it is much more about listening and ensuring that people feel they are being heard.

Understanding the existing internal networks can facilitate high-speed ripples within the business, because if you know who's connected to whom then you can identify how to spread an operational, cultural or strategic message rapidly by engaging the most influential people in those networks.

Network analysis is based on complicated social networking theory, but we use a much simpler approach that illuminates some very powerful data in just a few minutes. We ask nine simple questions to define three critical networks:

- *Operational network*: Name the people you typically get work-related information from. Name the people you regularly collaborate with. Name the people who you go to in order to get things done or achieve faster progress.

- *Cultural network*: Name the people you feel energized by. Name the people you feel you can be open and honest with. Name the people you turn to for support when things are tough.
- *Leadership network*: Name the people who stretch your thinking. Name the people to whom you turn for leadership and guidance. Name the people who actively support your development at this organization.

With these answers and some big data analytics we can flush out a lot of really critical information about the structure, leadership, talent pool and performance of your organization. For example, I worked with a global leadership team where one individual's quality of thinking and innovation abilities were really strong, but his leadership network revealed that very few of his peers turned to him for guidance on the big points where he could have added a lot of value. In addition, his cultural networks were weak, despite his having strong operational networks. This was an eye-opener for him and caused him to significantly change his behaviour towards his peers. He realized that he did not have anywhere near the influence he hoped for or needed in order to 'land' his brilliant ideas.

Another executive had very strong cultural connectivity but was moved sideways in a political reshuffle. This caused significant unrest in the division and a sudden drop-off in performance. This person was culturally important to the community and the move caused many other people in the division to become very uneasy and lose trust in the leadership.

Because network analysis can also identify hidden talents, when we do this across a whole team, division or company we see all the dendrites that spread out and can easily identify who the key players are. It therefore exposes how the business really functions, rather than how we might want it to function or think it functions. The insights generated can be incredibly useful for succession planning and driving improved performance.

For example, we did a network analysis across the whole executive team within a company in Eastern Europe. They had appointed two new senior executives to the board, both starting in the business on the same day – a new financial director and a new commercial director. Both candidates had been brought in as potential successors for the CEO position.

After just six weeks we clearly identified that the financial director had become the most highly connected person in the whole executive team. I told the CEO that neither of his new recruits were successors. The new CFO would be a peer inside a year and the commercial director would be let go. The CEO didn't believe that we could know this after just six weeks of these executives joining. But our prediction was totally accurate and that was exactly what then happened. We had mined the wisdom of the crowd and just six weeks after these executives joined, the crowd already knew what the outcome was for these two leaders. Having now analysed over a million relationships in 60 countries and in 16 languages, we have seen our Network Analysis predict the future in many organizations. In one Middle Eastern bank for example, we predicted 17 senior resignations in a row. This enabled us to then help the bank address their cultural issues that were significantly undermining their ability to grow the business.

The evolution of value systems

Trust is the glue that holds teams together. In fact, if we look at the stages of team development, trust is a central ingredient that increases as a team evolves from a collection of 'talented individuals' to an 'executive fellowship'. Understanding another person's motives is a crucial part of the trust recipe, and one of the fastest and easiest ways to understand motives and make serious headway in the development of highly functioning teams is to ensure that everyone in the team knows and understands their own and everyone else's motives or value system.

Numerous academics have published research on culture and values. In our work, we've integrated the research of Gert Hofstede, Shalom Schwartz and Clare Graves and a few other academics to enable us to profile how a leader's value systems vary depending on their situation. Of the three main academics mentioned above, Graves's work is perhaps the most commercially useful, not least because it has a vertical developmental or evolutionary dimension.

Graves was a psychology professor at Union College in Schenectady, New York. In setting his students various essay assignments, he noticed that the students' responses could be grouped into four main types of answers. He concluded that there were four 'world views' that determined the way students wrote their essays and what they emphasized. His model developed over time to identify eight world views, or value systems, each emerging from the previous one.

Two of Graves's students, Chris Cowen and Don Beck, went on to build on his work and named the framework 'spiral dynamics', and it is now one of the most widely used and cited cultural assessment models on the planet.

Graves' model defines a series of evolutionary levels that transcend and include each previous level. Thus, as people 'level up' they retain access to the behaviours, values and capabilities of all earlier levels. We may become more sophisticated with each new level but that doesn't mean we are in any way 'better' than people who operate at earlier levels, and it certainly doesn't

FIGURE 6.3   The evolution of value systems

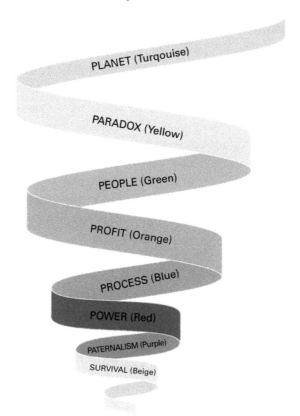

mean people at the higher levels will be happier or more successful. People operating from higher levels simply access more potential. Some of the most effective leaders operate from value systems at a lower level because what they can bring can be exactly what the situation requires. Whereas someone who is more sophisticated may massively over-complicate things and therefore be disastrous in a business setting.

Overall, there are positive and negative aspects at every level, but it's the negative aspect that always provides the upward evolutionary momentum. The impact of each value system is also affected by the maturity of the individual involved. Each level is depicted by a colour that is relevant to that level. As we level up the spiral, the focus of each level oscillates between the individual and the collective.

What's especially interesting about the values spiral is that, regardless of scale, the model still holds true. Thus, we can predict the likely behaviour of an individual, a team, a division, a business, an industry, a nation, a region or the entire population of the planet (Figure 6.3).

BEIGE: SURVIVAL (INDIVIDUAL FOCUS)

At the Beige values level, the prime focus is on individual survival.

There are many parts of the world where individual survival is still the primary focus. During the global pandemic, many people retreated and were forced to focus on short-term survival once again. We can see people operating from this level in modern society: furloughed individuals, people who have been made redundant, are unemployed, sick or marginalized all exhibit this value system. In times of economic hardship, Beige-driven behaviour even occurs in organizations as survival motives kick in.

What drives people operating at the Beige value system is their immediate basic needs. Once basic needs have been met, action tends to stop for the day. Tomorrow is another day and individuals think they will cross that bridge when they have to. As such, people at this level tend not to plan ahead very much at all. They live from day to day.

The upside of Beige is that the individual survives but the downside is there is very little progress or forward momentum. And it is this lack of progress that ultimately triggers individuals to start to wonder if they would survive better if they ganged together. This is what pushes individuals and cultures up the spiral to Purple.

PURPLE: PATERNALISM (COLLECTIVE FOCUS)

Purple emerges when people realize there is safety in numbers so the paternal 'tribe' emerges.

Tribal value systems are quite common in business during the early stages of a company's evolution, during mergers and acquisitions, in specific functions or in geographically separate offices. In many organizations, people start to identify with the sales tribe, the IT tribe or the London office or the New York office. Often, people's loyalty to these smaller tribes or cliques is greater than it is to the company itself. It's this value system that fosters silo behaviour. Induction to the various tribes is often reinforced by certain rituals, superstitions, a special language or a 'uniform'. For example, city traders wear coloured jackets.

Those operating from Purple are motivated by psychological safety and a secure working environment. They seek to develop a strong bond with their colleagues and prefer that no one rocks the boat too much or creates too much change. They may be mildly hostile to the company itself and can quickly sense a personal or commercial threat. As such, they easily fall into victim mode and can react strongly to protect their own position and the security of their work family.

The upside of Purple is that people operating from this level can create a great sense of belonging and will be happy to follow a good leader, especially if that leaders makes life safer and more comfortable. The downside is that tribe members can be very reactionary, fail to think things through thoroughly, and don't provide much direction themselves. It's this lack of direction at Purple that eventually spawns the evolution up the spiral to Red.

RED: POWER (INDIVIDUAL FOCUS)

At Red the focus swings back to the individual. These individuals like to take charge. In military recruitment processes, Red leaders are actively flushed out. Often, recruits are dropped into uncertain situations and then the recruiters wait to see who steps forward to take the reins – they are the Red leader. The same happens in business: out of the group steps a Red leader who spontaneously starts to provide direction to the tribe. This sort of leadership often takes an individual all the way to the top.

Red leaders are one of the two commonest value systems we see in the C-suite of global multinationals, and Red leaders are also particularly widespread in the new markets, start-ups, telecoms, the tech sector and, of course, entertainment and politics. Red leadership can be very helpful in the early stages of a company's evolution or in divisions that are opening up new territories. Certain functions, such as sales and PR, are often stuffed with people operating from the Red value system.

Red leaders are often charismatic, 'larger than life' individuals with a great deal of energy who often have a vivid sense of humour. However, they can also lead by fear, intimidation or force of will. They can be dictatorial and take a 'Just do as I say' stance. They tend to operate a 'hub and spoke' command-and-control model of leadership. They are great at simplifying and clarifying priorities and like to cut to the chase.

However, the downside is that progress is often dependent on the individual leaders themselves. The Red leader can become a bottleneck for decisions, and the excessive responsibility taken by a Red leader can create passivity in those around them as the team starts to believe there is no point in making a decision themselves because the leader is likely to overrule it anyway. This excessive ownership of every item on the agenda has been called a 'responsibility virus' and can itself stifle growth.[8] The intoxicating nature of ultimate power can fuel a sense of omnipotence in the Red leader and start to drive a whole range of unhelpful behaviours or egomania. It is this power lust that starts to create unrest in the collective, which begins to gang together to curb the excesses of Red leadership and the next level, Blue, emerges.

BLUE: PROCESS (COLLECTIVE FOCUS)

Blue is the colour that represents order, conservatism and loyalty, and it illustrates a swing back to the collective. Doing the right thing is important to someone operating from a Blue value system. Meaning emerges for the first time, and the search for a higher principle or authority, be it government or God, becomes important at Blue.

Government departments, bureaucracies and public-sector partnerships often have a Blue process-orientated culture. These are systems built on rules and order. All businesses must go through a Blue phase to build some infrastructure and a stable platform for growth.

In an attempt to create order, Blue often puts a whole raft of rules and regulations in place designed to instil some discipline and prevent the Red excesses from derailing the organization. Infrastructure and process start to emerge.

Trade unions are often a classic example of crystallized Blue organizational value system. They can often bring much-needed stability and fairness to an industry. But they can also become rigidly constrained by their own rules and processes, and drift into unhealthy 'jobsworth' thinking, as evidenced by the UK public-sector strikes in 2012. The fact that public-sector pensions far outstripped the average private-sector workers' and the country just couldn't afford them didn't matter to the offended principles of the Blue value system and the people striking. They couldn't see that a small reduction now might help to secure jobs and pensions in the long term.[9]

The upside of Blue is stability. But too much Blue and the business can become rigid and inflexible. Like all levels, it is this downside that eventually creates the conditions for the evolutionary push up into the next level and Orange emerges.

ORANGE: PROFIT (INDIVIDUAL FOCUS)

Orange marks a swing back to an individual focus.

Most businesses are run by leaders from a Red or Orange value system. In many ways the Orange leaders represent a more mature version of the Red leader because they've acquired an understanding of the importance of process and principle, and are less inclined to 'shoot from the hip' than the Red leaders. Remember, Orange transcends and includes Red and Blue.

Free from the stifling constraints of too many Blue rules, the Orange leader looks to build on the best parts of the Blue infrastructure and system whilst being more flexible in order to compete, grow the business and deliver results. The ultimate goal of Orange is Profit – to make money and win.

They take a pragmatic no-nonsense view of the world and they are happy to do whatever it takes to achieve the targets they set for themselves.

Margaret Thatcher almost single-handedly broke the Blue union mindset of the 1970s in the UK, and her policies pushed the country into an Orange flourish.

Many people consider Orange to be the pinnacle of success. This is the ultimate destination and wealth is the ultimate prize. Needless to say, Orange, like every other level, has a dark side – greed and manipulation. When we deregulate markets and sweep away too many rules, we start to create the conditions that foster extreme Orange behaviour. People start to 'play the system' for their own personal benefit. The global financial crisis of 2008 was a banking-driven economic disaster that can be traced back to some extreme Orange behaviour on the bond desks of a few firms on Wall Street who saw the chance to 'game' the whole mortgage market and knowingly sold 'toxic assets' to naïve purchasers because the system allowed them to.[10]

As a result, an increasing number of people, particularly Generation Y, have spotted the flaw in this value system and many have begun to seriously wonder or explore what lies beyond.[11] They seek a way of moving forward that doesn't favour the few at the expense of the many, that doesn't worsen the already considerable gap between the haves and the have-nots. Whilst the upside of Orange is wealth creation, it is polluted by the excessive greed of the few, which acts as the next evolutionary stimulus and Green emerges.

GREEN: PEOPLE (COLLECTIVE FOCUS)

Green sees a swing back to the collective. Green businesses or Green leaders often emerge as an antidote to Orange profit-focused excess. They are motivated by finding a more caring, inclusive way of proceeding that benefits all people, not just shareholders. Such businesses are rarely in the FTSE 100, although there are companies whose internal culture has a strong Green orientation. Proving that it is possible to transcend and include the best performing share in the FTSE 250 in 2020 was Pets at Home, who have a strong Green culture.

Green leaders have realized that the 'winners and losers' mindset is ultimately a zero-sum game. Exploitation detonates strong forces that eventually cause a tsunami of suffering, recrimination and a backlash. Green leaders make a different choice. They take a more people- and customer-centric approach. And their care extends from people to the planet. They are interested in their carbon footprints, genuine fair trade, local produce, sustainability and the whole green agenda. They are also much more sensitive to the needs of the collective.

Green CEOs and leaders are often ambassadorial in style. They are generally more emotionally intelligent and are driven by a desire to help. They attempt to include a wide section of opinion and have an intense dislike of hierarchies.

All the levels from Beige to Green are known as first tier. The biggest problem with the first tier is that, at each level, those at that level think they are right and everyone else is wrong. Many team or cultural tensions are rooted in this mistaken belief that 'I am right' and 'You are wrong'. A great deal of time is wasted in business and government as 'sides' argue their case.

Green is particularly conflicted around this point. They want to make everyone correct and equally valid. All are welcome, all are included; there is no 'better/worse'. Green abhors better/worse suggestions and is the most likely to reject the vertical nature of development. Green thinkers seek to bring everyone to the same level playing field. But in doing so the Green value system is blind to its own hierarchy and belief that the horizontal ('We are all equal') is better than a vertical hierarchy. Such blindness typifies the Green contradiction.[12] On the one hand very caring and inclusive, and on the other hand myopic and judgemental.

Green leaders focus on taking people with them and will slow down to make sure no one is left behind. They try to achieve win–win relationships and will often 'go the extra mile' to make sure people are able to contribute. They are motivated by human contact and achieving results through the team. Being liked is often more important than competitive advantage. Employee engagement and net promoter scores are seen as important sustainable metrics that will ultimately drive EBITDA.

One of the downsides of Green leadership is that leaders are so busy being inclusive that no one gets anything done and the business loses momentum. The key distinction between a Blue leader and a Green leader is that the Blue leader is guided by principles and doing the right thing, whereas the Green leader seeks to keep everyone on board and leads by consensus.

The upside of Green is collaboration and care, but ultimately the failure of the tier 1 value systems, of which Green is the last, has provided a stimulus to accelerate the emergence of the tier 2 value system, the first of which is Yellow.

YELLOW: PARADOX (INDIVIDUAL FOCUS)

Yellow is a swing back to the individual. When Yellow emerges, it grows out of the understanding that all of the previous first tier value systems have some validity but that they are all flawed in some way. If you take the inclusivity of Green and the creativity that such inclusivity enables and put it 'on steroids', the result is Yellow innovation.

Yellow is disruptive and is comfortable with paradox – the idea that something can be better and worse at the same time. There is much more nuance. Not in a Red maverick way but in a much smarter, more sophisticated way.

Yellow businesses are innovation engines coming up with smart solutions to complex problems. They succeed by changing the game, creating a paradigm shift or establishing clear blue water.[13] Yellow businesses are usually small, or if large they are organized on a small scale. They are competitive because they are fast, agile and able to 'hack' around older, less optimal structures.

Globally, only 1 per cent of the population is operating at Yellow.[14] However, amongst the more senior population of ~15,000 business leaders whose value systems we have assessed in the last few years, this figure is closer to 10 per cent. The Yellow value system is much more common in Generation Y. They do not follow a traditional career path. If it is not working, they will often leave and try their hand elsewhere.

Yellow leaders know that the world is not black and white and they accept that they may be simultaneously part of the problem and part of the solution. To paraphrase business consultant and author Jim Collins, the first six levels of tier 1 'look out the window' for the source of the problem and someone to blame, and tier 2 leaders 'look in the mirror'.[15]

Yellow leaders don't wait to be asked, they take responsibility for the solution. They see multiple perspectives and can easily handle conflicts of interest. They are drawn to complex problems and see them as challenges. They are excited by new ideas and want to have an impact beyond their company.

The upside of Yellow leaders is that they take personal responsibility; they are innovative, disruptive, very focused on learning and their own development. On the downside, the Yellow leader can be way too conceptual, far too complex for most people to understand, and can consequently appear 'aloof', dispassionate or even detached. And it is this apparent disconnection that fosters the emergence of the final value system that has emerged – Turquoise.

TURQUOISE: PLANET (COLLECTIVE FOCUS)

Turquoise signals a swing back to the collective again. Turquoise organizations tend to be movements rather than formal businesses. Their focus tends to be evolutionary and long-term – focused on the good of the planet, not just individual or even corporate pursuits. Such movements look for ways to create cultural and social change for the benefit of all people without falling into the trap of being too prescriptive or patronizing. A Turquoise leader is therefore much more interested in a social mission and the greater good.

Turquoise CEOs and leaders are very rare, and when found they are normally at the helm of social or public enterprises.

They can often appear distracted because they are much more attuned to the long term and the unintended consequences of their decisions rather than the short-term result. They are able to compute a massive number of moving variables and look for patterns and balance within complex data sets. Such live calculations and assessments can be baffling for others as it is not always clear what their motivations are or if they are just sitting back and allowing things to happen.

Globally, only 0.1 per cent of the population operate from a Turquoise value system. This means that less than 2 per cent of the global population are operating from a tier 2 value system of either Yellow or Turquoise.[16]

Turquoise leaders are not afraid to turn a profit if this helps the cause. They are also interested in being of service and living their lives as an example. System harmony, increasing maturity and natural emergence all invigorate their actions. They are focused on leading beyond their authority and look for ways to be of service to everyone.[17]

VALUES SPIRAL IN ACTION

We have found that helping team members understand their own and other team members' value systems can significantly enhance connectivity, mutual understanding and performance. The team is better able to explore differences of opinion and perspectives without descending into a battle or a stalemate. Difficulties that seemed intense and complex dissolve when each person realizes their 'argument' is little more than a reflection of their individual value system and the way that value system plays out within the team. It's no longer personal.

In addition, built into the Complete Values Profile are various sub-scales that reveal how people's value systems vary depending on the task they are engaged in. For example, when leaders are working on strategy their profile may be Yellow, suggesting that they are innovative and can contribute new ideas. The same leaders may shift to Orange or Red for implementation, suggesting that when they are executing strategy their approach is much more pragmatic.

Similarly, the values within the team can shift depending on what the team is working on. How a team interacts when they are strategizing can be quite different from how they function when they are in operational mode or when they are managing people. In other words, the Complete Values Profile can reveal why a team functions better in one conversation than another.

When we have a much deeper understanding of the subtlety of our value systems, we can explain ourselves better to others. In a meeting, for example, a Yellow leader is able to say, 'Look, I am motivated to spend a lot of time exploring ideas but I know you are more Red, which means you will get frustrated by that, so why don't we compromise and agree on a set time-frame for strategic discussion before we get into action?' That way the Red individual doesn't get so frustrated and they collectively agree a plan that both honours their respective Yellow and Red strengths while mitigating their weaknesses. This mutual understanding and value-specific language alone can massively improve the quality and output of relationships, and a lot of the arm wrestling and power struggles just disappear.

Imagine the Red and Yellow person have their meeting and get five or six good ideas. They now need to access the Orange value system in themselves, if they have it, or in another team member in order to effectively convert those ideas into something workable. Once they've decided on the best idea and how it might work in the business, they need to build a more detailed plan and a process that can deliver that idea. If there is insufficient Blue capability, there is a gap and they need to invite a Blue person into the conversation who can help build out a detailed plan, rules and principles to enable execution.

This is why so many meetings fail: because the team doesn't have access to all the necessary value systems that can deliver what's required. What happens is that people operating from Red value systems do their best to plan and bring attention to the detail that is required. But they are nowhere near as effective as people who operate from the Blue value system at doing this. The result is that the outcome is significantly less effective.

Once the Blue person has worked out the best process, other people in the business need to buy into the strategy for successful execution, and that's a Green strength. If there is no Green in the team, a Green person is invited to join and their job is to determine how to get everyone engaged with the idea. If the new group is spending too long debating the finer details, Red's restless impatience brings passion and drive to make it happen.

Knowing which team member can contribute which value system and at which point to drive a successful outcome is incredibly useful within a team. All of this detail can be revealed by the Complete Values Profile. Each leader becomes much clearer about what values they have when building a strategy, implementing the strategy or managing others. They also know this information about everyone else in the team, too.

The value system that human beings operate from offers profound insights about the motivations of individuals, teams and organizations. Being able to accurately profile values across the business can be a commercial game changer. For example, some years ago we did some work with an Australian logistics company, who were trying hard to win a large account from their main rival. They had tried everything to lure the customer using incentives – buy one get one free, 5 per cent off, 15 per cent off, free Fridays. This business was very Orange in its approach and the fact that Orange financial inducements did not work was baffling to them. 'We are cheaper than the competitor, why isn't the customer switching?' was the question they just couldn't answer.

We explored what the customer's values system was and concluded that it was probably Purple. And Purple companies are not remotely interested in Orange messages. What matters to Purple is safety and maintaining the status quo. Purple is about group survival and security (the customer was actually an IT security company) so the most important thing to them was to avoid change. All our client's messages were focused on what they did differently from their competitor, when they should have been saying how similar they were. And that's exactly what they did; they explained their similarities first but then added that, unlike their competitor, they could guarantee the security of the parcel to the destination in ways that their competitor could not match. As security was critical for the customer, the new sales narrative completely changed how the customer saw what was being offered and they instantly switched their business – without discounting.

The Exceptional Organization

When all four quadrants of the Exceptional Leadership model are activated, Exceptional Organizations become possible. One of the key areas we help organizations with is step changing their governance processes. More specifically we teach them a whole series of new governance processes. The aim is to replace a top-down, predict-and-control default with a new way of distributing power and increasing engagement. Installing high-quality governance is like installing a new 'operating system' that can deliver rapid evolution in the core processes of the organization.

When an organization commits to embedding dynamic steering principles at its core and invests properly in developing leadership teams that can distribute authority and establish bi-directional feedback loops across the organization, it can pick up significant speed and go much further, faster. As part of this organizational upgrade, we install integrated decision making (IDM), which gives everyone a voice and overcomes the tyranny of consensus.

IDM delivers high-speed decisions and complete alignment on complex issues. When combined with a whole range of other developmental processes, there is a real sense of a company properly set up for the future. This fundamental transformation, or vertical leap forward to a new type of organization, involves:

- clarifying and aligning purpose at every level of the organization;
- establishing all decision-making forums and new sub-forums;
- defining the remit and limit of authority of all forums;
- setting up reporting process, frequency and quality standards;
- establishing clear accountabilities at every level;
- creating new roles as required;
- assigning new accountabilities to existing roles;
- establishing new policies or changes to existing policies;
- defining the ways of working within teams;
- establishing meeting discipline and communicational efficiency.

Helping an individual leader become exceptional is one thing, developing a group of senior leaders to become an integrated fellowship is a much more complex and sizeable task. Building an Exceptional Organization requires a much greater investment. We have seen time and again that the return on such investment is more than 1,000 times, and there is virtually nothing, not a new IT system or business process reengineering, that can deliver that sort of sustainable change.

An integrated programme that upgrades individual, team and organizational capability in this way establishes a deliberately developmental organization (DDO) and is a huge leap forward in organizational evolution.[18]

And whilst it delivers breathtaking results, it's not for the faint hearted. It requires a level of open-mindedness that may not be familiar to many leaders and senior executives. To prevent it all falling apart in a clash of egos, the organization will need a compelling purpose that invites everyone to serve something larger than themselves, and a purpose-driven executive team to anchor it. Sustaining this over time will require new language and meaning making in the culture, to help uproot deeply entrenched mental models (such as predict and control) that are limiting the organization's potential.

Beyond predict-and-control

Most modern leadership and management techniques are based on a predict-and-control paradigm. Such an approach asks leaders to anticipate the future and design the best path to achieve a set of pre-defined goals. The core practice here is scenario planning. Such an approach matured through the first half of the 20th century and worked well enough in the relatively simple and static business environment. But in a rapidly accelerating world such tactical reductionism struggles to keep up with the increasing complexity and volatility that we are now witnessing. Predict-and-control also fails to ignite the passion and creativity of a new generation of employees who demand greater meaning. In today's environment, steering an organization using predict-and-control ignores the unpredictable nature of the commercial and global environment. It also inhibits the development of agility, which most organizations now recognize is key to success in the future.

The DDO processes we are suggesting here help an organization find a more dynamic approach that can guide its work, gradually shifting the company through 'experiment-and-adapt' to a 'sense-and-respond' mindset. A sense-and-respond approach is much closer to the 'dynamic steering' we use when we ride a bicycle. We have a general aim and adjust continuously in the light of real data that we sense as we progress.

Organizationally, dynamic steering means establishing tight feedback loops and frequent steer points throughout the company's operations. This allows planning and decision-making processes to focus on quickly reaching a workable decision and letting reality inform the next step. This stops us agonizing about what 'might' happen and stops us trying to conjure up the theoretical 'best' possible decision. Dynamic steering frees teams to move swiftly from excessive planning to testing decisions in real time and adapting rapidly as the results come in. Plans that start out imperfect become well aligned with needs through a continuous process of facing reality and incorporating the feedback.

This mindset shift is critical; however, transitioning from static control to dynamic steering takes quite a bit more than just new principles. It is necessary to embed this shift into the core of an organization by installing a more organic structure, along with new decision-making and management processes that embody dynamic steering principles. This provides several immediate benefits, such as ultra-efficient meetings, and it sparks a process of organizational evolution that generates deeper learning and transformation over time.

Upgraded governance

Whilst governance is widely used and frequently talked about in business, what most companies currently consider to be governance is little more than legal compliance and operational oversight. Governance practice must be upgraded right across the organization.

Every leadership team faces a few critical questions that must be answered for the members to work together effectively. For example: What activities are needed to achieve the group's goals, and who will perform them? How much autonomy will each team member have, and within what limits or requirements? How will various decisions that the team needs to make get made? How will tasks be defined and assigned? What overarching guidelines or policies will be followed?

These are all questions of governance, about how the group will organize their work together – their answers define authorities and expectations within the group. An explicit governance framework to answer these questions only exists, if it exists at all, at the top of an organization. But these questions are just as relevant on the shop floor as they are in the boardroom. Without an explicit governance process for each team at every level, the opportunities to improve organizational patterns will remain unresolved or largely stuck at the top.

GOVERNANCE MEETINGS

The way the game of business is currently set up means that most executive teams spend 80–95 per cent of their time focused on short-term commercial performance and operational issues in the top left-hand quadrant of the

Exceptional Leadership model (Figure 1.6). What time remains is usually consumed by strategic debate and the occasional cursory nod to 'governance'.

For most organizations, their decision-making and accountability agreements are not properly defined. Even if they are, which is rare, they are never universally understood and applied up and down the business. Leaders are constantly wrestling with issues that are fundamentally caused by a lack of clarity around who makes what decision and why, where these decisions get made and who is really accountable for delivering certain aspects of the business plan. In addition to setting up the necessary decision-making forums and establishing the limits of executive authority, it's also necessary to fully define the feedback loops. What are leaders and executives expected to communicate and to whom? Are they expected to circulate minutes, everything or just the decisions? These issues are no longer 'something to discuss informally at the off-site if we have time'. They are fundamental to business survival in a complex world. Successful businesses are no longer run by a few people at the top; globalization, technology, the nature and speed of change, not to mention the increasing complexity, mean that the rules of the game need to be redefined, clarified and aligned behind robust, upgraded governance.

Most businesses already realize that they need to address operational, strategic and governance issues, but most will try to have all three conversations simultaneously. One of the core principles of upgraded governance is therefore to establish separate meetings, frequencies and meeting disciplines for operations, strategy and governance. Chris Hope, ex-Head of Operations Strategy and Change for easyJet, explains the profound impact greater meeting discipline had on meeting time and productivity:

> We mapped out all the meetings that involved two or more senior managers from the team. This also established how much time we spent in meetings and showed that even a small improvement in our efficiency and effectiveness in those meetings would deliver a significant benefit to the business... We looked at all our meetings to decide which were working well, which needed to be improved and which didn't really need to happen at all... Having set out the structure for the meeting and being clear about what we were trying to achieve, we then focused on behaviours by adapting ground rules for each section. In one section of the meeting, which involves going through action items, it could take us an hour just to check if the items were open or not. We found ourselves having the same discussions again and again. By setting ground rules for that section of the meeting, we could avoid those behaviours.

And the outcome was significant – cutting meeting time by half – and best practice started to spread throughout the business.

The reason that meetings are such a bone of contention for most business leaders is that they can often take hours without any resolution. What we find when we work with leaders and their executive teams is that often those involved in the meetings are not individually or collectively clear about what conversation they are having. For example, in the middle of an operational meeting someone will raise a point that has strategic implications, so the team diverts off to discuss strategy for 20 minutes before someone realizes that they have drifted off the original issue. A few moments later, someone mentions a governance issue and the same thing happens, largely because there is insufficient differentiation of the three types of meetings. Once people appreciate the distinction and can differentiate between the different types of conversation, they can maintain focus and park things in the right place. Meetings that used to take three hours are wrapped up in 30 minutes because as soon as someone raises a strategic issue at an operational meeting or a governance issue at a strategic meeting the team reminds that individual to raise the issue at the appropriate meeting and the agenda stays on course. What we've found is that just by clarifying these distinctions companies leap forward in productivity and results can improve almost immediately.

On a human level, regular governance meetings can also transform the emotional tone of a team. Lack of clarity around governance leaves everyone with implicit expectations about who should be doing what and how they should be doing it. Without a defined governance process, the tendency is to make up negative stories about others or blame each other when these unspoken assumptions clash, neither of which helps move the organization forward.

When genuine governance meetings are introduced, team members have a forum for channelling the frustration of misaligned expectations into organizational learning and continual improvement. Playing politics loses its utility, and personal drama gives way to a more authentic discussion of how to consciously evolve the organization in light of its goals and broader purpose.

ROLES AND ACCOUNTABILITIES

One of the key early outputs of upgraded governance is the detailed clarification and definition of roles and accountabilities. Again, this sounds obvious and most executive teams believe this is already done well enough or covered in their job description. However, in our experience, when we look at executive accountabilities in detail it's possible to identify a number of gaps where no one is clearly responsible as well as a number of areas where roles overlap. I am continually surprised by how much we are able to improve a team's clarity around their accountabilities even when they have already spent a lot of time working on their RACI (responsible, accountable, consulted and informed) frameworks.

In defining roles and specifying accountabilities, it is critical that this is done regardless of who is available to fill such roles and whether they have the skill set to deliver. Many organizations try to fit the role to the person rather than deciding what the business really needs and recruiting or training people to that requirement.

A PURPOSE-DRIVEN LEADERSHIP TEAM

As the 'war on talent' continues to get even fiercer, it is increasingly apparent that the financial ambition of a company is insufficient to attract, retain and motivate the best people. Mission statements outlining 'visions of future desired states' are often seen as too abstract. Companies and boards need to uncover a more emotive cause if they want to truly motivate their talent and unlock discretionary effort. A corporate cause should draw on the evolutionary purpose of the organization, ie what purpose does the world need that business to serve? Why does that company exist?

Profit is a metric, not a purpose. But with a leadership team composed entirely of executive shareholders, profit is very likely to get mistaken for a purpose. Exceptional Organizations are first and foremost purpose-driven, with all activities designed to deliver the organization's mission.

The needs of shareholders and other stakeholders remain important constraints, but with upgraded governance installed it's the inspiring vision and deeper evolutionary purpose that ultimately pulls the organization forward. Although we've only explored a small part of the full spectrum of what upgraded governance really looks like, it's important to appreciate that each aspect dovetails with all the others to create exceptionally strong organizations that are able to adapt in real time and make faster, better informed and aligned decisions so as to deliver Exceptional Leadership – not just at an individual leadership level but as a collective force for good in the world.

How to be more *influential*

Building on all the physical and personal skills from previous chapters, the skills in this chapter are focused on other people and culminate in elevated emotional and social intelligence (ESQ).

According to a 1995 *Time Magazine* article, IQ gets you hired, but emotional intelligence (EQ) gets you promoted. Of course, we all know individuals who have got to the top without either! But if we wish to succeed in a complex world, we need social intelligence. It is social intelligence that inspires others and makes Exceptional Leadership possible.

Although some people are more naturally gifted socially than others, social intelligence is a natural consequence of internal vertical development. When we have access to more energy, when we become aware of our emotions and can self-manage and regulate those emotions, we have greater access to our very best thinking, which in turn makes us more socially intelligent. When we mature as adult human beings and expand our perspectives so that we understand our own and other people's value systems, we become even more socially intelligent. And when we learn the last two interpersonal skills of Enlightened Leadership, our ESQ is significantly increased, which in turn facilitates the development of high-functioning teams and executive fellowships.

In previous times it may have been possible to rise through the ranks on IQ, business smarts and hard-nosed aggression alone. But today it is impossible to build a great company without ESQ. A coherent, exceptional leader is distinguished by the application of emotional and social intelligence to sustain positive relationships, drive success and create genuinely brilliant future-proofed organizations.

Relationships coherence – social intuition, empathy and rapport: MAP skill

When two people are in dialogue, they are usually in dialogue with themselves rather than each other. We see this in business in the form of endless circular meetings. No one is listening to each other. Everyone is just having a conversation with themselves: 'I just said that!' 'Did you? Oh, I wasn't listening.' We even say that to each other! And in a digital world with a day full of Zoom meetings it's even worse, because we now spend a lot of our time looking at ourselves as we speak, too. Not only that but we are often so desperate to get our point across, before someone else does or before we forget it, that we interrupt others' transmissions all the time. Men tend to do this significantly more than women and it's usually a control play or a tool to manipulate the conversation to get primary positioning. It's common to hear phrases like 'Let me stop you there...'. Even if the interruption is for good reasons, to clarify the message, it still breaks the transmission and therefore often sets up confusion and miscommunication.

THE MAP SKILL FOR HIGH-QUALITY LISTENING

The MAP skill is an acronym for the process you go through to ensure that you are really listening at the deeper meaning Level 3.

Move your attention away from your own thinking and drop into the body and BREATHE.

Appreciate the speaker.

Play back the underlying meaning.

Rather than immediately focusing on what you are going to say or interrupting the other person when a transmission starts, move (M) your attention away from the noise in your own head. Consciously and deliberately move your attention away from your own thoughts, preconceived ideas, judgements about yourself or the other person, the meeting or the pile of work on your desk, and shift your focus to the centre of your chest and your breath. Using the BREATHE skill from Chapter 2, breathe rhythmically, evenly and through the heart. Stop thought-chasing.

When I first teach this skill to executives, they are concerned that if they move their attention away from their own thoughts, they won't hear what the other person is saying. But words are only a tiny part of the transmission. It's not necessary to 'actively listen' to every word. Our brain still processes most of the words anyway.

Next, activate a state of appreciation (A) for the transmitter. This is the critical step. Influential psychologist Carl Rogers referred to this state as an 'unconditional positive regard'.[19] Turn on a warm glow of acceptance and support for the person talking with you. Rogers believes that unconditional positive regard is essential to healthy development, and when we do this properly the transmitter feels it – they feel a sense of unconditional acceptance that can be extremely moving.

When I'm teaching this skill it's usually one-on-one or to a group of tough, hard-nosed business executives and leaders, so it can be quite funny. To help break down their initial resistance and discomfort I usually go overboard in the instruction and ask them to 'bathe each other in the warm glow of appreciation'. It's such an unusual request and one that is never heard in business that eventually everyone starts laughing and we can move on without any resistance. What is remarkable is that once leaders put down their prejudices around this process and just try it, without exception they feel the difference it makes to the depth and authenticity of the interaction and communication. Both as the person doing the 'bathing' and the person receiving the unconditional positive regard, we instinctively feel more peaceful, less resistant, the judgements slip away, and we feel supported and nurtured.

When we do this, two really profound things happen.

First, it changes the transmitter. As a result of the warm acceptance and lack of judgement that is radiating toward them, they often open up and tell the receiver things they hadn't planned to share, which increases the information flow. In addition, when the transmitter feels encouraged and appreciated, the quality of their transmission also improves. So not only do we get more information, but the information we get is much clearer, more precise and more succinct. This enables us to get to the heart of the issue much faster than we ever would with our normal impatience, interruption or restlessness. When we radiate impatience or negativity, which is often what happens in business, listening is much worse. Our frustration or judgement simply closes the transmitter down. We get less information and it's poorer quality. When the transmitter doesn't feel listened to or is frequently interrupted, he or she starts to mumble or stumble over their words and become hesitant. This in turn can make the receiver even more frustrated and negative, which shuts the transmitter down still further.

The second incredible thing to occur when receivers put themselves in a state of appreciation is that it completely changes the capability of the receiver. The reason this happens is because at a biological level the fluctuations in our heart rate variability change from chaotic to coherent. Think of it like manually tuning into a radio station; when we are in a negative incoherent emotional state there is too much interference and static in the connection so we can't fully make out what is being transmitted. Once we tune in to exactly the right frequency and create coherence at a biological level, the transmission becomes crystal clear and we can start to understand the communication at a much deeper level. The level of meaning. With a coherent internal signal, the receiver starts to hear things that would have been impossible to hear from a place of frustration or judgement. When we do this well, it enables us to hear things that the other person didn't even say! It feels to the transmitter that we're reading their mind – but we're not, we're just tuning into them so brilliantly that it feels like we're reading their mind.

I remember coaching a guy who managed a number of well-known professional golfers for a sports management company. I explained how there is always more going on in every conversation than just the words, tonality and body language. There is always, even in the most fleeting conversations, a deeper level. He didn't believe me. He was adamant that in some conversations there was no deeper meaning and gave me the example of one of his golfers who had called him to give him flight information and ask him to organize taxis to and from the airport. The manager said, 'He told me he was landing at Terminal 2 at 10 o'clock, and needed a taxi back the next morning to get a flight to the Copenhagen Open in time for practice rounds. That was it.' He believed the conversation was a straightforward information download. I disagreed.

What this golfer was really saying at the meaning level was, 'Take care of me', and if you wanted to go into even deeper meaning beneath that what he saying was, 'You're not taking care of me.' I shared this insight with the manager. I said that at much deeper levels still the golfer thought the manager was taking better care of the other golfers in his stable and the player was pretty upset about it. I could hear this even though I wasn't on the original call. I suggested that he call his client the next day and make a real fuss of him because in my view the golfer was clearly upset.

The manager didn't believe me and did nothing. Within a week the problem was all over the sports pages of the national press. The golfer was threatening to leave the management group and it took the manager three months to fully repair the damage. If he'd just listened properly in that first conversation, he would have saved everyone time and upset, not to mention the reputational damage to his management group.

Once you've detected what's going on at a deeper level, you then have to play back (P) what you've received. Until you get good at this, you can't be sure that what you think is going on is actually what is really going on.

Often, we mistakenly assume we have accurately detected the meaning, but often what we have detected is just our own internal noise. Quality playback is vital. It must be distinguished from just repeating, summarizing or précising what the other person said. And it absolutely is not about providing our own view or answer. It's about playing back what we feel the other person meant at the deeper level.

There are two rules to playback to make sure it achieves the desired quality:

1   When playing back what you believe the receiver meant, you need to play back the meaning as your subjective 'felt' sense rather than playing back an assertion or the meaning as an objective observable fact. In other words, play back in terms of 'I' rather than 'IT'. You could preface your playback with: 'You said a lot of things, but it feels to me that what you really meant was…' or 'I got the sense that this is about…'. Playing back

to someone, 'I get the sense that this is about your boss' is a lot less confrontational than asserting, 'This is obviously about your boss.' When you play back your subjective sense of the transmission, the transmitter can't argue with you because they can't dispute what you are feeling. Plus, even if you are right in your assertive 'IT' statement, being so direct can often simply push the receiver into a defensive stance and no real progress will be possible. But if the statement is about what it feels like to you, they can't disagree – you're not saying it is something, you're just saying it feels like it might be something to you.

2 For playback to be successful it must always be presented as an offer or question, not an assertion. Offering it as a question for them to confirm or deny is much more inclusive and allows you to mutually decide if your subjective sense was accurate or not. This approach therefore invites them into the interpersonal space with you, and your question creates a connection that they can choose to engage with or not. If your subjective sense is accurate, the transmitter will usually confirm your assertion; if not, they will deny it and give you more information so that you can fine-tune your playback. In the moment of confirmation, you are suddenly aligned in a shared place of understanding. The transmitter knows for certain you understand them: you've played back, and they've confirmed. This can be profoundly moving for the receiver, who can feel genuinely heard and listened to – often for the first time. It is also the moment when the transmitter's view of you, the receiver, is suddenly transformed. It's a moment of supreme influence because the transmitter feels that you have taken the time to really understand them. When you as the receiver play back something so insightful and accurate that the transmitter wasn't even aware of it until you said it – that's the moment your relationship is transformed, and you have established profound influence.

This is the ultimate goal of the MAP skill – to create an experience for the transmitter of being completely understood. This is such a rare experience that it can be incredibly motivational to the transmitter and can unlock a huge amount of discretionary effort. 'Finally, my boss gets me', 'Someone is listening', 'They finally understand me'. When employees and members of your senior team experience this with you, loyalty and engagement increase.

The MAP skill is a simple yet deceptively powerful technique that can transform interpersonal dynamics. But it does come with a warning. This technique allows us to understand what's really going on for someone – even when they themselves may not be sure what the issue is. As a result, we must always share any insights we may perceive with care and consideration.

One of the big advantages of this technique is that when we realize the dynamic between two people or two opposing groups, we have a choice about how to resolve the conflict, and that's incredibly powerful.

We used this MAP skill in negotiations between management and the unions to break through months of stalemate with one client. Every year, prior to our involvement, these groups would negotiate on terms and conditions, and every year it would be fraught, protracted and both sides would emerge feeling bruised. Eventually, some compromise would be agreed upon, but neither side was that happy and the process would be repeated the following year. It was a very expensive and time-consuming process. Both sides were taught the MAP skill, which meant that everyone fully understood and recognized each other's position. By installing a foundation of common understanding, management were able to facilitate a negotiated settlement that the union was happier about in much less time and with a fraction of the angst. That's the power of the MAP skill.

Relationship coherence – social intelligence: appreciation of others' skill

We explored how to create an optimistic outlook using the appreciation skill in Chapter 5. This skill is also fundamental to social intelligence because it allows us to appreciate someone else. When we sincerely appreciate something in another human being that is also meaningful to them, it can be motivating and inspiring for the other person.

I remember speaking to a commercial director of a top retailer about appreciation. He told me he could remember the single day, ten years earlier, when the CEO of that company had said something nice to him. In the same way that everyone remembers where they were when Princess Diana was killed or when John Lennon got shot, this moment was so significant and so rare that he remembered the date. They had worked together for 25 years!

Unfortunately, appreciation in any form is not common in most organizations. This skill is, however, especially useful when we meet and must work with someone we would not normally or naturally resonate with.

For us to really connect with another human being, we have to shift our own perception and find something about that person that we can sincerely appreciate. When we like someone or naturally gravitate to them or feel as though they are 'on the same wavelength', that process is easy and largely unconscious. We instinctively trust them. Or at least trust is made possible by that initial acceptance and connection. It's a virtuous cycle. Remember the four component parts of trust – personal connection, understanding motives, consistent delivery and working style. If we can appreciate some-one, we are much more likely to spend time with them and personally connect; if we do, we are more likely to understand their motives; we already resonate with their working style so as long as they deliver consistently, trust is likely to develop and the relationship will prosper.

On the other hand, if we find it difficult to appreciate someone, we won't want to spend time with them and will instead avoid them. We therefore won't get to understand their motives, and as we don't like their work style it actually won't matter much whether they deliver or not because there is little trust and almost no relationship. This creates a barrier that effectively stops the relationship working before it's even begun. And that barrier can be a serious hindrance to the development of trust and the creation of an effective working relationship. The appreciation skill can therefore make a massive difference to building successful working relationships.

With elevated ESQ we can learn to connect with anyone and create a productive relationship – even if the only thing we can appreciate is that the individual in front of us isn't a twin!

THE APPRECIATION PROCESS

To appreciate another person, we must find some quality within the other person that we can sincerely appreciate, because if we can't appreciate them, we can't make an effective connection. And if we can't make an effective connection, we can't be an influential Exceptional Leader.

Many leaders are so busy focusing on the tasks they must complete to deliver their quarterly targets that they can easily forget that their success is entirely dependent on others. Learning to notice what is special about those others can be a very valuable practice to sustain motivation throughout the day.

Create a list of the people you are in contact with most in your life, personal and professional and list what you appreciate about each one. Think too about when that characteristic shows up, where it shows up and how. Take the time to notice at least one of these every day and talk to the person about the characteristic you appreciate.

It's a general principle that all positive emotion is transformative. This is why the SHIFT skill from Chapter 4 is so useful, because it allows us to induce positive emotions and alter brain function. Appreciation is a power-ful antidote to judgement or any negative emotion and can radically influence our ability to create strong working relationships.

Developing social intelligence starts with breathing skills and the emotional awareness to recognize that someone is irritating us. When we are more emotionally skilled, we can actively move into a different, more constructive emotion such as patience. When we are in a more appropriate emotional state, we ensure that we keep our frontal lobes on and don't become reactive. Instead, we take a more expanded perspective and seek to understand the other person's motives and values. ESQ therefore makes all the skills outlined in this book more effective.

Relationship coherence facilitates complete coherence

Relationship coherence is the final piece of the Exceptional Leadership puzzle. And it is deliberately positioned that way because relationships and connections inside and outside work are the biggest determinants to a happy, successful and fulfilled life. Success of any type without people to share it with is pretty hollow.

When experienced palliative care nurse Bronnie Ware started to document what people in the last weeks of their life really felt remorse over, she discovered five common themes – 'I wish I'd had the courage to live a life true to myself, not the life others expected of me', 'I wish I hadn't worked so hard', 'I wish I'd had the courage to express my feelings', 'I wish I had stayed in touch with my friends' and 'I wish that I had let myself be happier'.[20]

When we have developed physiological and emotional coherence, we have more energy and can experience any emotion we wish – including courage. We will by definition find it easier to express our feelings and let ourselves be happy. When we embrace the power of relationships and build cohesive high-performing teams or executive fellowships, we won't need to work so hard. The efforts of the many toward a common purpose finally liberate all of us from the tyranny of overwork so we don't need to lose touch with friends and neglect loved ones. When you add to that cognitive coherence, better-quality thinking and elevated maturity, you will find that improved performance and abiding deep-rooted success – professionally and personally – is finally possible.

Summary of key points

If you don't remember everything in this chapter, remember this:

- Relationships are the hardest thing we do as human beings. This is because we were only taught the transmission side of communication, not the reception. As a result, most people's definition of communication is 'waiting to speak'.

- We don't understand the component parts of trust, namely personal connection, understanding motives, consistent delivery and work style. Trust is therefore absent, lost or eroded, and we don't really know why.

- Without communication and trust, strong, enduring relationships – inside and outside work – are virtually impossible.

- Real business transformation will only emerge when we do the personal inner developmental work ('I'), step-change the top right-hand long-term quadrant ('IT') and also truly attack the bottom right-hand quadrant of people leadership ('WE').

- It's possible to develop leadership teams into high-performing units or even executive fellowships that we trust enough to take care of the vast majority of commercial performance.

- There are nine stages of team development from a collection of 'talented individuals' that is largely inert or dysfunctional to 'united fellowships' that can radically alter the business and the results.

- The values spiral offers a profound insight into personal and collective motivation that can allow everyone in a team to understand their own and each other's drivers which in turn can radically improve productivity and performance.

- Values also shed light on the power struggles in business and the unsatisfactory and dysfunctional decision-making and governance dilemmas that so often impair organizational growth.

- Upgrading governance is vital to dealing with the incredibly complex dynamics at play inside and outside many modern multinational organizations, offering a way to fully activate all four quadrants of the Exceptional Leadership model, thus creating Exceptional Organizations.

- When we combine interpersonal skills with physical and personal skills, we facilitate superior emotional and social intelligence and complete coherence.

- Exceptional Leadership is achieved when the leader is physiologically, emotionally, cognitively and behaviourally coherent and able to create successful relationships in all areas of life.

Notes

1 Csikszentmihalyi, C (2013) *Flow: The classic work on how to achieve happiness*, New Ed Rider, London

2 Christensen, C M, Alton, R, Rising, C and Waldeck, A (2011) The big idea: The new M and A playbook, *Harvard Business Review*, March

3 Ornish, D (1998) *Love and Survival: The scientific basis for the healing power of intimacy*, HarperCollins, New York

4 Cockerill, A P (1989) The kind of competence for rapid change, *Personnel Management*, 21, pp 52–56

5 Schroder, H M, Driver, M J and Streufert, S (1967) *Human Information Processing: Individuals and groups functioning in complex social situations*, Holt, Rinehart and Winston, New York; Harvey, O J, Hunt, D E and Schroder, H M (1961) *Conceptual Systems and Personality Organization*, Wiley, New York; Driver, M J (1960) The relationship between abstractness of conceptual functioning and group performance in a complex decision-making environment, unpublished Master's thesis, Princeton University; Dold, A W, III (1964) The effects of group composition and stress on heterogeneous teams in a simulated industrial setting, unpublished senior thesis, Princeton University.

6 Cockerill, A P (1989) *Managerial Competence as a Determinant of Organisational Performance*, Unpublished doctoral dissertation sponsored by the National Westminster Bank, University of London; Bales, R F (1951) *Interaction Process Analysis: A method for the study of small groups*, Addison-Wesley, Cambridge, MA; Cartwright, D and Zander, A (1968) *Group Dynamics: Research and theory*, Harper and Row, New York; Fisher, K (1999) *Leading Self-directed Work Teams*, McGraw-Hill, New York; Katzenbach, J R and Smith, D K (1993) *The Wisdom of Teams*, Harvard Business School Press, Boston, MA; Peterson, R S, Owens, P D, Tetlock, P E, Fan, E T and Martorana, P (1998) Group dynamics in top management teams: Groupthink, vigilance, and alternative models of organisational failure and success, *Organisational Behavior and Human Decision Processes*, 73, pp 272–305; De Dreu, C K W and Weingart, L R (2003) Task versus relationship: conflict, team performance, and team member satisfaction: A meta-analysis, *Journal of Applied Psychology*, 88, pp 741–49; Lencioni P M (2002) *The Five Dysfunctions of a Team*, Jossey Bass, London

7 Mishra, D (nd) The org chart is dead. Welcome to the age of networks, Complete Network Analysis, https://complete-network-analysis.com (archived at https://perma.cc/7AA7-9UWZ)

8 Martin, R (2002) *The Responsibility Virus: How control freaks, shrinking violets – and the rest of us – can harness the power of true partnership*, Basic Books, New York

9 Lewis, M (2011) *Boomerang: The biggest bust*, Penguin, London

10 Lewis, M (2010) *The Big Short*, Penguin, London
11 Tapscott, D (2009) *Grown Up Digital: How the net generation is changing the world*, McGraw Hill, New York
12 Wilber, K (2017) *Trump and a Post-Truth World*, Shambhala, Boston
13 Kim, W C and Mauborgne, R (2005) *Blue Ocean Strategy: How to create uncontested market space and make the competition irrelevant*, Harvard Business School Press, Boston, MA
14 Wilber, K (2001) *A Theory of Everything: An integral vision for business, politics, science and spirituality*, Shambhala Publications, Boulder
15 Collins, J (2001) *Good to Great: Why some companies make the leap and others don't*, Random House, London
16 Wilber, K (2001) *A Theory of Everything: An integral vision for business, politics, science and spirituality*, Shambhala Publications, Boulder
17 Middleton, J (2007) *Beyond Authority: Leadership in a changing world*, Palgrave MacMillan, New York
18 Watkins, A and Dalton, N (2020) *The HR (R)Evolution: Change the workplace, change the world*, Routledge, London
19 Rogers, C R (1967) *On Becoming a Person*, Constable, London
20 Ware, B (2011) *The Top Five Regrets of the Dying*, Hay House, London

Conclusion

Most business leaders are under enormous pressure and are understandably completely immersed in their industry. They rarely have time to reach out beyond the constraints of their market sector or read books on subjects that are not directly and obviously relevant to their industry or their results. If they did, they would discover a vast treasure trove of science and research-based knowledge that could radically alter the performance of their organizations, if only it were known and applied. The problem is that most of this knowledge is not 'commercial knowledge', neatly packaged and personalized to organizations in the form of business or leadership books, an MBA course or a management journal. It's knowledge of the human system, biology, brain function, adult development, behaviour or human relationships. And, sadly, much of this knowledge is packaged and delivered in a range of dry, dull academic or scientific papers contained in obscure publications that are almost incomprehensible to anyone who is not also an academic, scientist or medical professional.

This book therefore tries to cut through all that and present some of the key secrets that can, if properly applied, consistently elevate performance and results. When applied, this information leads to nothing short of a complete transformation of the lives of leaders, their organizations and the world.

Exceptional Leadership is an invitation to re-imagine a new future. A future that is not just measured by materialistic rewards but that redefines the very purpose of business itself. Our goal is to encourage the business community to support humanity and human evolution. This means we need to find a new way of keeping score in business, a new bottom line that accounts for the return on financial capital and also the return on natural, social and human capital. Only then can we really know the true value of a business.

The reason I know about this research is that I originally trained as a medical doctor and before leaving the profession I spent 11 years in many of the front-line medical trenches around the world in hospital-based roles, general practice and ultimately academic medicine. As a medical doctor and then a businessman, I realized that I was in the unique position of spanning two very different worlds that rarely meet except through the prescription of blood pressure medication, depression pills or post-operative care following a heart attack! In Chapters 2, 3 and 4, we explored how one of those worlds – neuroscience – has a profound implication on the other.

One of the reasons I decided to leave medicine was my inability to make a big enough difference to the scale of human suffering I was seeing. For example, the average GP may have 2,000 patients on their list, but they only see the same 200 patients on repeat. Although I enjoyed working as a cardiologist, oncologist or obstetrician, I still wasn't able to reach *enough* people. I wanted to work with people whose actions affected the lives of thousands or hundreds of thousands. That meant working with big multinational corporations.

Some of our 90-plus clients employ hundreds of thousands of people, and if we manage to improve leadership in those companies, we may positively improve the lives of the entire employee base. If we take the employee's family and friends into consideration then we may be able to reduce the suffering in some small way of one or two million people. If we include customers and supply chains, then we're talking about millions of people. Big business has the potential to improve the lives of millions, or billions. This is what excites me every morning of my life – the possibility of reducing the scale of human suffering for millions of people through more compassionate, more enlightened Exceptional Leadership. If we encouraged people to apply the advances in understanding of the human condition across the globe. I believe, we could finally solve many of the so-called 'wicked problems' currently facing society.[1]

I have had the good fortune to meet and work with some great leaders over the last 25 years. In this book I have attempted to share some of their key insights. In examining the many, largely agreed upon, 'facts' from multiple, often obscure fields of science and medicine, as well as the research from business schools and leadership journals, some astonishing conclusions become clear; conclusions that, extraordinary as they may seem, consist of no more than pre-existing knowledge. But when these insights are taken together, something remarkable emerges. These insights, when properly applied, can change all our lives for the better.

The complexity of the human condition and the potential inherent in that sophistication inspired me from an early age, and I hope that some of what I have shared has inspired you. Please find time to practise a few of the skills, experiment with the ones that resonate most strongly with you, and apply the knowledge in this book to your life. Pay attention to what happens. These insights, which I have accumulated over many years of study, have certainly helped me to understand that we are all so much more than we realize or have been led to believe. And they also made me realize that if enough organizations change, it *is* possible to reduce human suffering on a global scale, because when applied these insights can transform our experience of ourselves, how we relate to each other and the very nature of the lives we live.

Note

1 Watkins, A and Wilber, K (2015) *Wicked & Wise: How to solve the world's toughest problems*, Urbane Publications, Kent; Watkins, A and Stratenus, I (2016) *Crowdocracy: The end of politics*, Urbane Publications, Kent; Watkins, A and Simister, M (2017) *Our Food, Our Future: Eat better, waste less, share more*, Urbane Publications, Kent

INDEX

Page numbers in *italic* indicate figures or tables.